Dedicated to the Messiah

"For unto us a Child is born, unto us a Son is given; And the government shall be upon His shoulder. And His name shall be called Wonderful, Counsellor, The Mighty God, Everlasting Father, The Prince of Peace." (Isaiah 9:6)

And my Mother & Father.

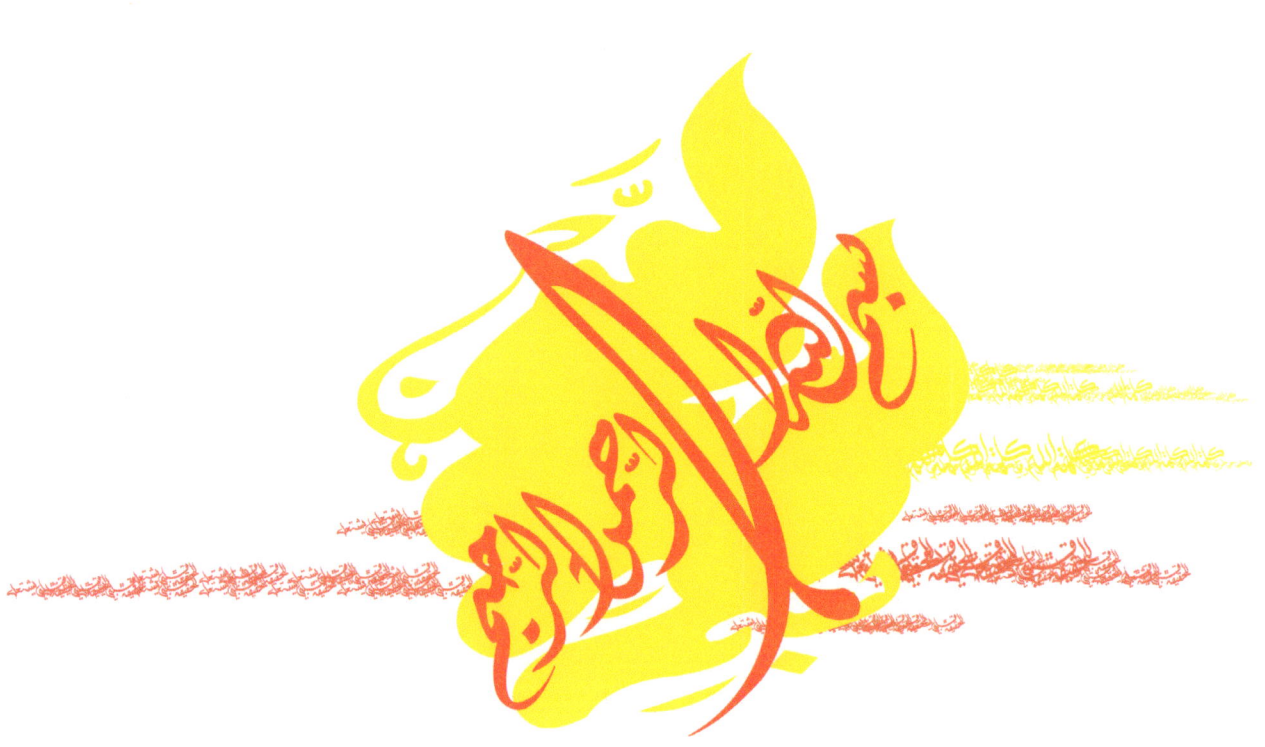

Introduction

I arrived in the Middle East full of inhibitions and with a mixed bag of notions about the region. This was in the full flush of the aftermath of September 11th, when clips of the Taliban and Al Qaeda atrocities were flooding the news on a daily basis. In a sense, those stories precipitated my arrival in the region. I wanted a crack at the action. Armed with one suitcase and about $1000 in cash, I began establishing myself as a journalist in the Gulf. This soon turned into a news anchor position with a local Dubai TV network—certainly the best place to live for an independent expatriate woman with gusto.

My life took another turn after covering the 2006 war in Lebanon. The stories I filed from there led to my being head-hunted by another leading network in Dubai and I became one of the faces of its daily news shows. This gave me much wider exposure, and the change occurred on both sides of the camera. As more people in the Middle East came to recognize me on their television screens, I developed a passion to better know and understand the Arab world.

I was certainly not a likely candidate for this awakening thirst for deeper knowledge of a region so ancient and complex, and one where religion has shaped every aspect of the culture. I'm from Australia, a wide open society where the line between church and state is firmly drawn and fiercely defended. Nonetheless, the longing to know more was planted in my heart and I became impatient with the smooth and comfortable life of the Gulf; however beautiful and easy, it was not enough. My passion to learn about these mysterious peoples and their ancient land led me to frequent trips across the region. Thus I began a unique journey across one of the world's most storied as well as most controversial places.

Awash though it may be in ancient archeology and historical revelations, one cannot become immersed in the Middle East and not be touched by the humanness of its rich diversity, and the humility found amongst the inhabitants of some of the oldest cities in the world. Out of the swirl of smells and tastes and cultural intricacies of the region and its people, have come more conflicts—and more peace treaties—than generated in any other section of our globe. Here in the birthplace of the world's three Abrahamic faiths, Judaism, Christianity, and Islam, many say is where the world began. And where it will end.

However, despite the religiosity and the controversy surrounding religion, it is in several cities across the Arab world where we see actual proof that the followers of the three great faiths can live together in peace and prosperity.

Furthermore as a result of my travels, I learned that the Middle East is home to a vast variety of ethnic groups who have contributed to the world and society at large, both culturally and economically in a plethora of ways.

Far from being the monolithic universe many in the West mistakenly believe it to be—the peoples of the Middle East include a diverse range of ethnic and religious groups. These people live here as well, and they have survived thousands of years of environmental, social and political change, occupation, and wars. Upheaval has also caused thousands of their number to immigrate and become absorbed into diasporas throughout the rest of our society, but the majority continue to call one of the most fraught parts of the world home. What's more, these ancient groups continue to survive amidst adversity and globalization.

I met them as I journeyed across the region, impelled by my longing to understand the world in which I found myself. I came across their rituals and religious practices, and I began to delve into their ways of life. Their faces tell stories of survival, hardship, displacement, loss and love. Discovering the place that was home to the great Patriarchs of the Old Testament, walking in the footsteps of Jesus, and listening to the daily calls to prayer from the mosques that dot the entire Middle East was a thing of wonder, but my travels also caused something unusual to happen inside me. The region caused me to confront myself and what I believed in.

It was during this process of breaking and humbling that I decided to examine my own beliefs and cross from my secular state to that of a believer in the one true living God. Furthermore, the love of God also caused me to examine a lot more than just myself, it also made me understand that there was far more to those who are biblically known as the children of Ishmael, than terrorists, burqas (and the bans against them) and angry bearded men.

As I travelled across the Middle East, I encountered the various ethnic minorities and social groups who reside throughout the region. Each country in the area includes small populations who over the centuries have found themselves under threat as a result of political and social tumult and in our time, globalization. Nonetheless, the common thread that unites us as human beings was evident in many people I met and who touched my life. It would be impossible to count the number of people who offered me shelter, friendship and food on a whim. The kindness of strangers made me believe there is still hope for bridging the gaps in the East-West equation.

This region has experienced more than forty wars in the past ten years: it's the place where the most blood has been shed globally. And while war seems to harden most people, what I found so special about the Middle East was that many people were able to keep trusting, loving and forgiving. And so my journey began. My thirst for knowledge and information led me to the mountains of Iraq; a country battered by tribal wars and sectarianism, not to mention one of the most ruthless dictators of the 20th century; to the inner quarters of Jerusalem. The city of all cities. The city where God told the prophets of old, His name shall always reside.

Far from compiling a definitive history or a political statement, I began to just engage and learn about people, and take snapshots of their daily lives. It was not too long before I began to gather a body of work that documented another face to the region, and the existence of a rich diversity within its boundaries. This discovery led me to a passion to expose this new dimension of an area so marred by an overload of terrorism, violence and dictatorships. That in turn led me to delve into serious debates, and to probe areas almost untouched by foreigners.

Perhaps ironically, in the West many are taught to avoid discussion of religion and politics due to the often heated consequences. In the Middle East one is constantly immersed in these two subjects. They bubble on a daily basis out of every newspaper, TV station, and from every mouth, from the least to the greatest. It's actually amid this chaos of opinions and heated debate that many individuals find their identity and they take comfort from voicing their thoughts; a mystery of madness, yet it all makes sense for those who call the region home.

Trekking across this part of the world for almost a decade, capturing the faces of the young and the old who reside here, my hope has been to reveal another side, another view. Their faces speak a thousand words, whether in moments of joy or sadness. Theirs are the stories I want to share with you. It's these very moments that helped me see and define who we are as individuals and which also unite us globally through a common thread of understanding and the human desire for peace.

I believe this common understanding and desire for peace can, if we try, unite us all.

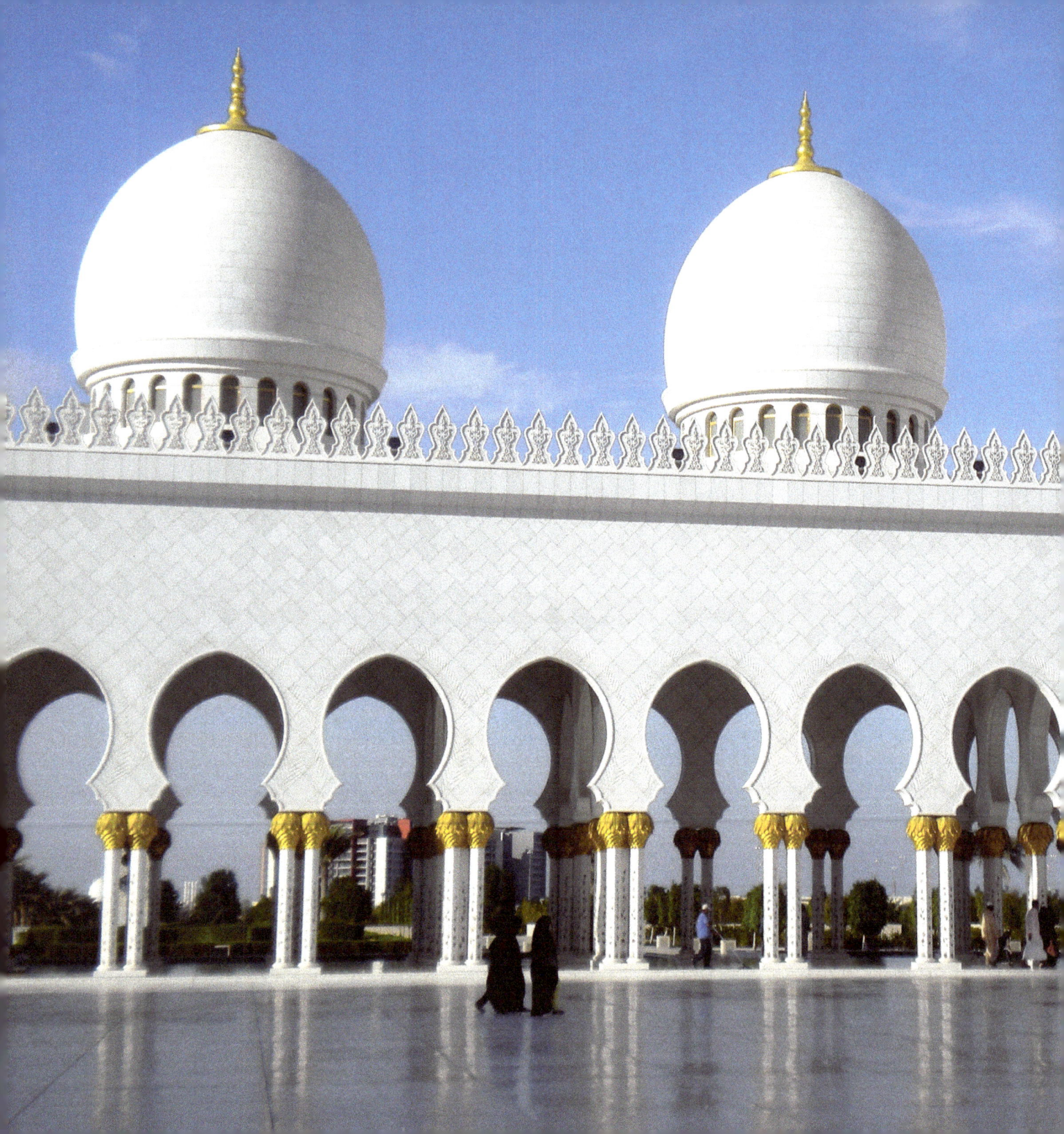

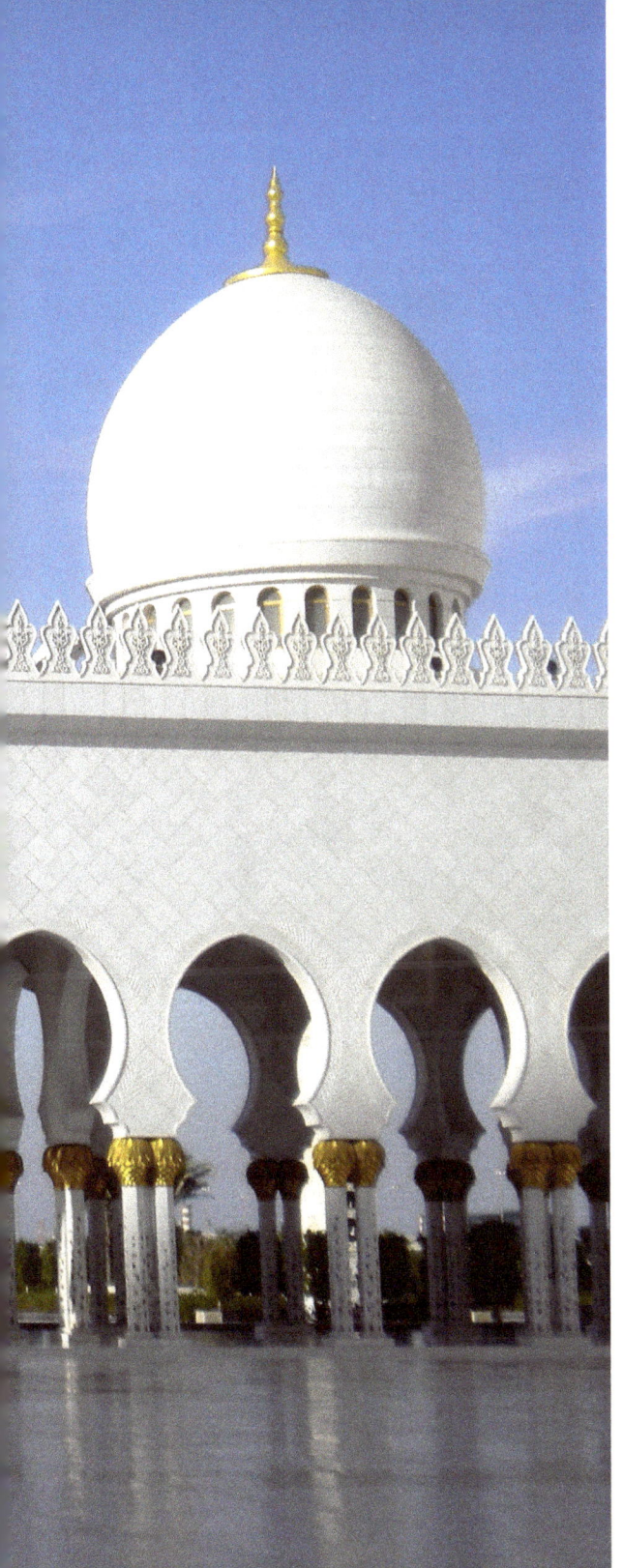

Sheikh Zayed Grand Mosque. Abu Dhabi, UAE.

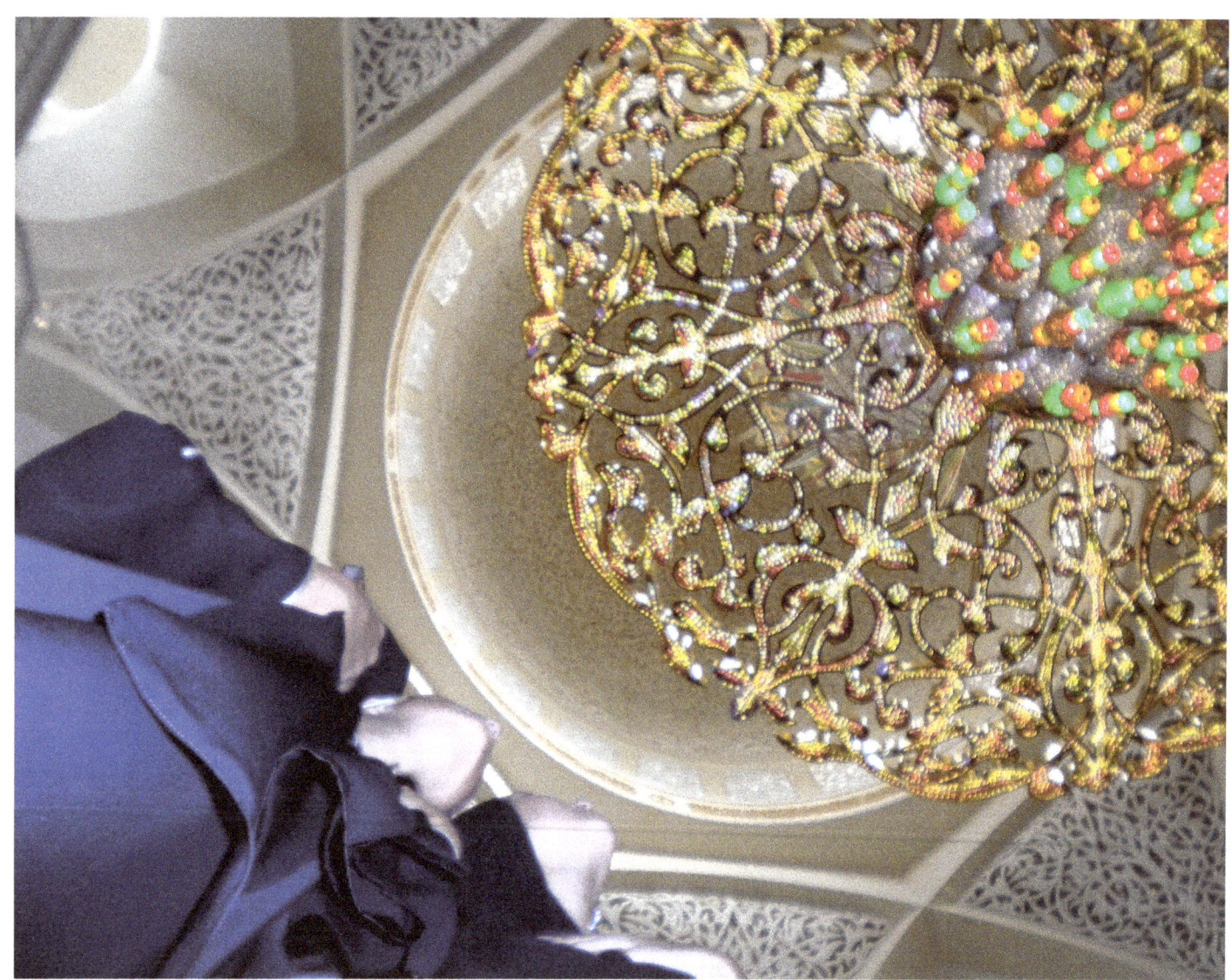
Two women admire a chandelier in the Grand Mosque. Abu Dhabi, UAE.

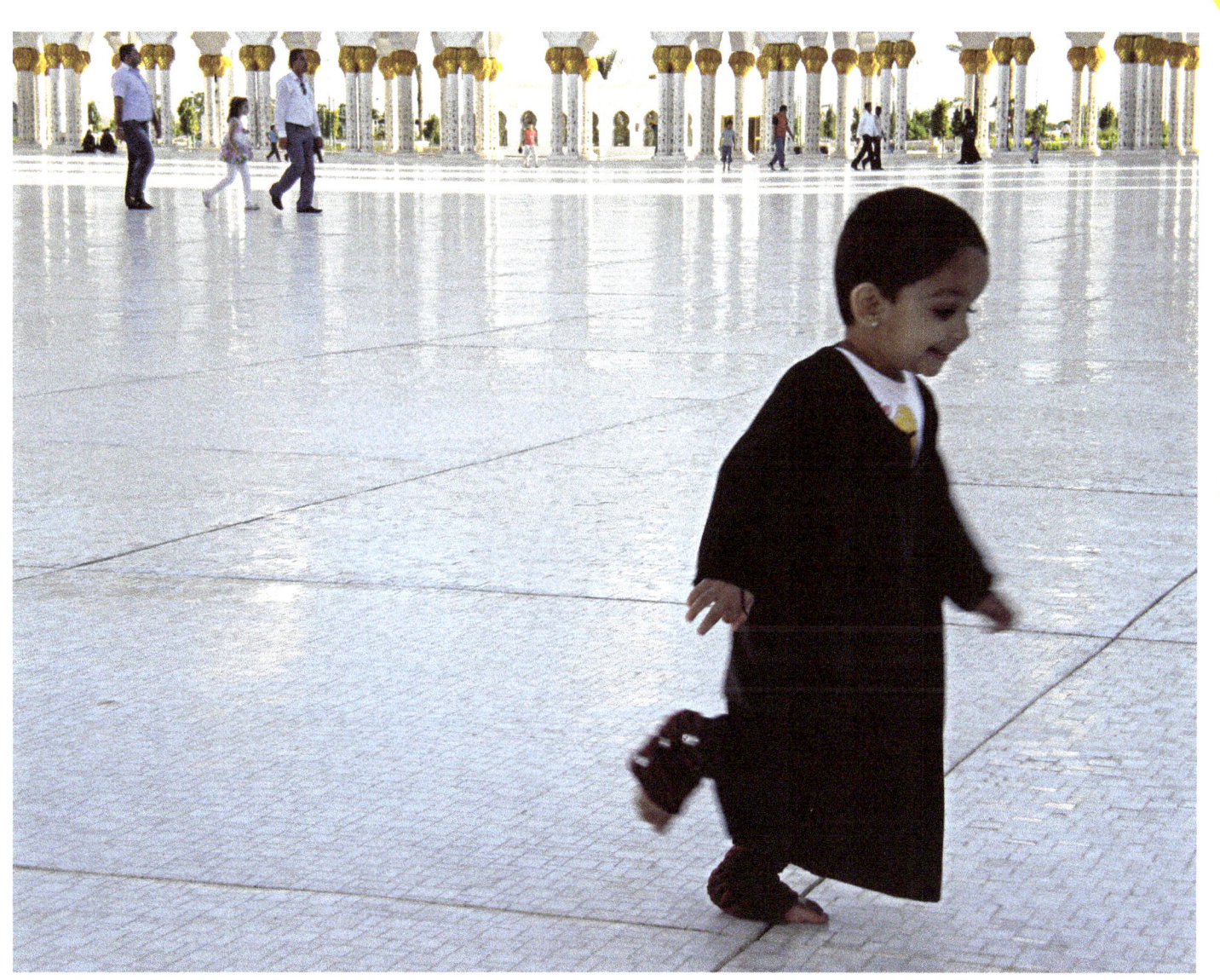

A child plays in the outer courts of the Grand Mosque. Abu Dhabi, UAE.

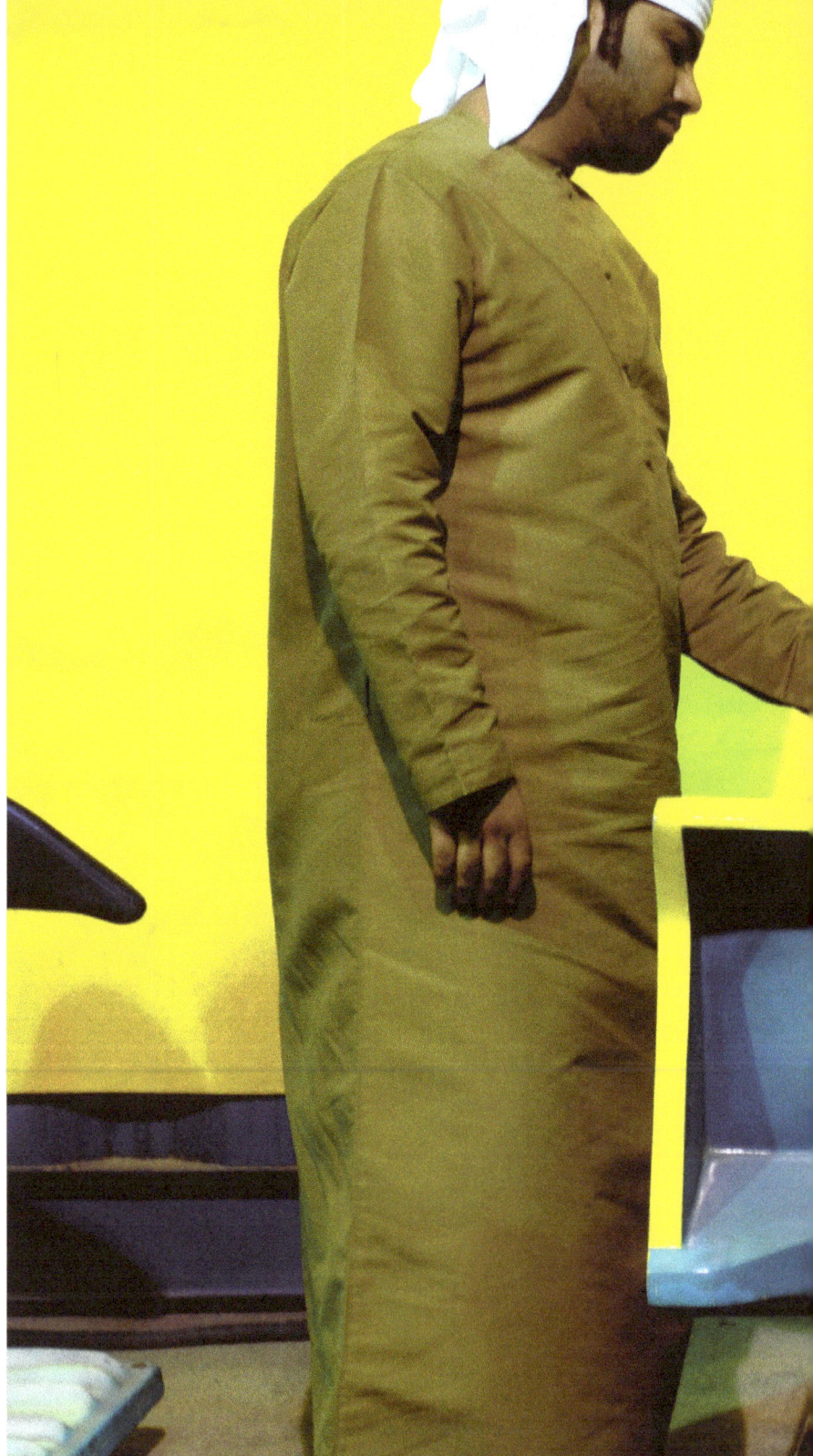

Whilst the UAE has a diverse cultural imprint, most Emirati males still prefer to wear a traditional Kandora, an ankle-length white shirt woven from wool or cotton.

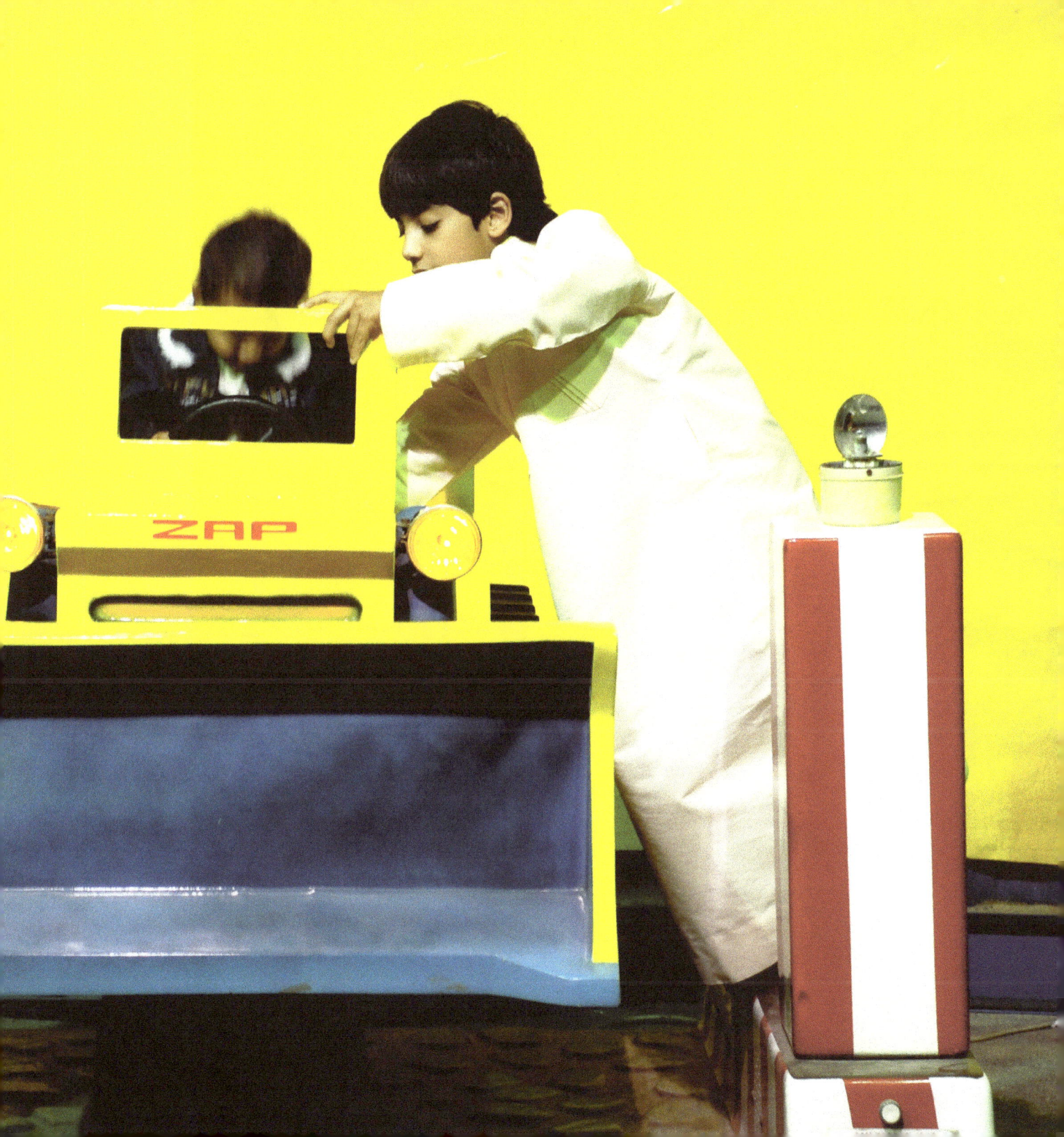

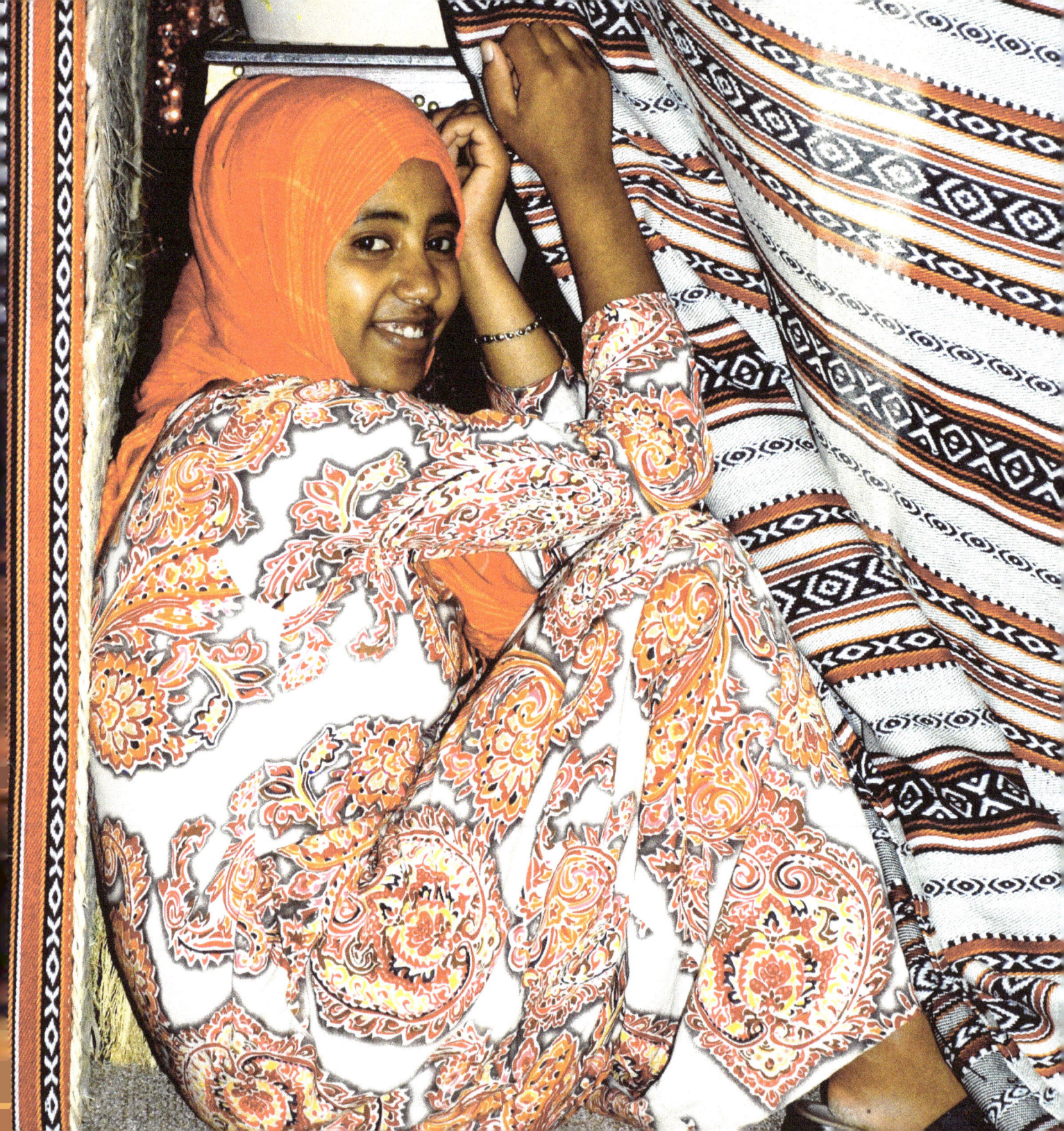

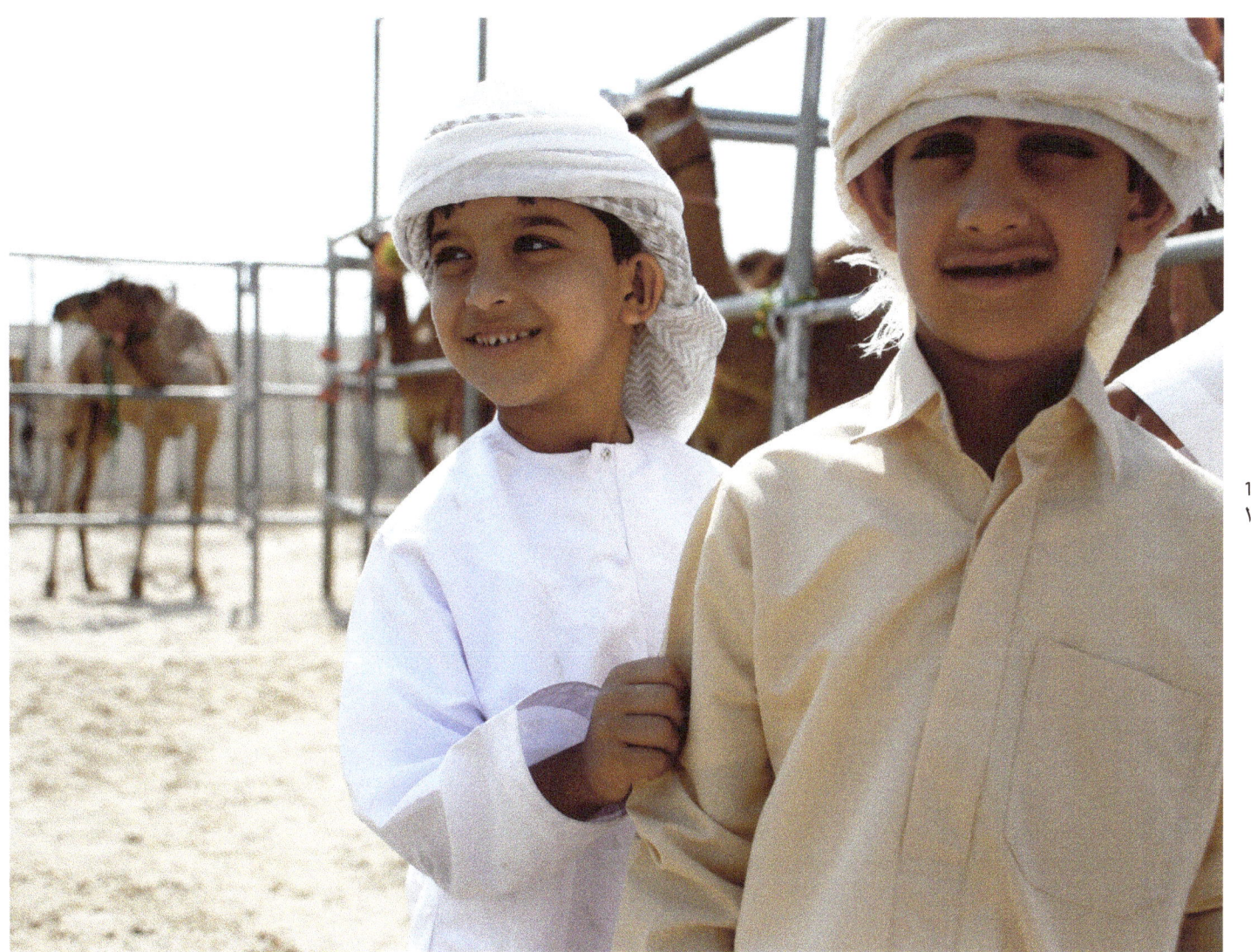

Emirati Children at a Camel Souk. Abu Dhabi, UAE.

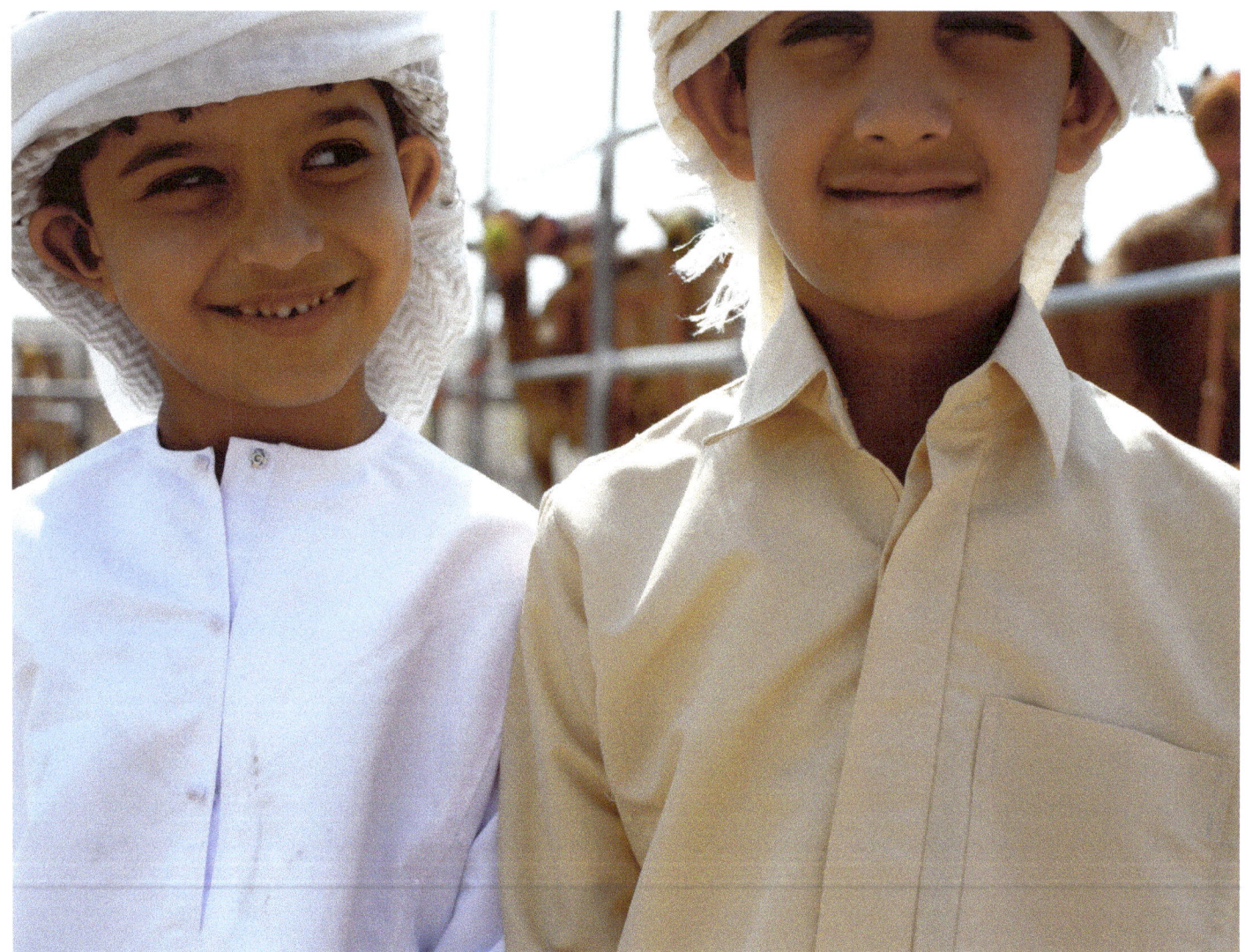

Featuring the world's seventh largest oil reserves, today the UAE is a bustling metropolitan hub stocked with everything one could possibly need in order to live and do business. Within four decades the Emiratis have become global players in business, trade and tourism.

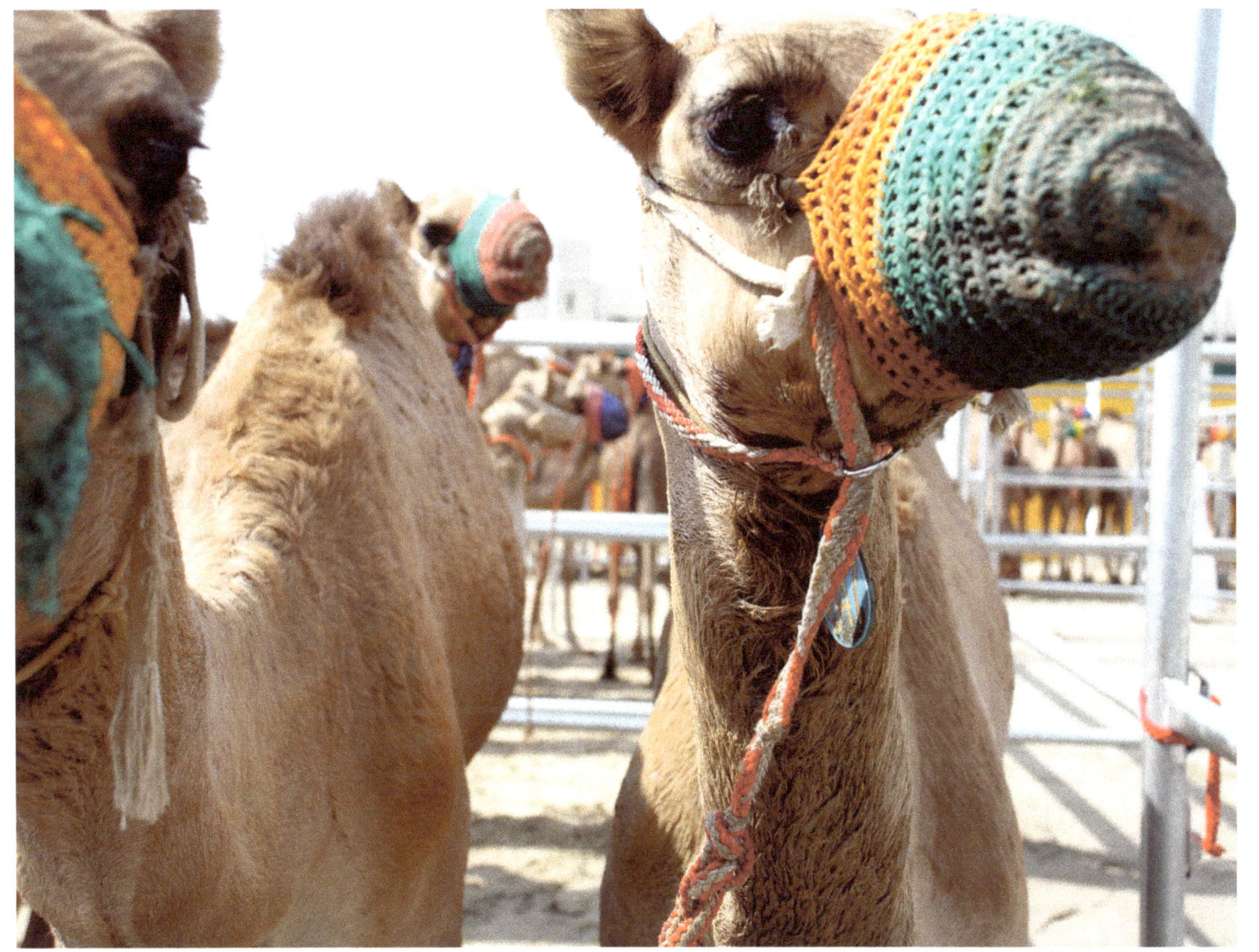

The progressiveness of the UAE has had very little effect on traditions such as camel racing which continues amidst the winds of change. Today, the camel has been moved from being a mode of transport and carrier of goods to a nostalgic symbol of luxury and the Arabian heritage. Camel Souk, Abu Dhabi, UAE.

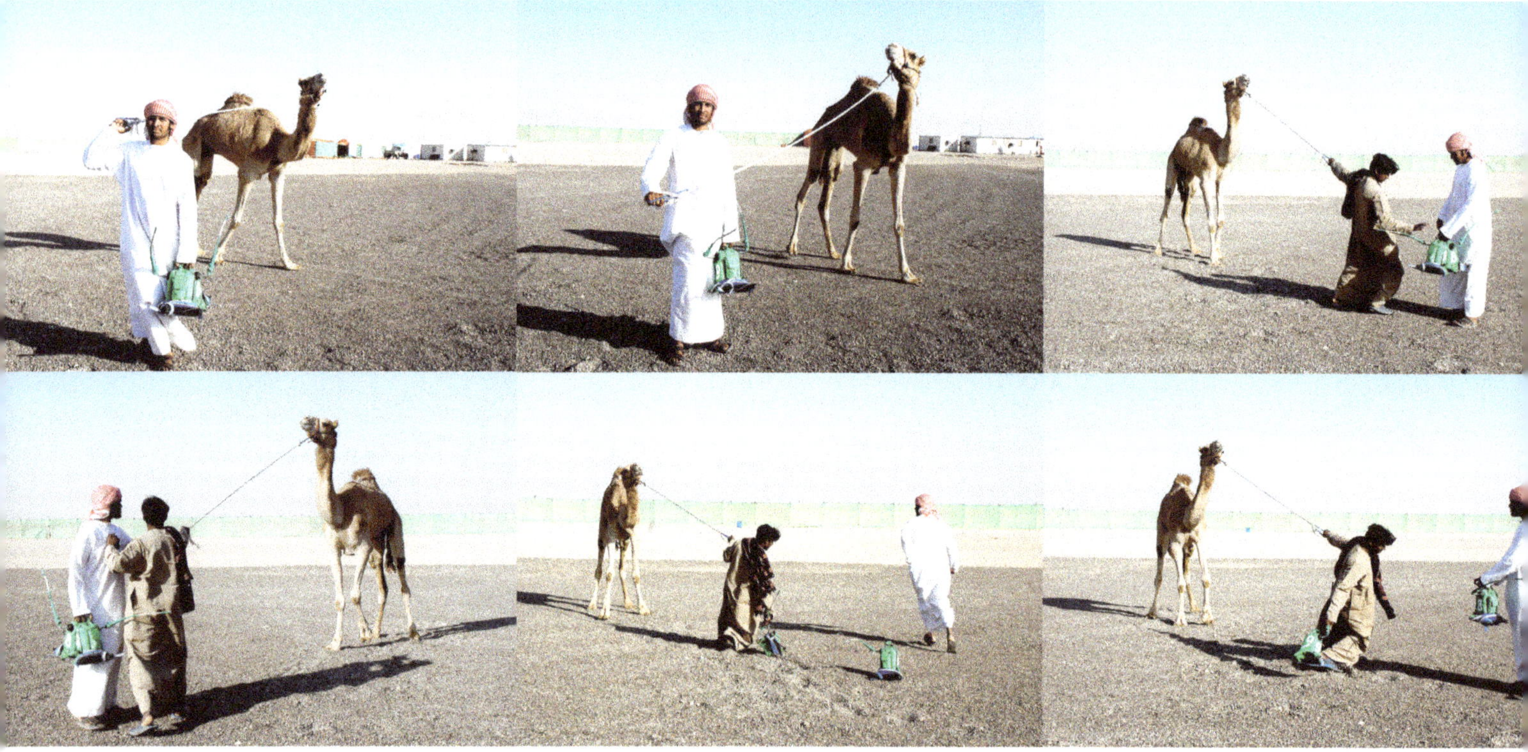

As for the races, in 2005, camel jockeys were replaced with robots in the UAE.

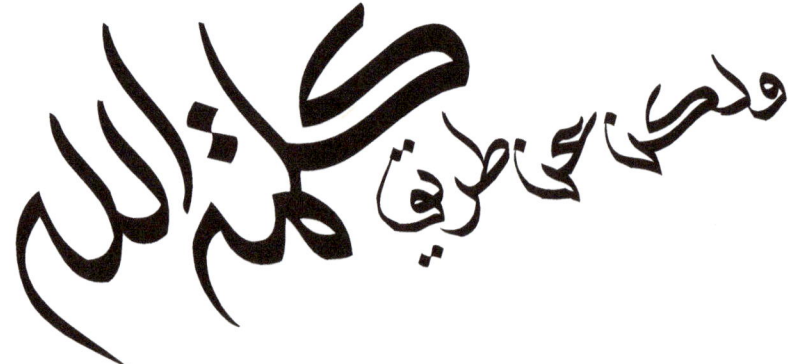

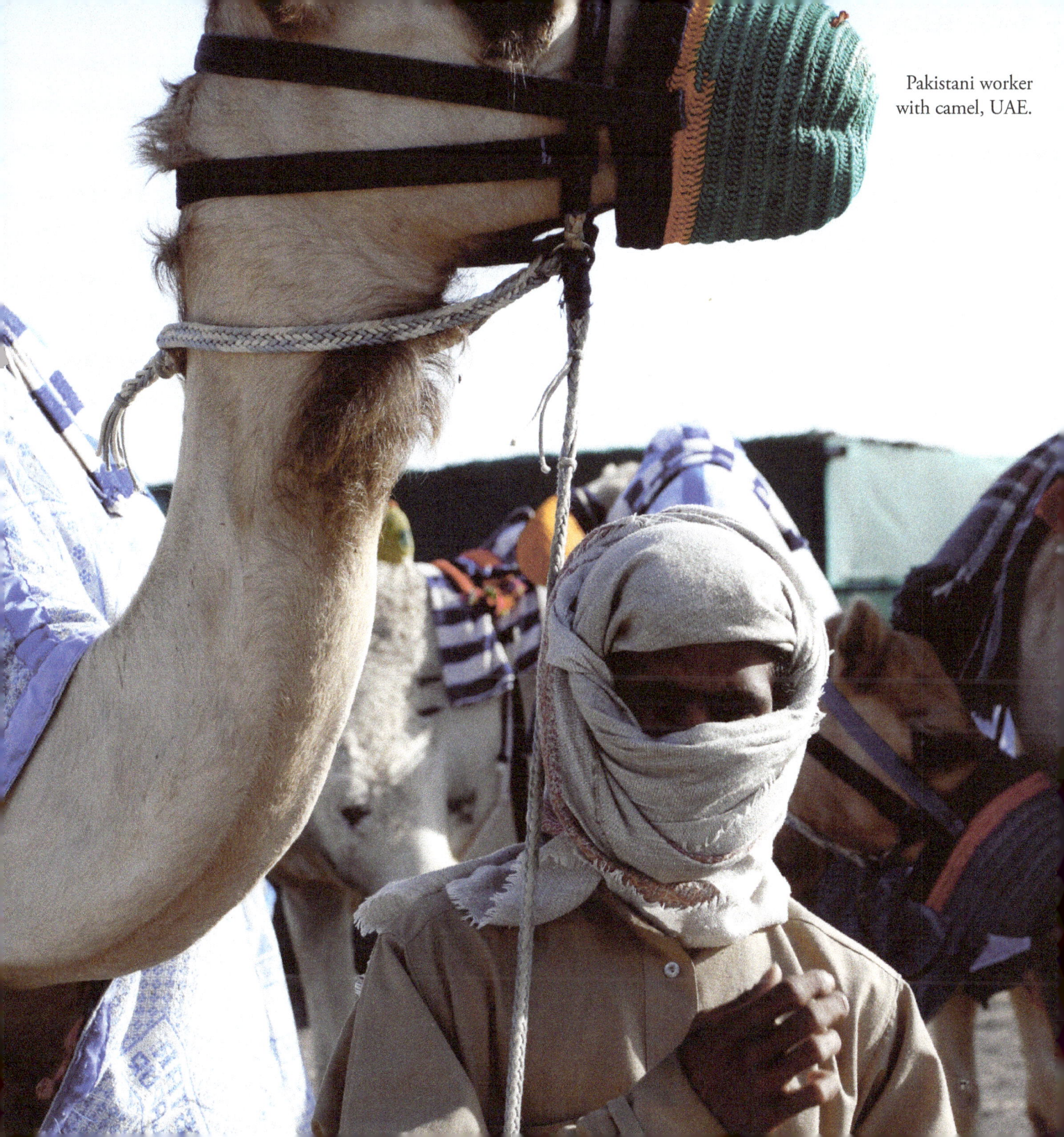

Pakistani worker with camel, UAE.

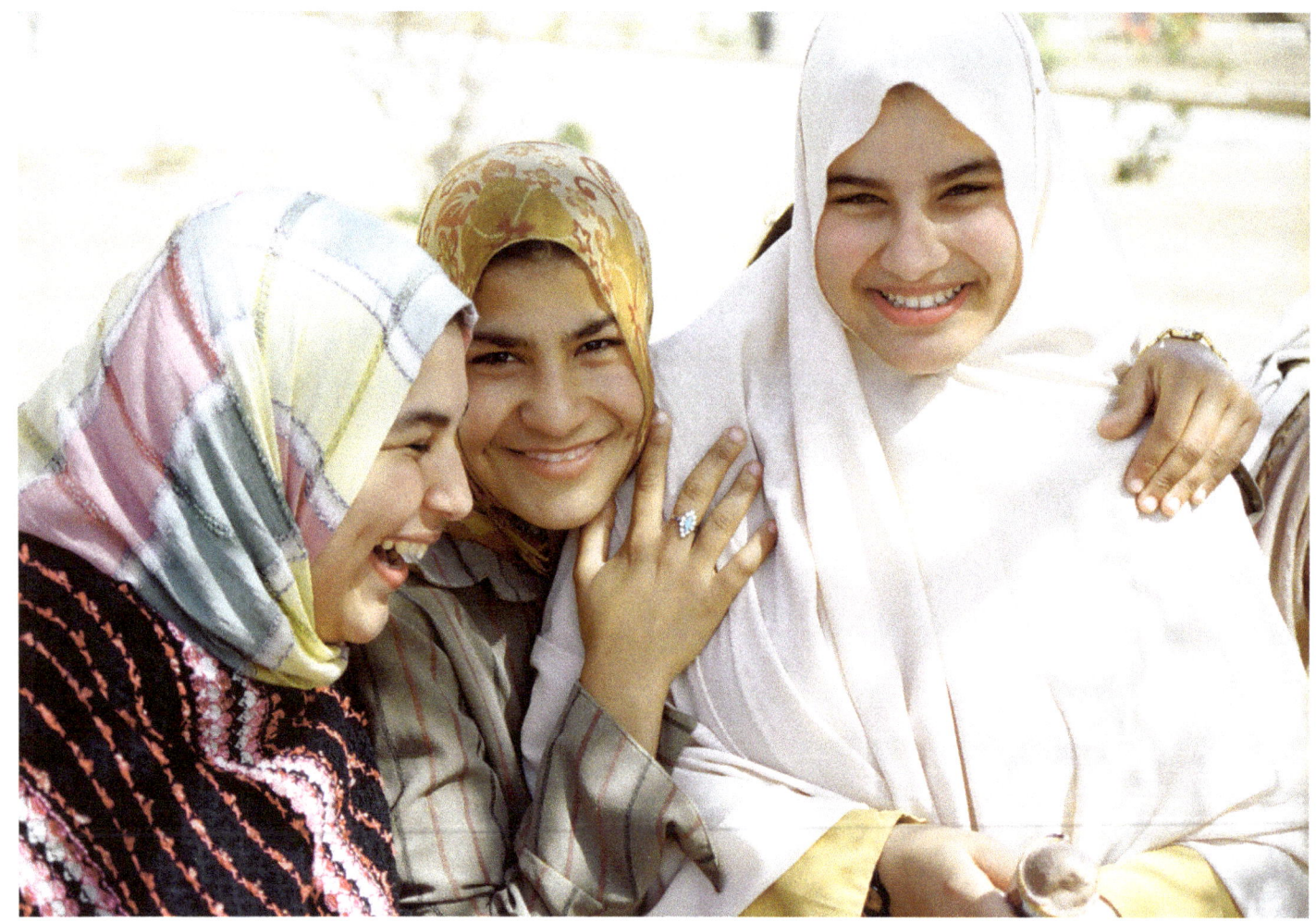
Most Muslim women wear the abaya over their clothes and a headscarf draped over their heads as a sign of respect. Considered a form of national dress, women who cover all their hair and wear the abaya are called muhajibba, meaning they are religious. Cairo, Egypt.

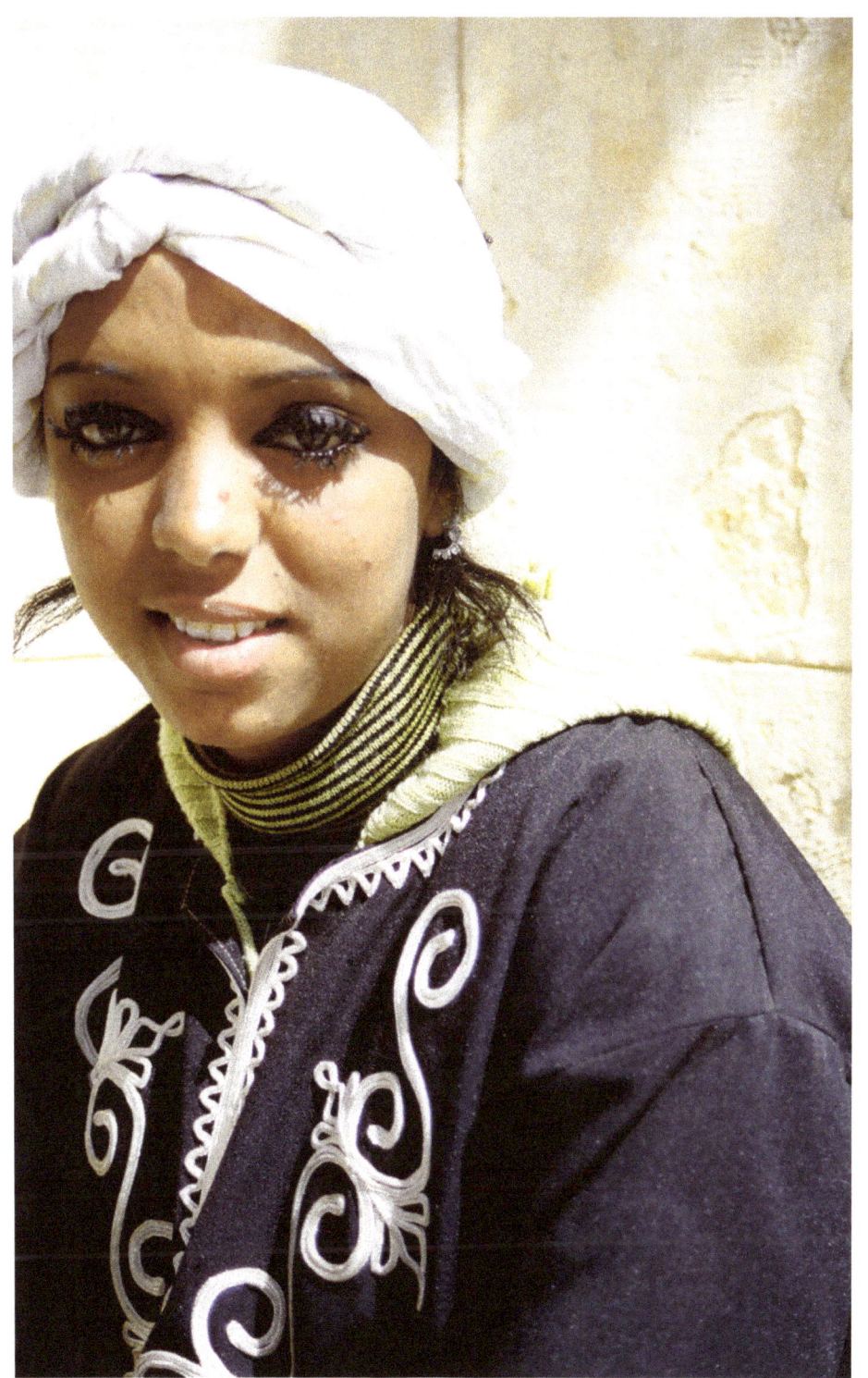

Cairo, Egypt.

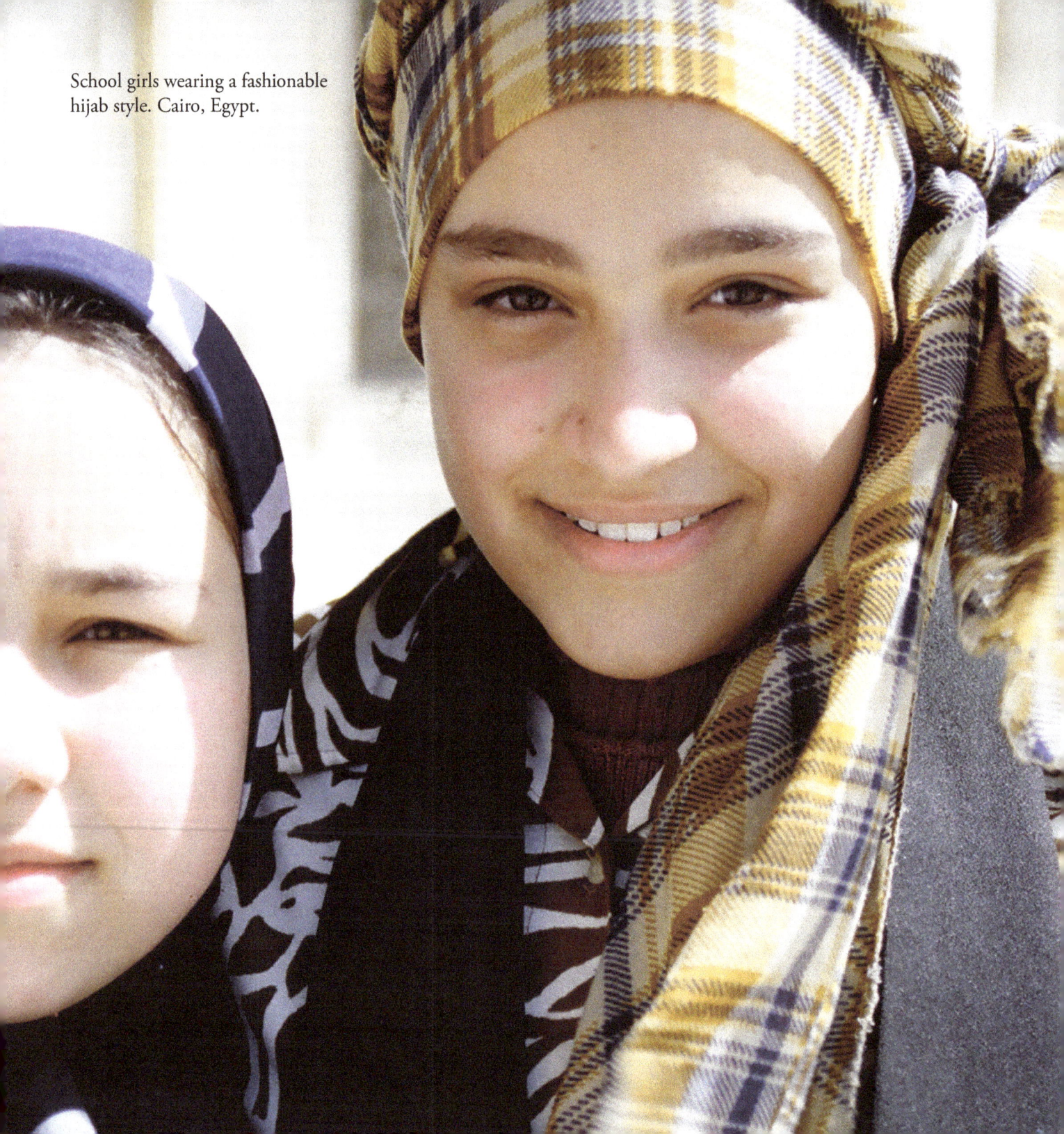
School girls wearing a fashionable hijab style. Cairo, Egypt.

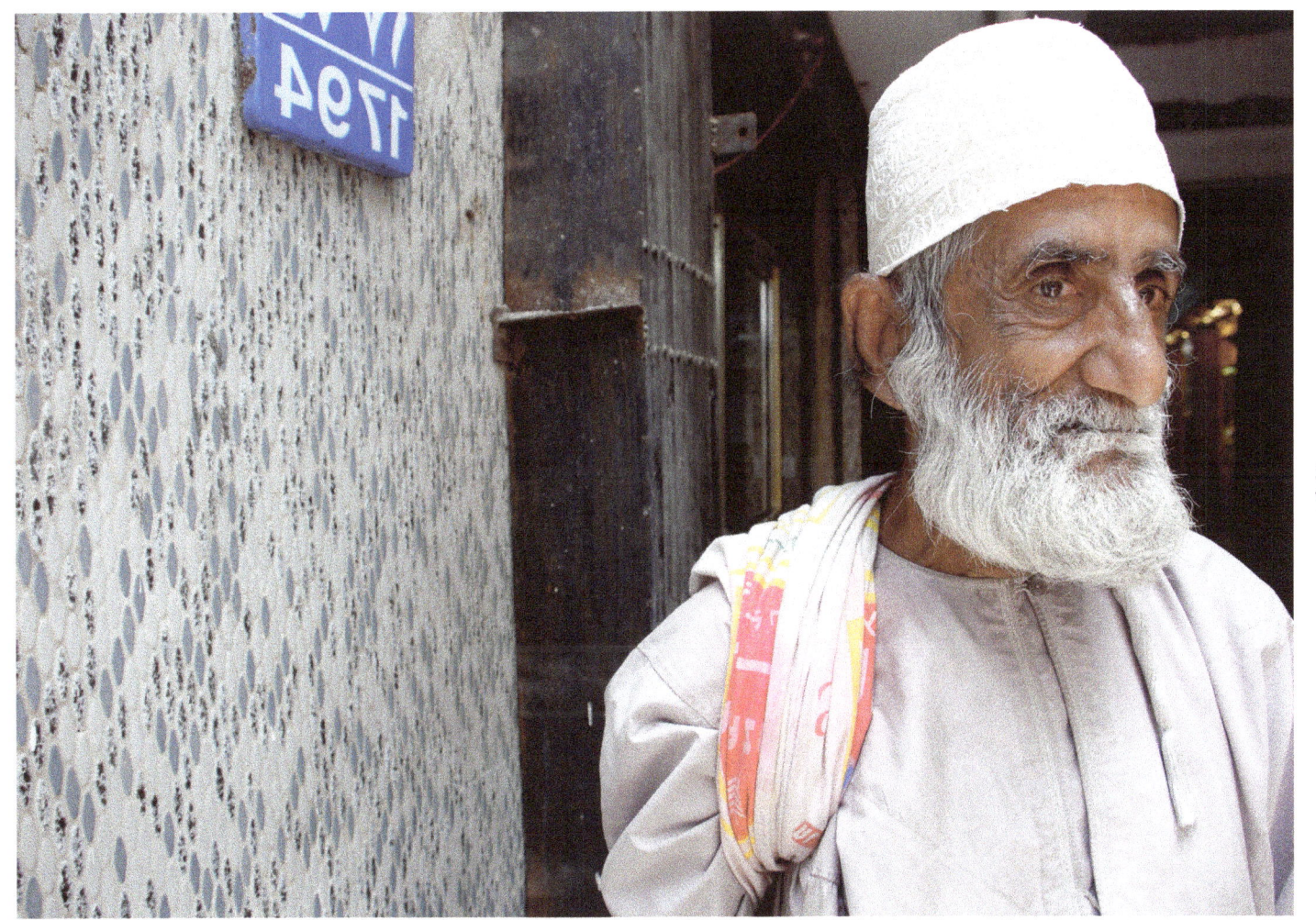

Oman's Bedouins continue to survive in freedom and peace; two values deeply entrenched in their ancient culture. In winter, when there are substantial amounts of rainfall in the Gulf, they migrate deeper into the desert, seeking refuge near secure water sources. For many, the city is the preferred location for the summer months.

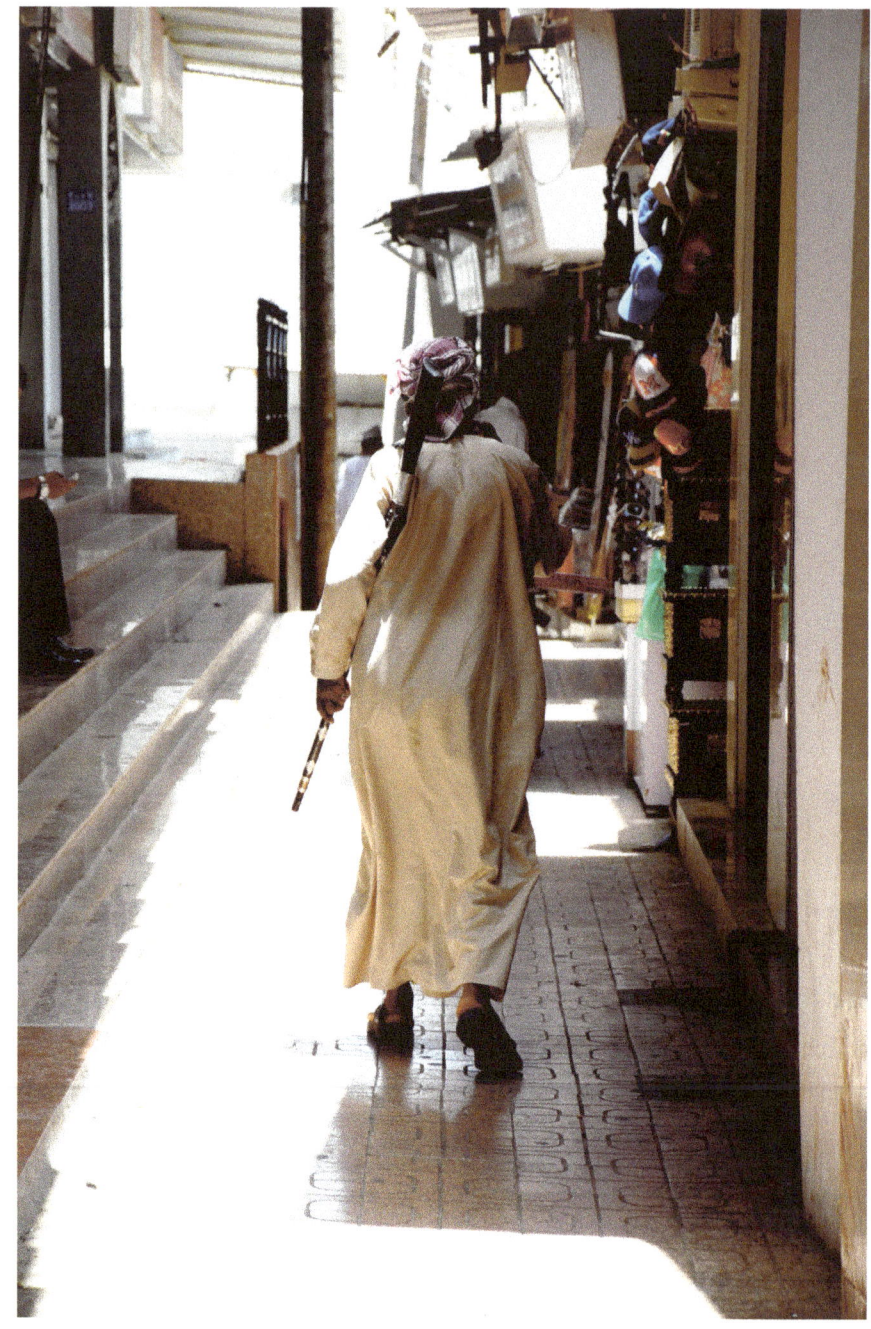

Bedouin men are easily distinguished by their traditional rugged Omani attire, and the rifles strapped to their backs. Wandering the souks, they need no introduction: Their faces are lined with a thousand tales of desert survival.

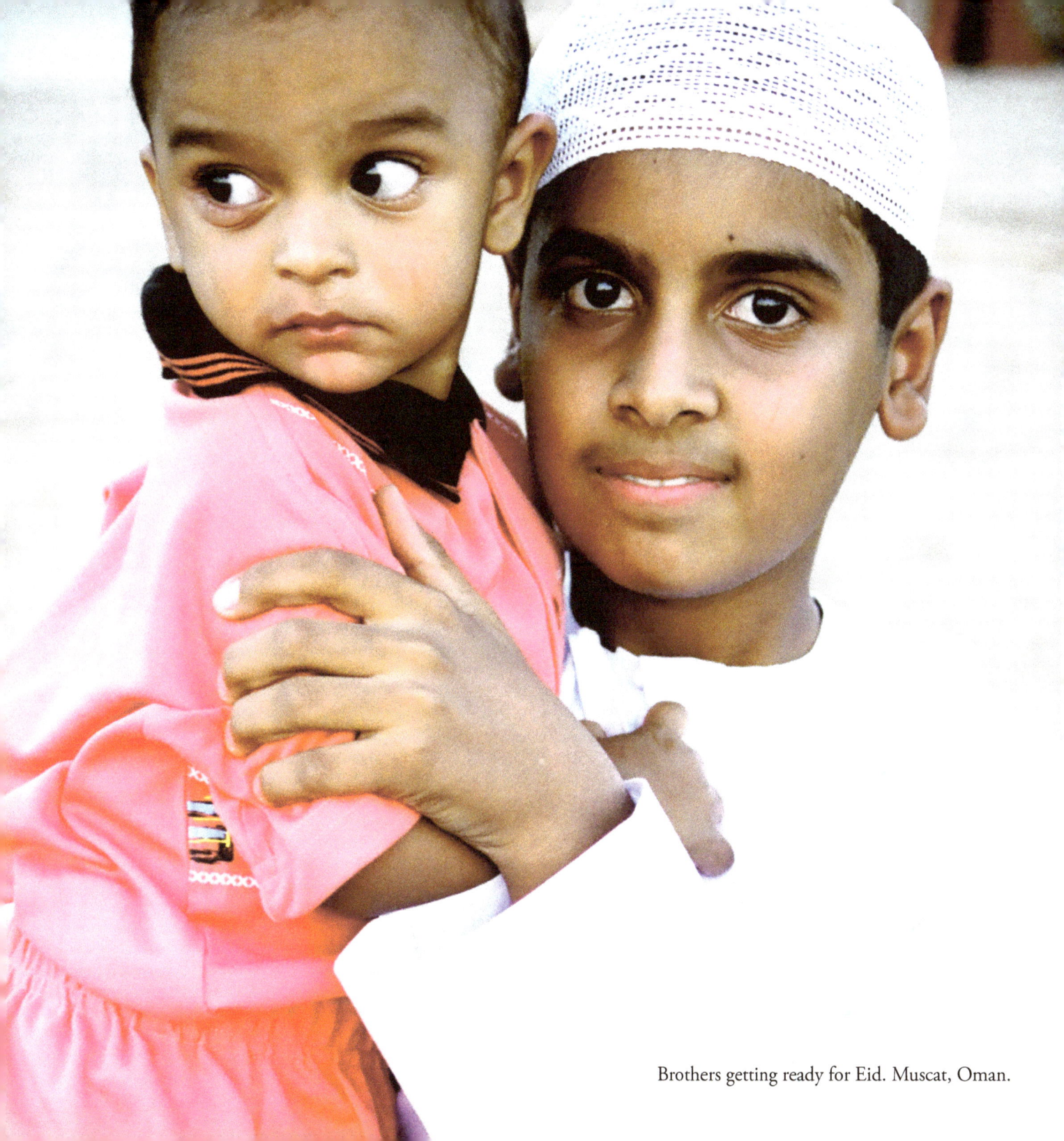
Brothers getting ready for Eid. Muscat, Oman.

نجاتك
وجة بالمرارة

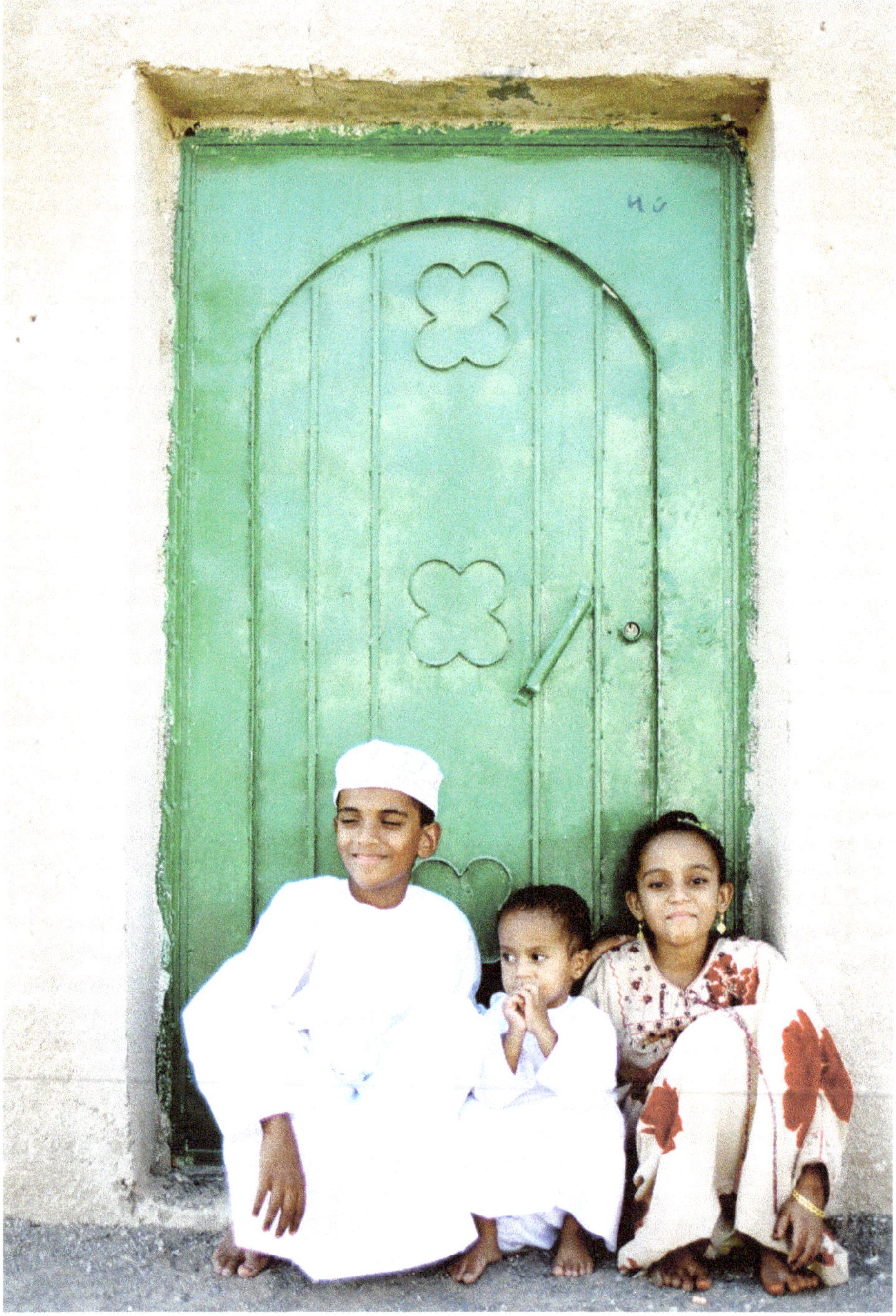

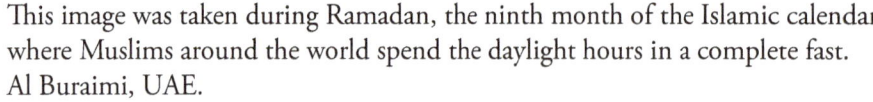

This image was taken during Ramadan, the ninth month of the Islamic calendar where Muslims around the world spend the daylight hours in a complete fast. Al Buraimi, UAE.

مليئة بالغم

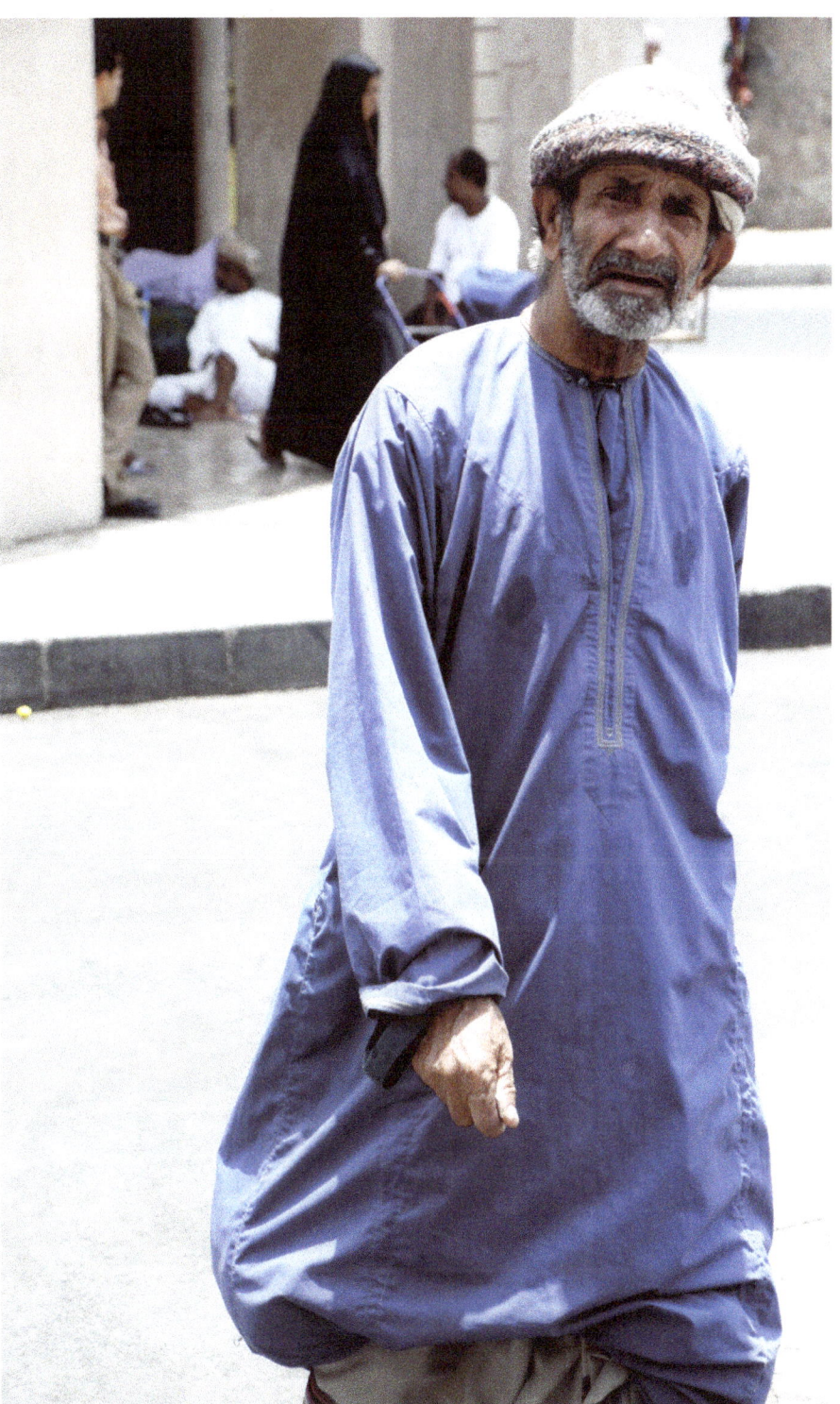

Omani man in traditional attire.
Muscat Souk, Oman.

معجونة بالصلاح
مدفوعة بالحب
تعطى مع السلام

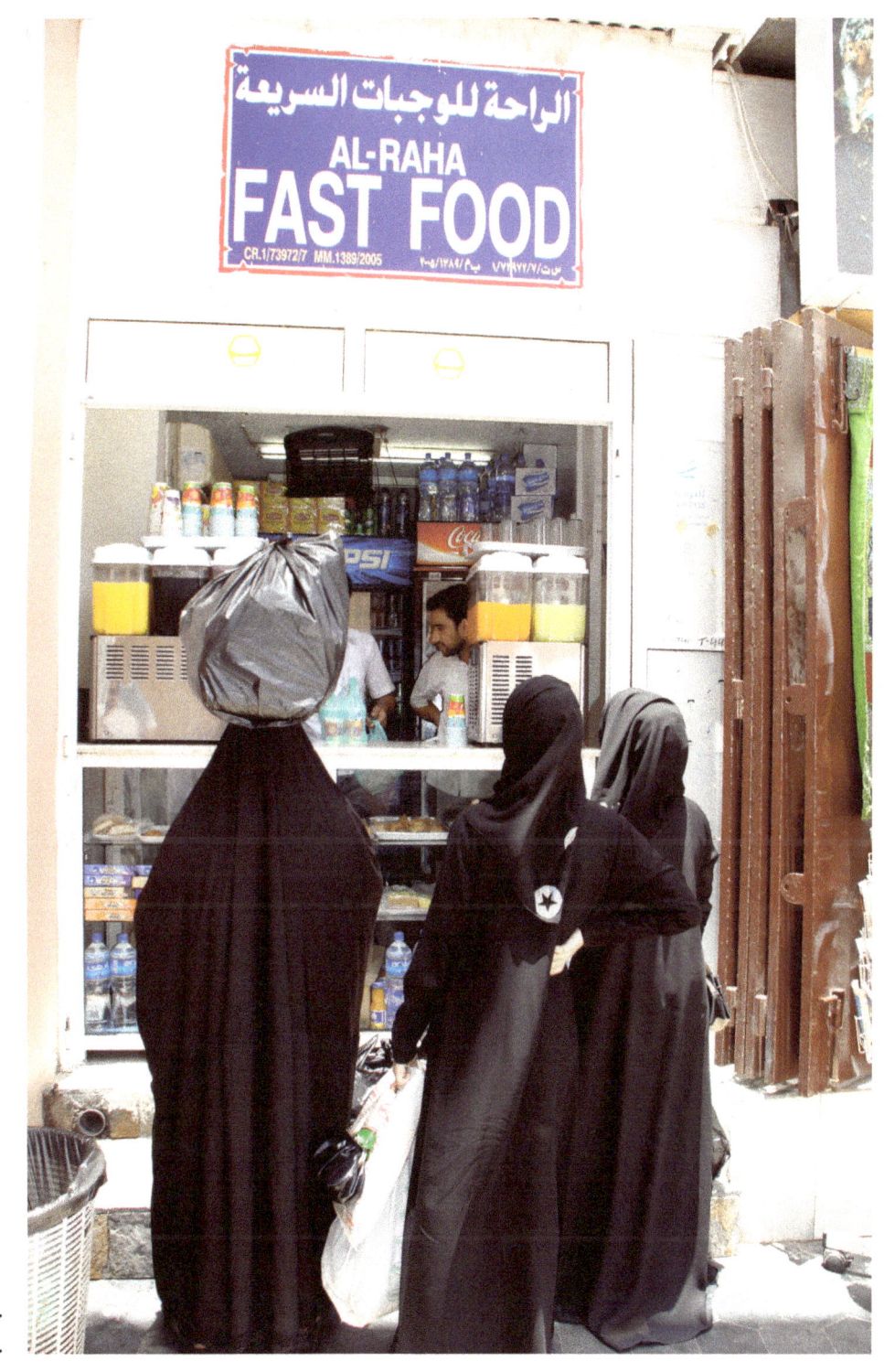

Local women shopping.
Muscat, Oman.

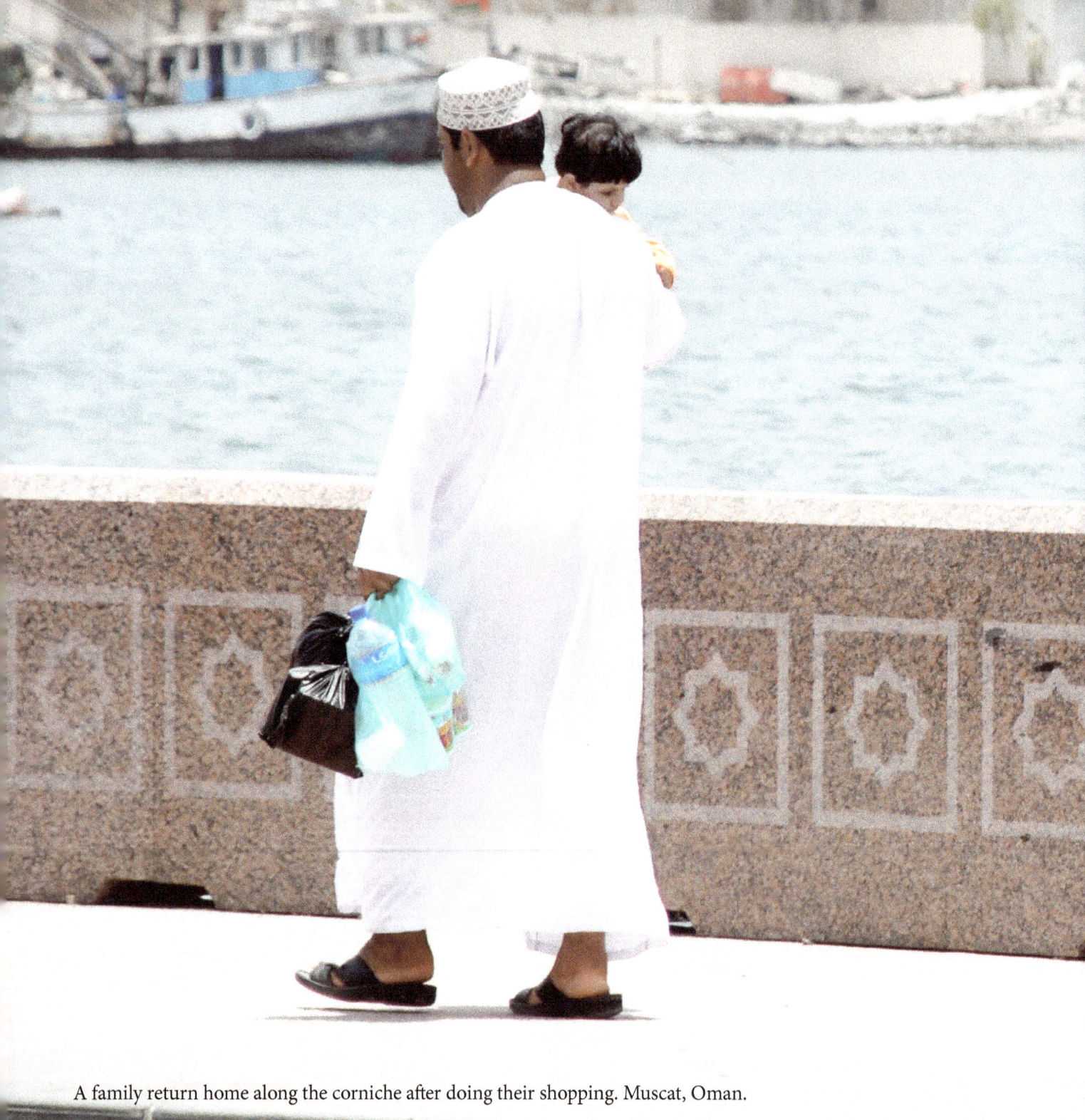

A family return home along the corniche after doing their shopping. Muscat, Oman.

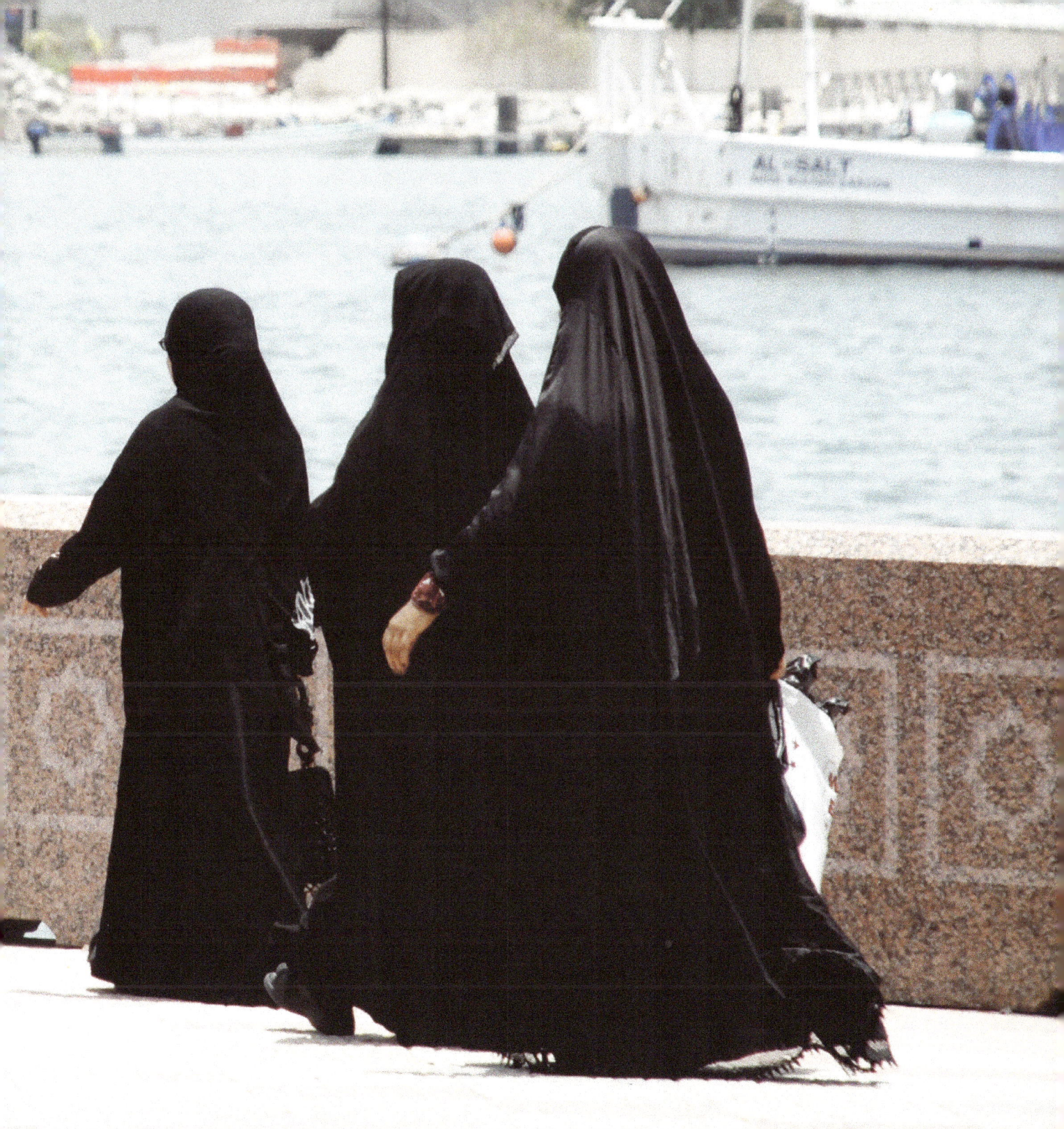

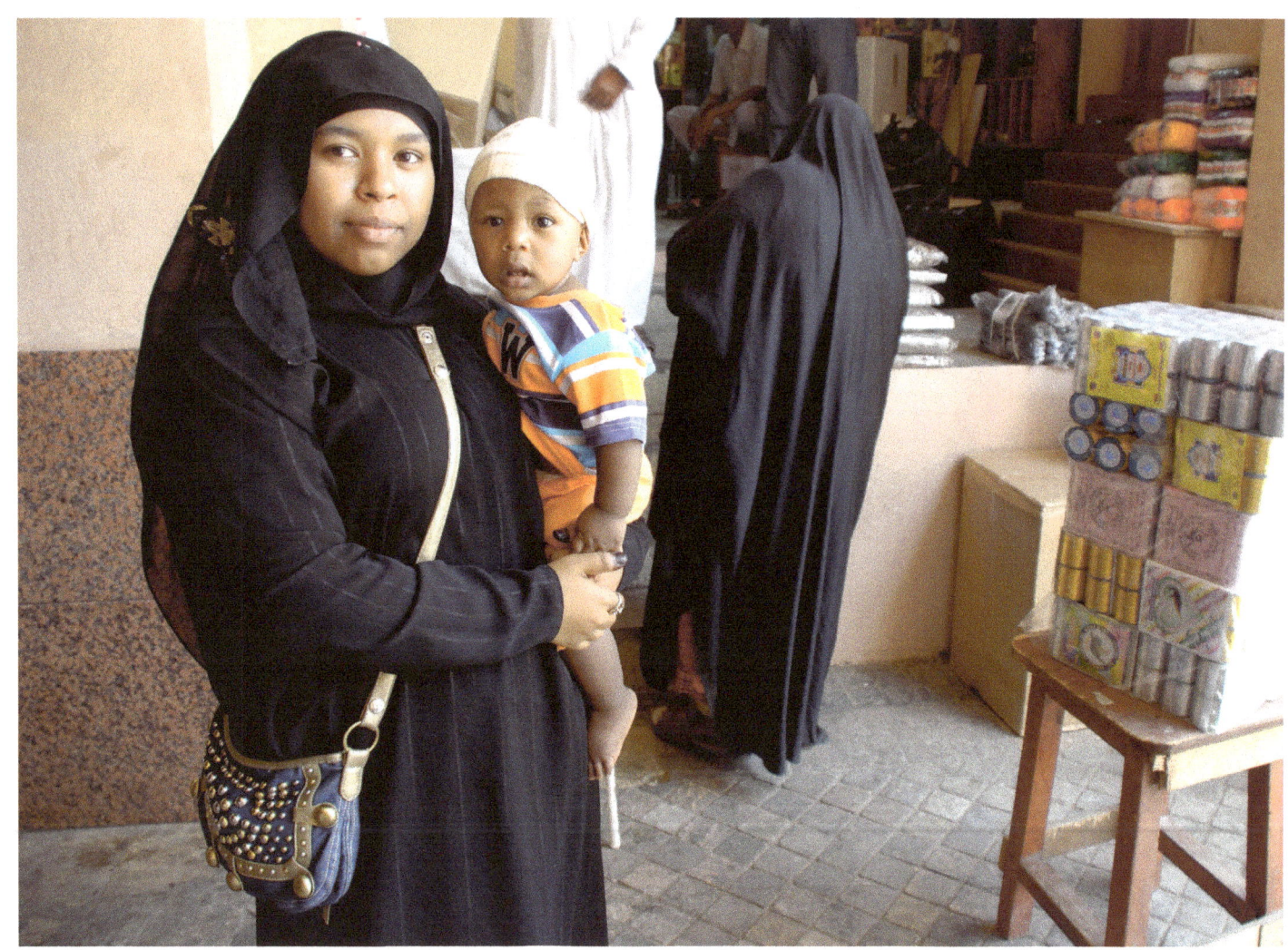

Scattered throughout Oman, the Ibadi Bedouins are living witnesses to the rapid transformation of a country that in a short time has gone from a total of two schools and an infant mortality rate among the worst in the world to being one of the most forward thinking in the Gulf.

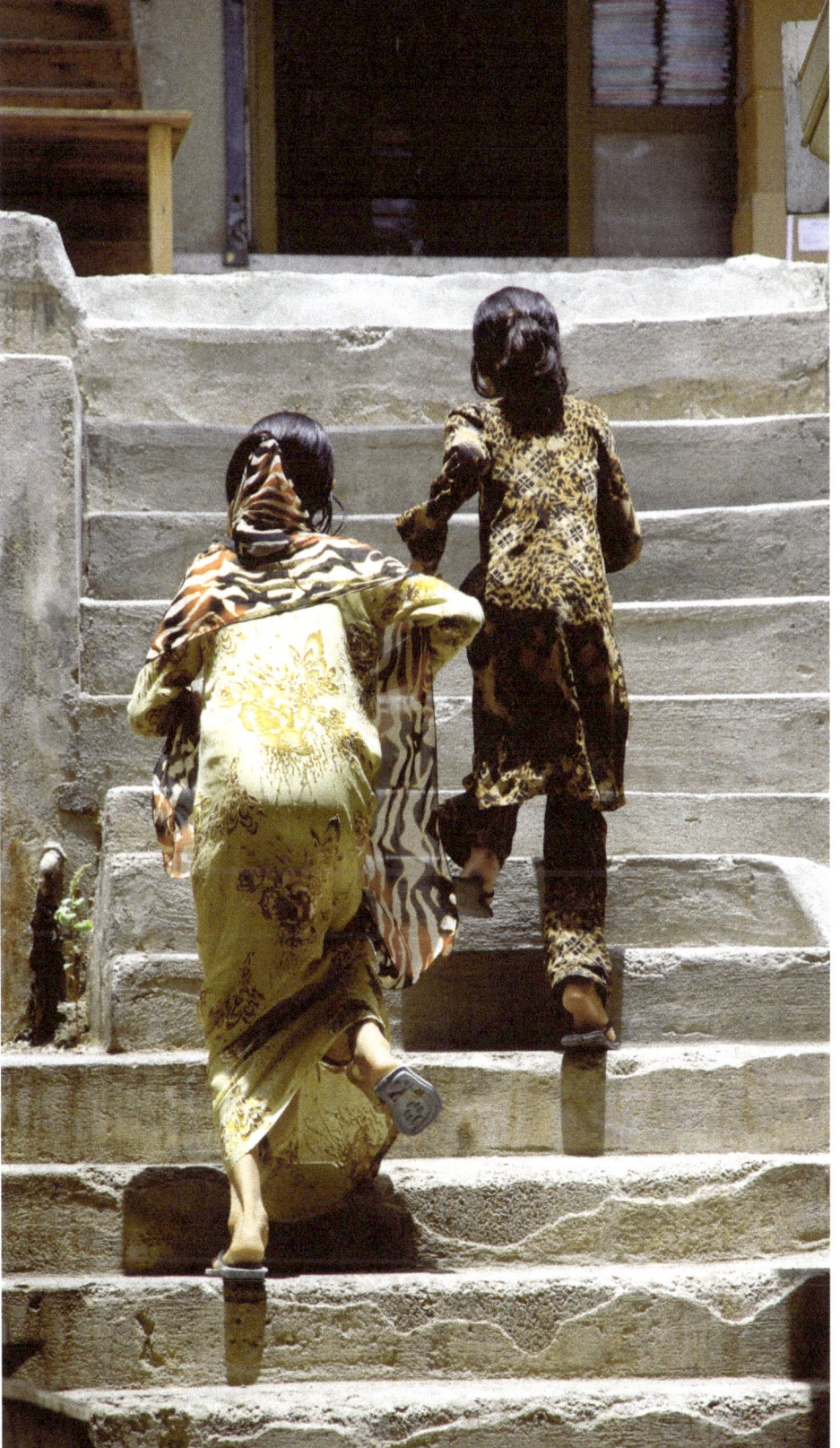

Two Omani girls play on the stairs. Muscat, Oman.

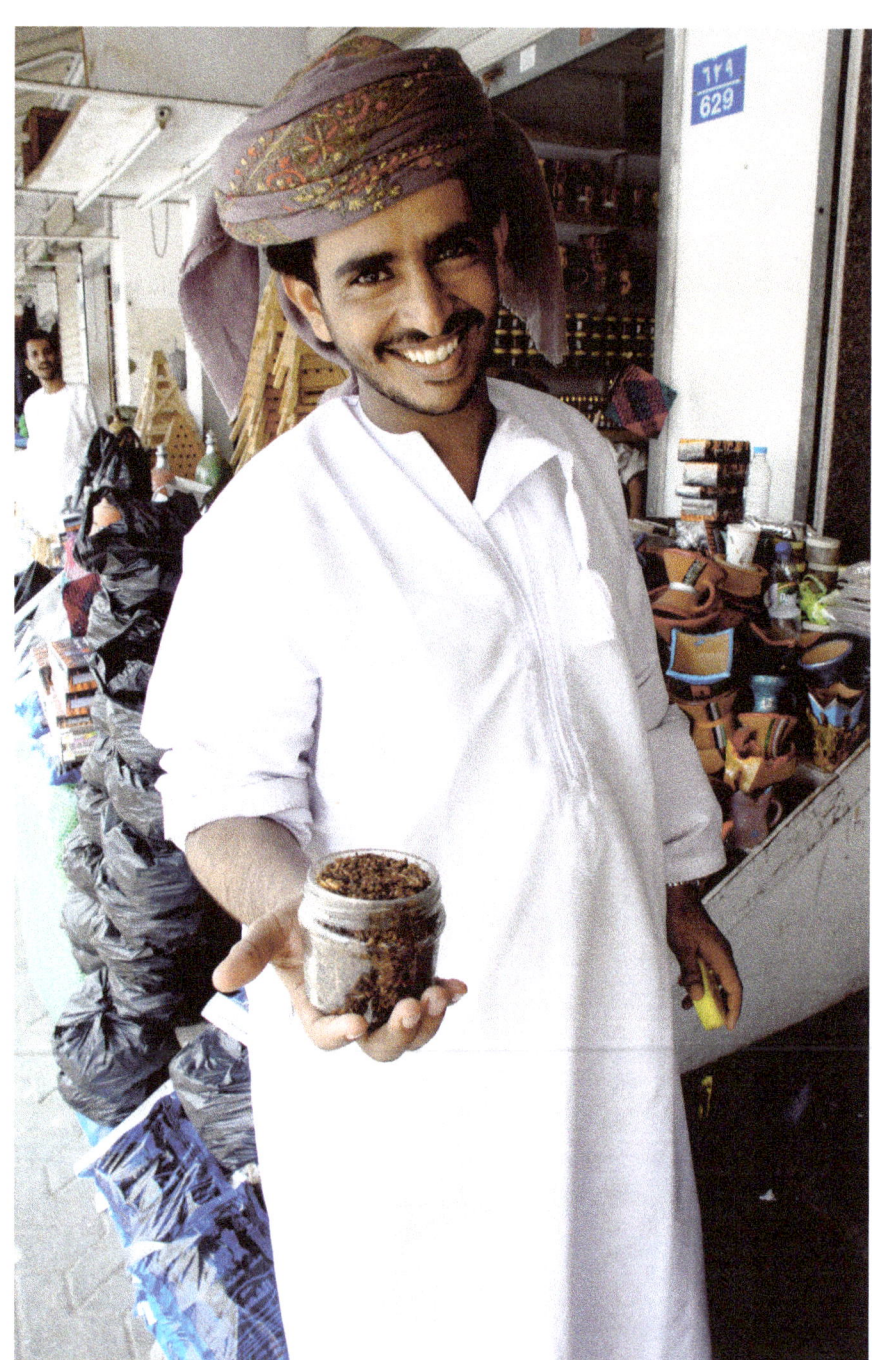

Many Omani men still trade frankincense, bitter coffee and very sweet dates, as well as their ancient solutions to the blistering heat.

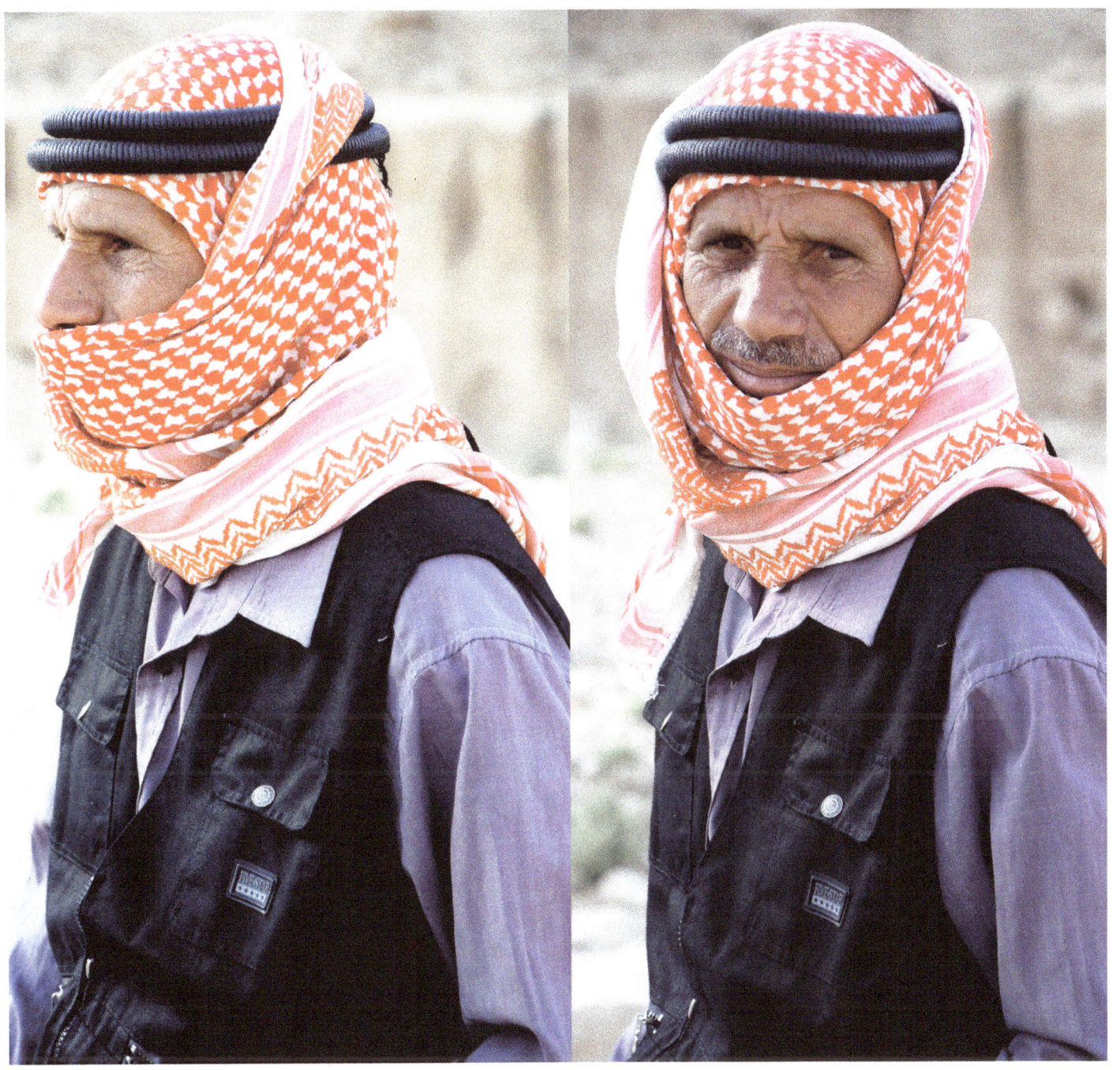

The Nabataeans who built Petra were traders, a tribe of Arabs who dominated the region from around 300 B.C. They were nomadic Bedouins. Petra, Jordan.

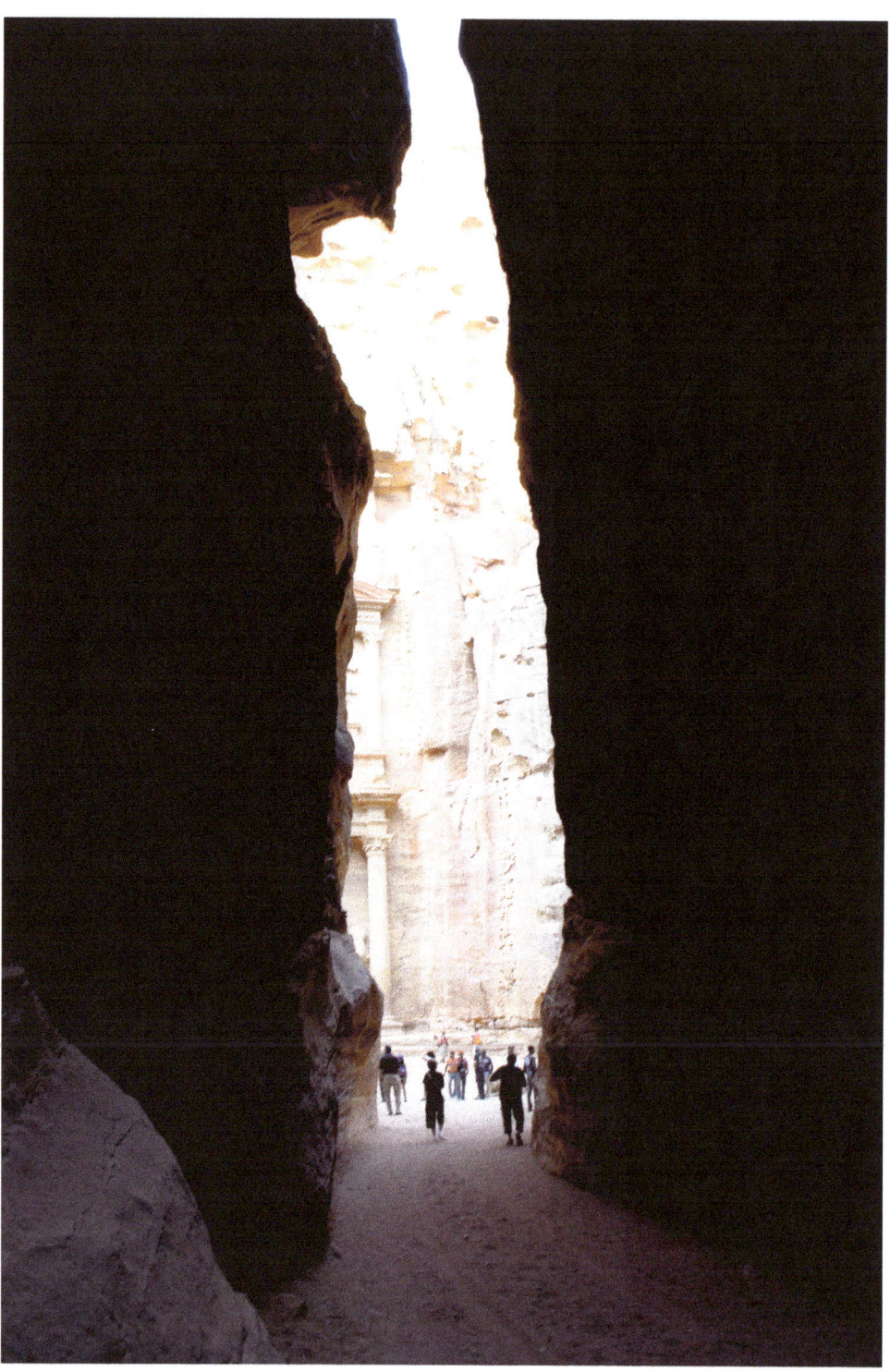

Roughly two miles square, Petra is a unique city carved from sheer red rock by the Nabataeans well over two thousand years ago. It is accessible only by a narrow, mile-long gorge called the Siq.

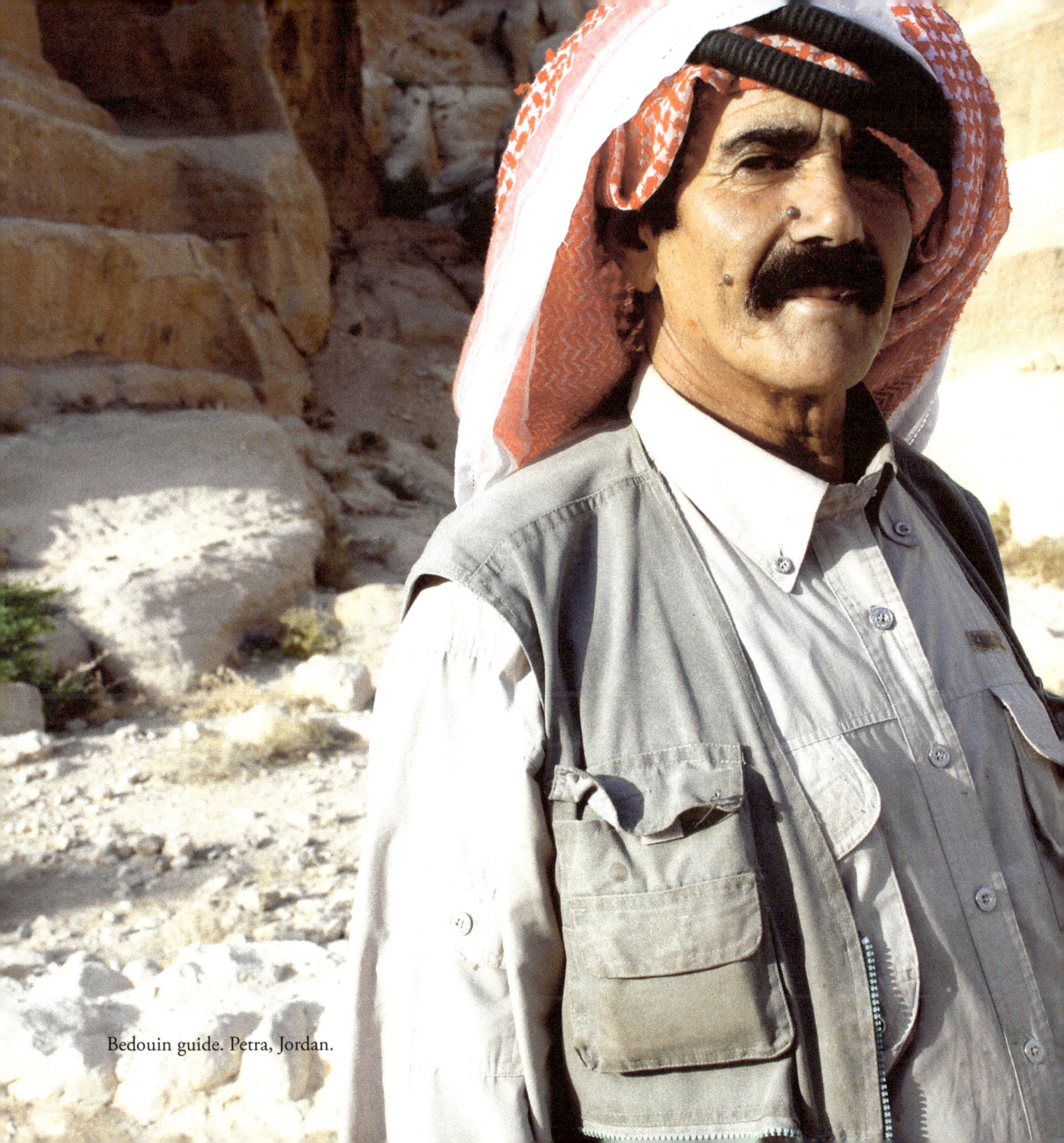
Bedouin guide. Petra, Jordan.

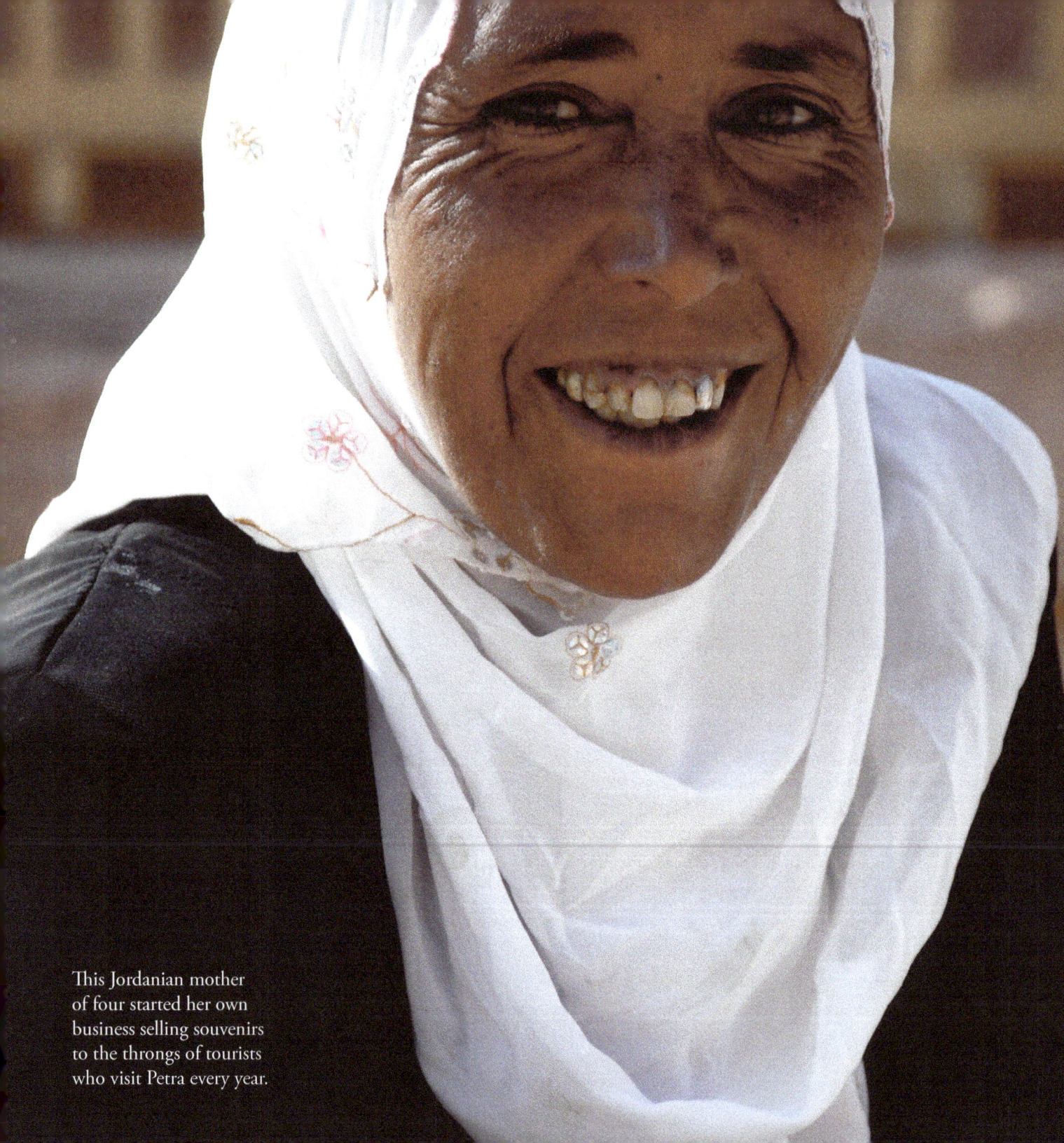

This Jordanian mother of four started her own business selling souvenirs to the throngs of tourists who visit Petra every year.

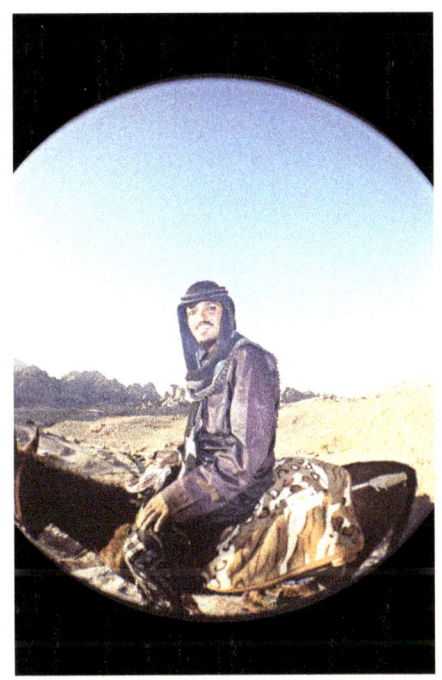 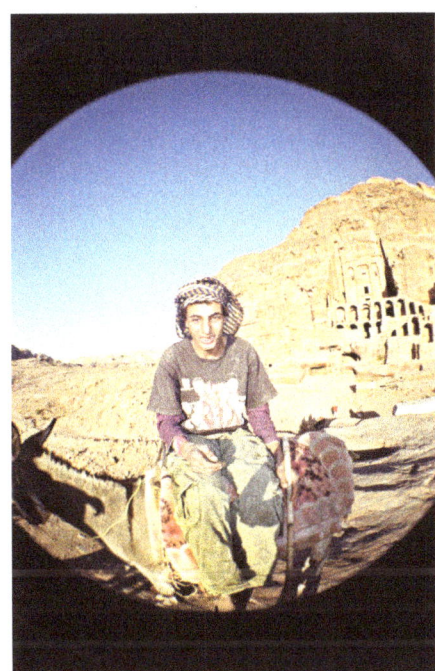 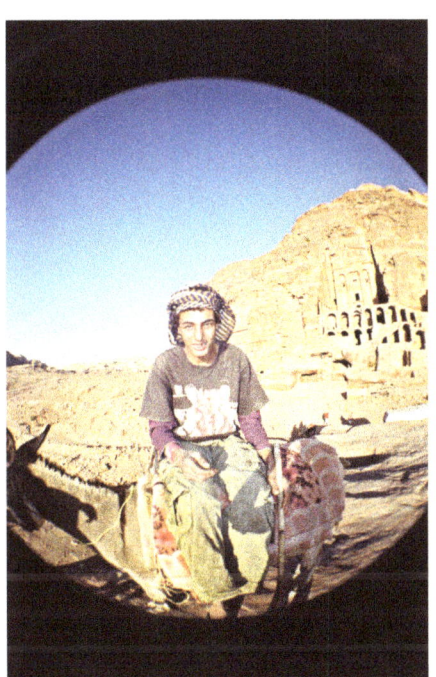

Today the Nabataean caves are home to only a few Bedul families. In the mid-1980s many of the Bedul agreed to move out of the caves and into a small village, Umm Sayhun, set on the edge of what is now designated as Petra National Park, Jordan.

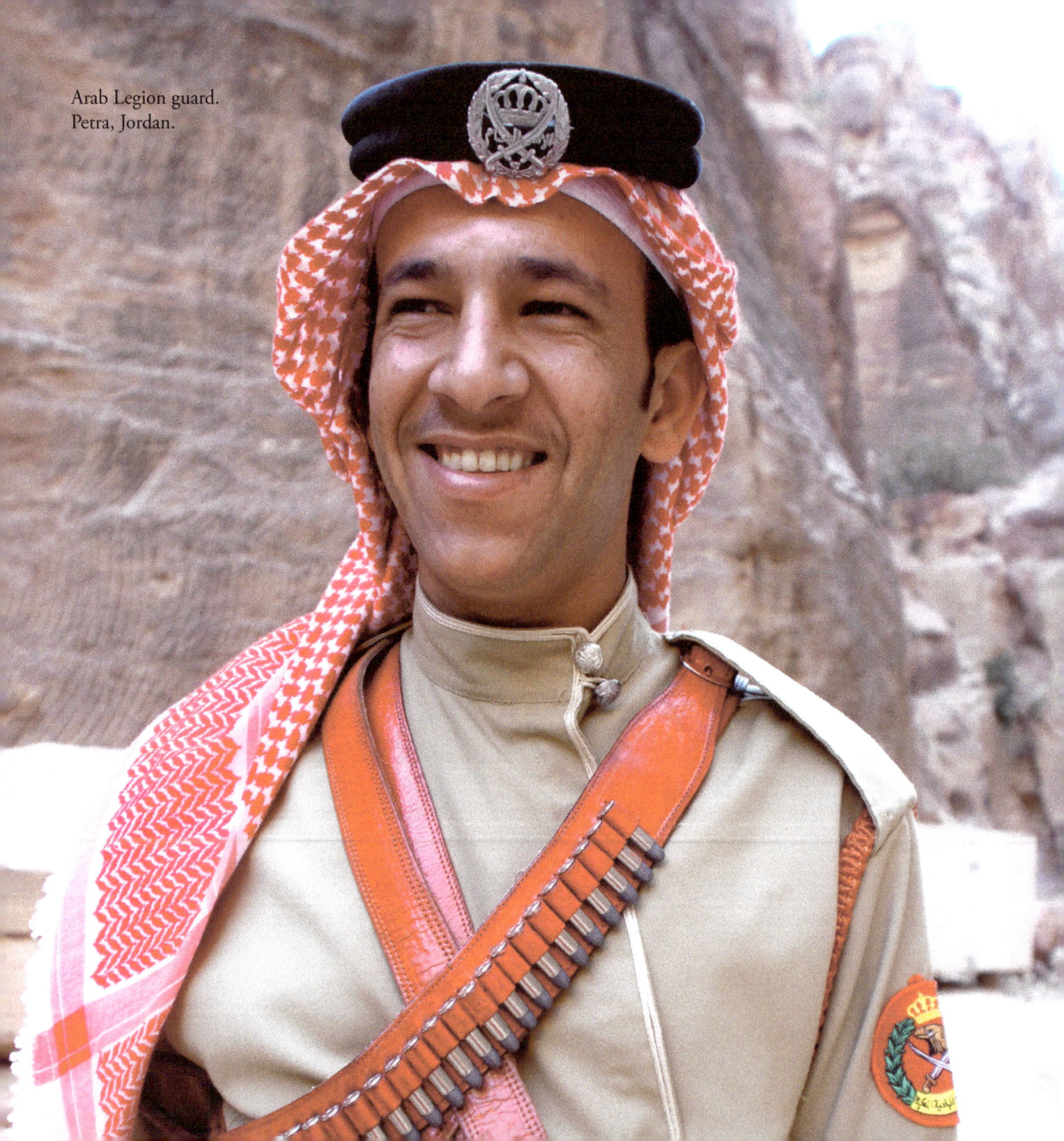

Arab Legion guard. Petra, Jordan.

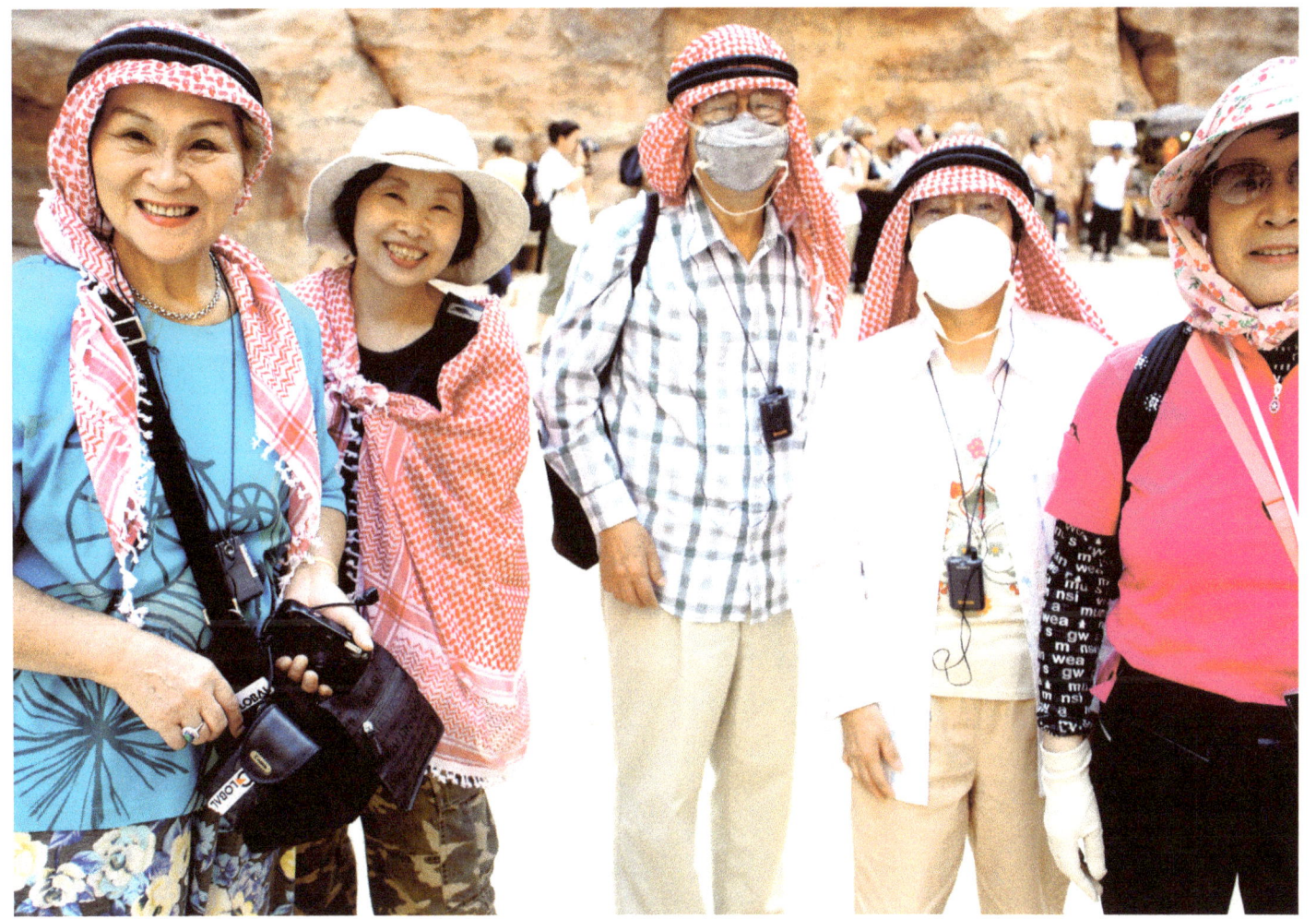

Throngs of tourists have caused most Bedul families to transition from their pastoral pre-market economy to a modern life in the government-subsidized village. The move has undoubtedly caused major erosions to their historical culture and way of life, and has thrust them into an uncertain commercial future. Petra, Jordan.

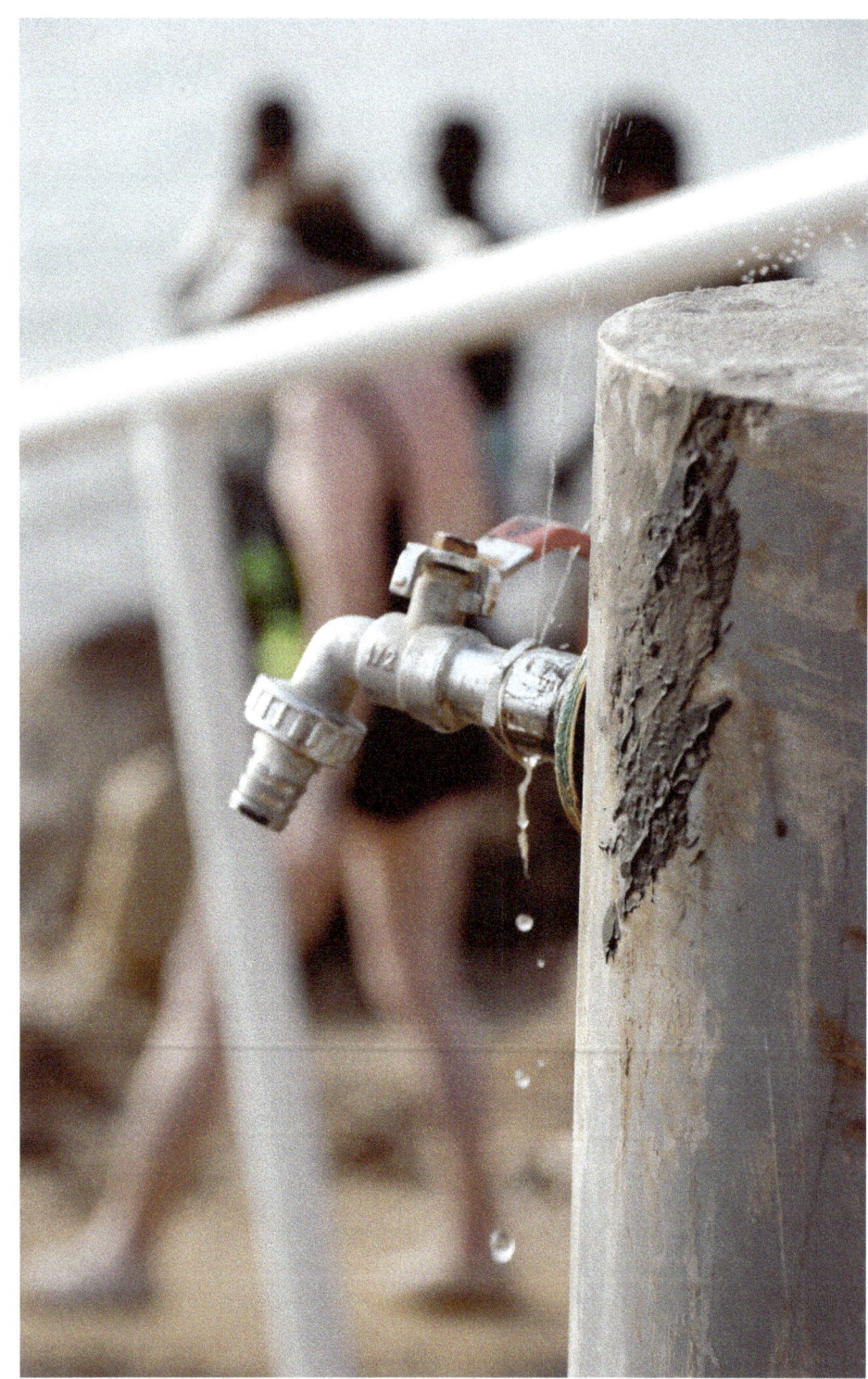

Dead Sea, Jordan.

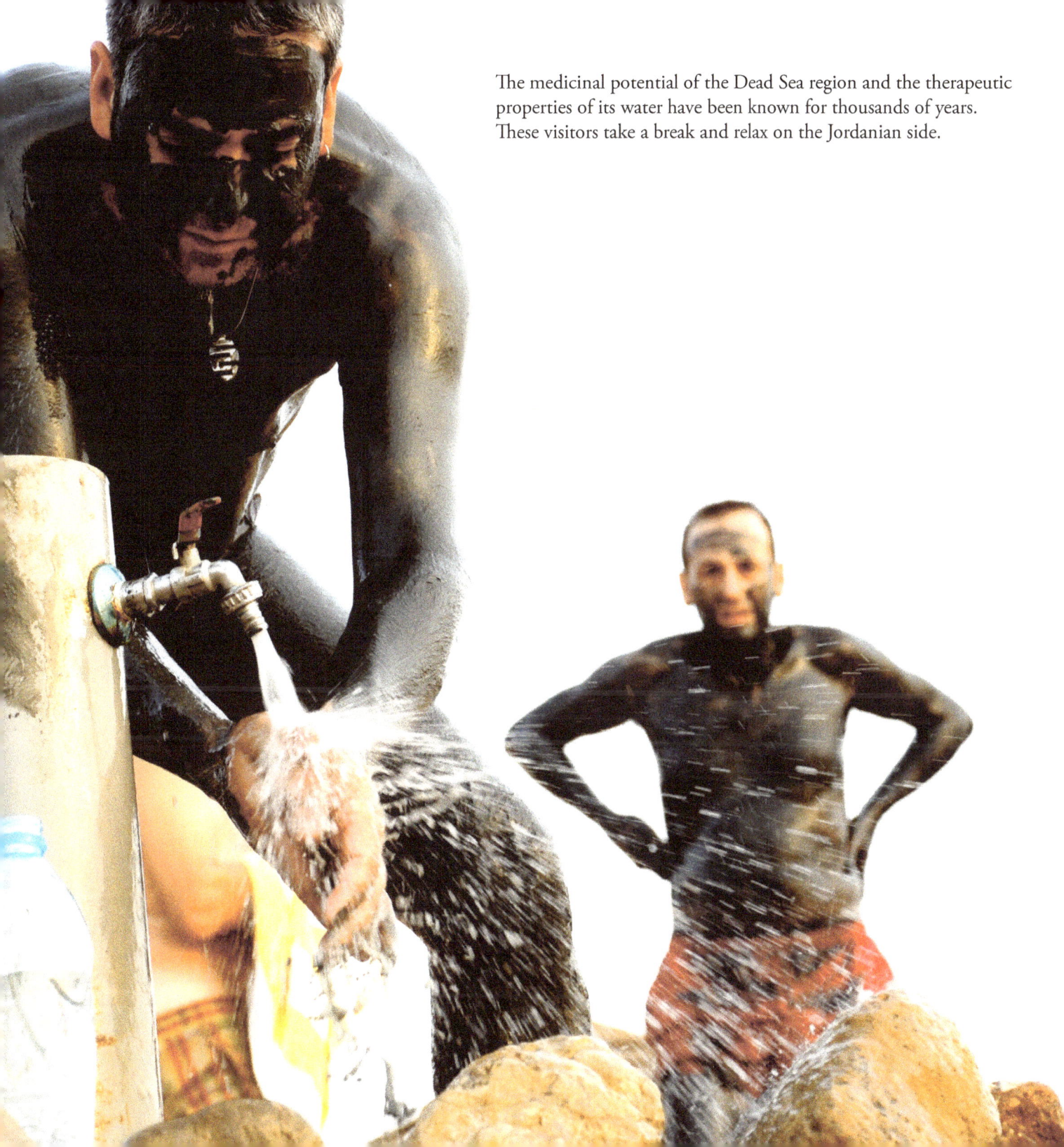

The medicinal potential of the Dead Sea region and the therapeutic properties of its water have been known for thousands of years. These visitors take a break and relax on the Jordanian side.

The high density of the Dead Sea makes swimming similar to floating. Here a father and daughter enjoy the daily papers while they float around in the Dead Sea in Jordan.

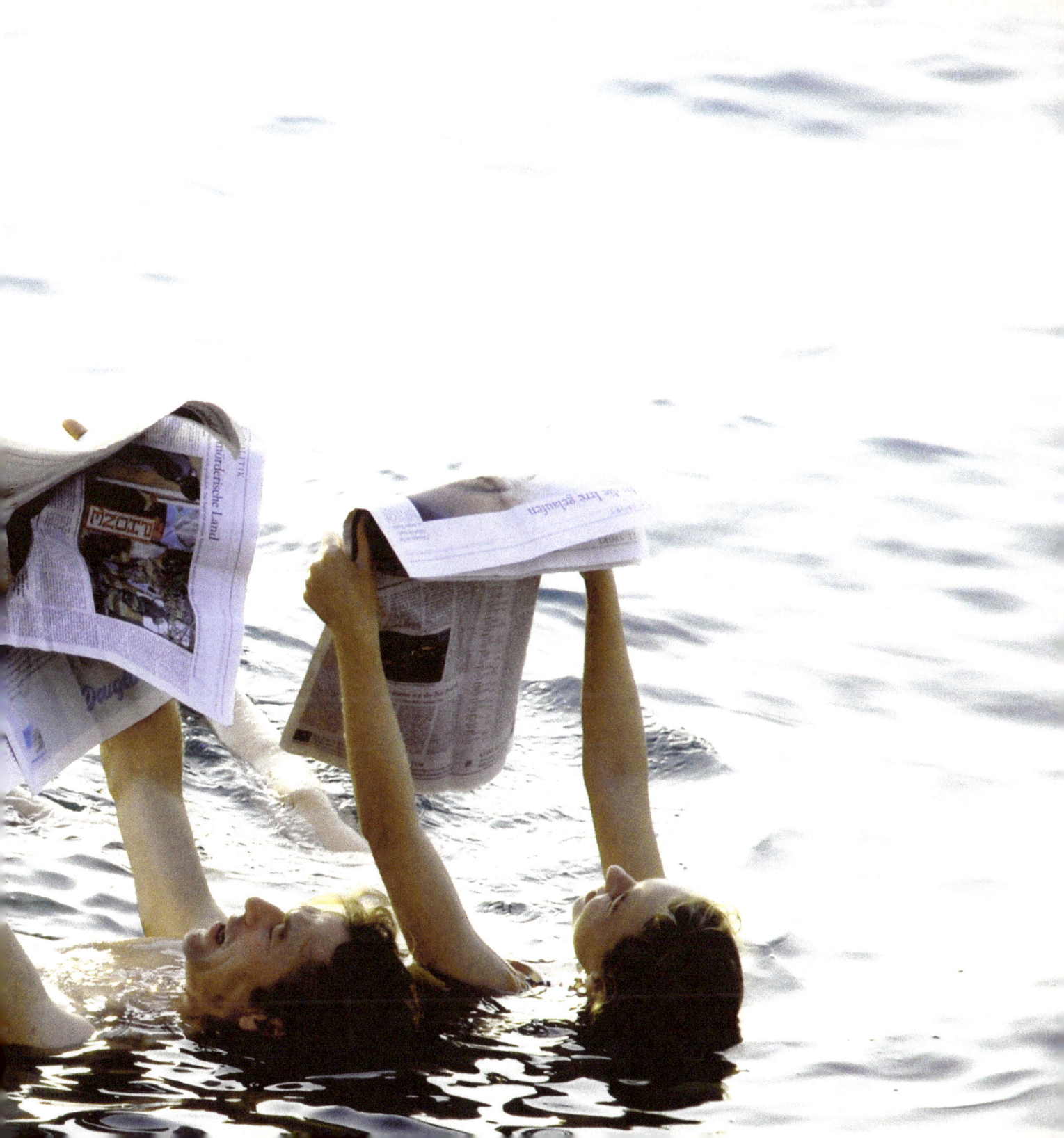

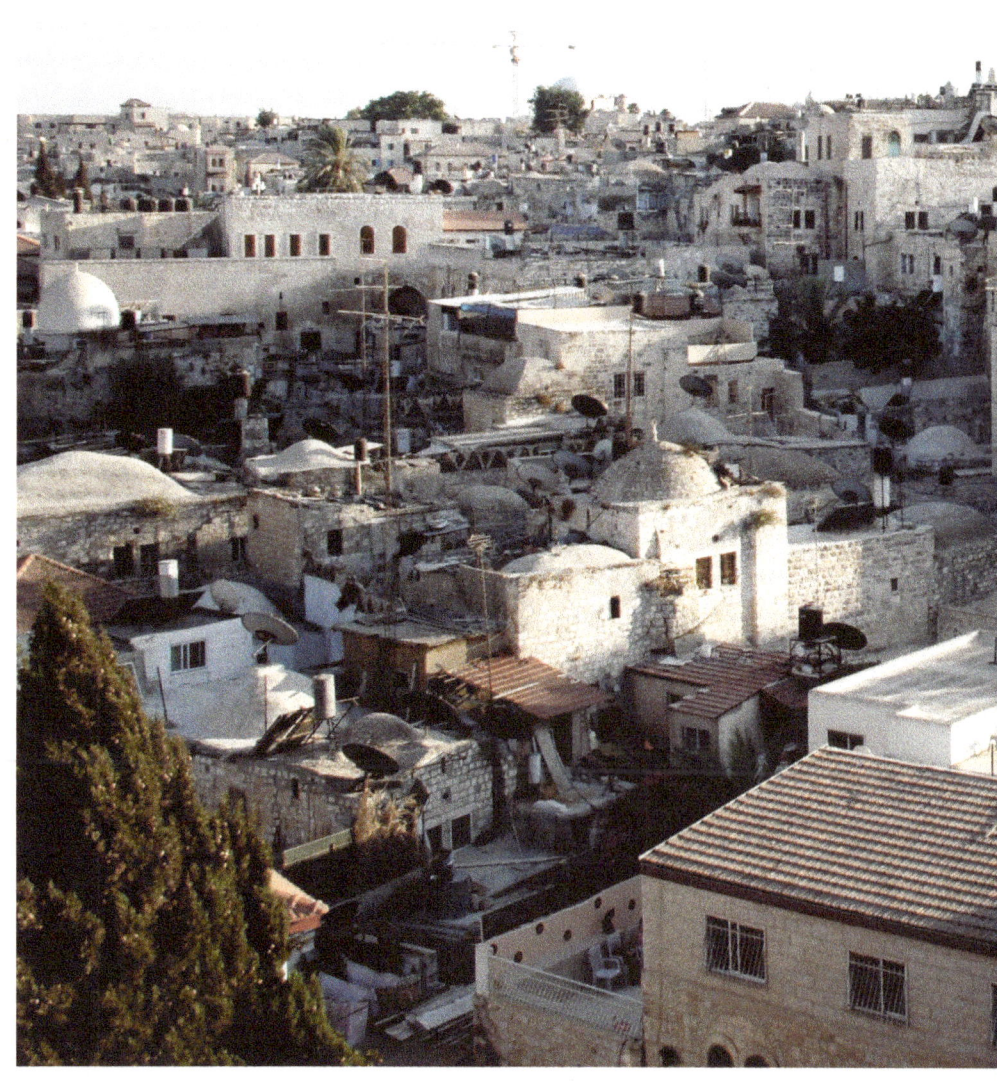

As the cradle of Christianity, the Middle East is home to some of the world's most ancient Christian denominations. Jerusalem, Israel.

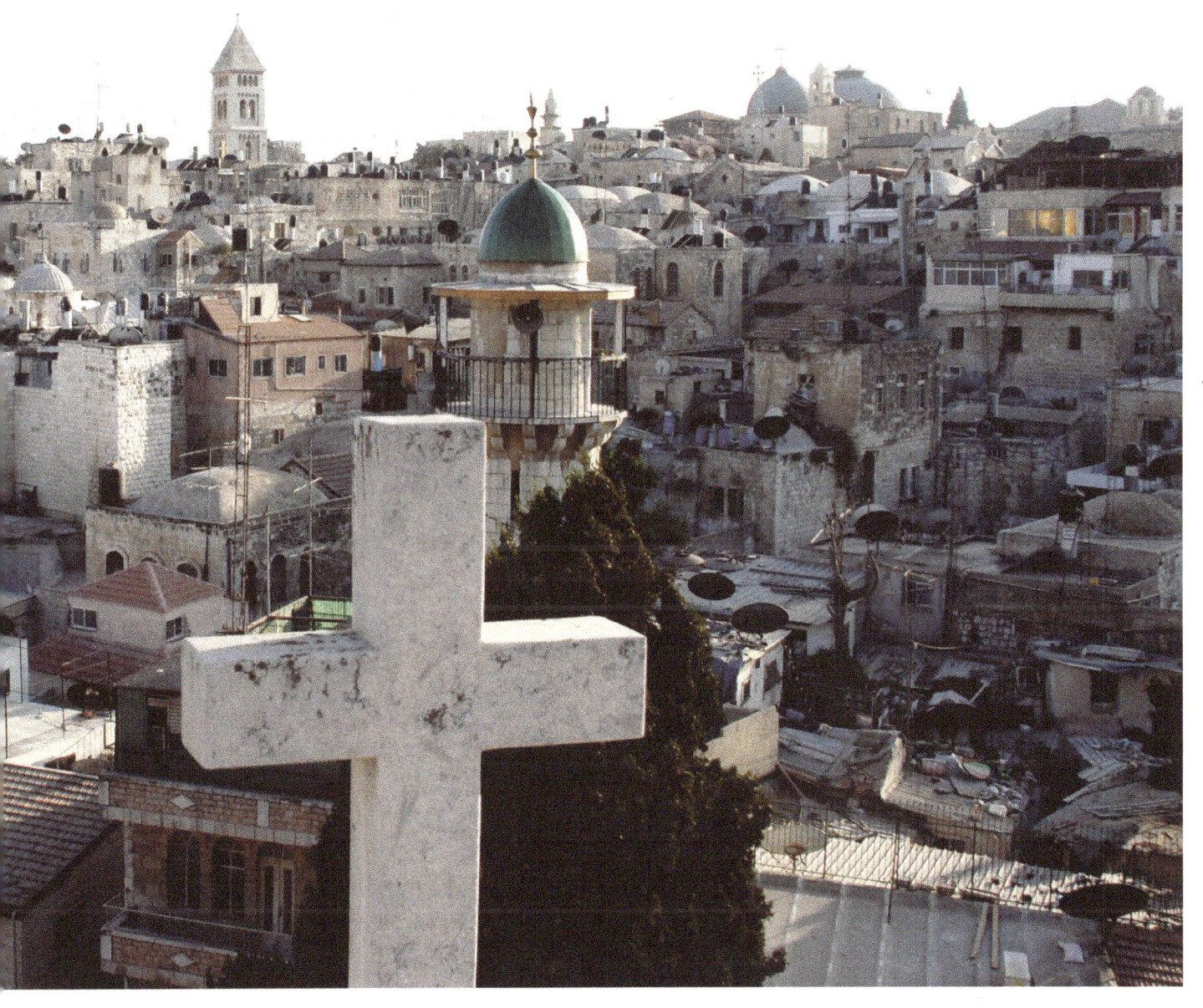

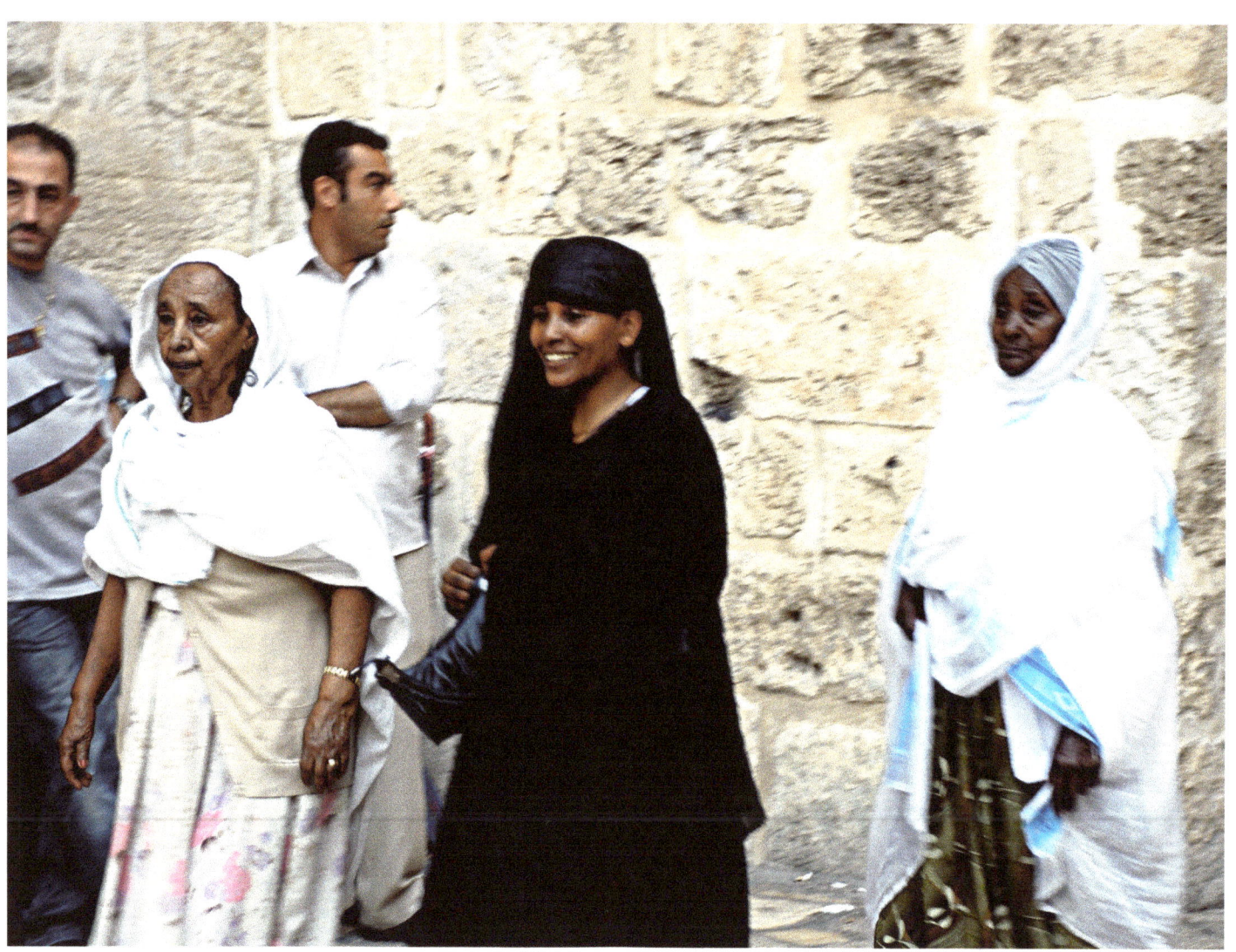

Ethiopian Christian pilgrims. Jerusalem, Israel.

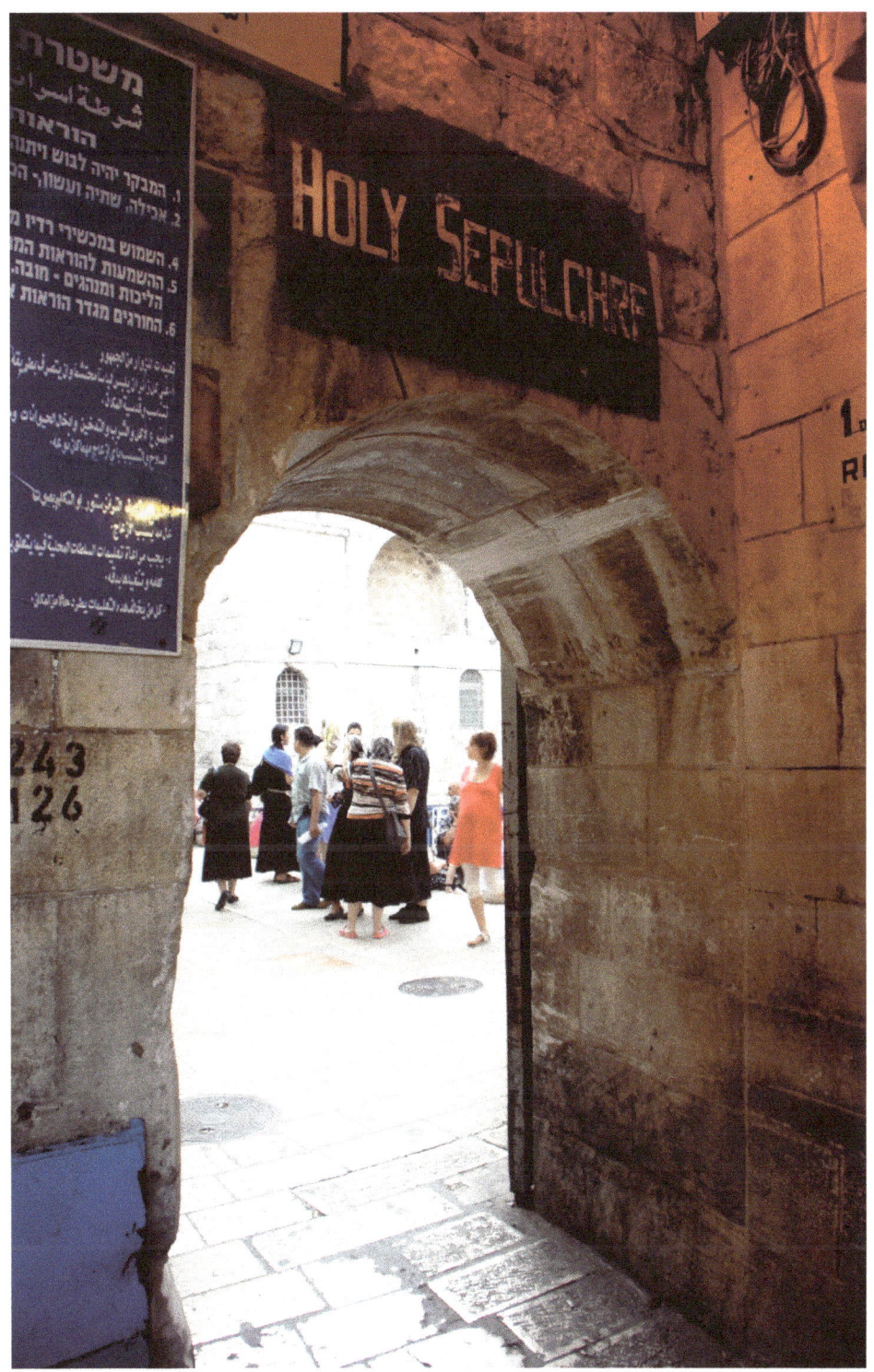

The entrance to the church of the Holy Sepulchre. Jerusalem, Israel.

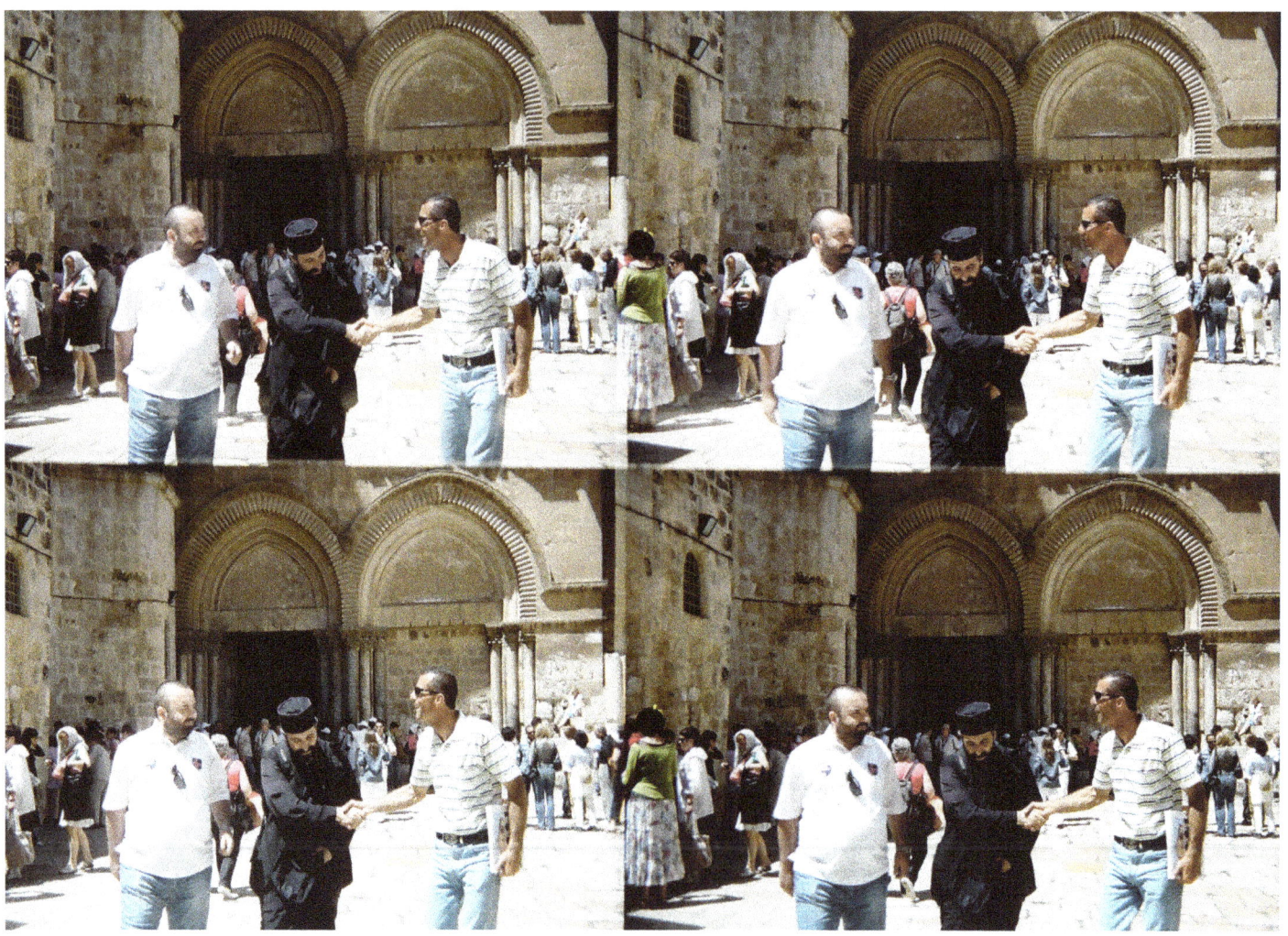

A Priest greets a worshiper outside the Holy Sepulchre which is also called the Church of the Resurrection. Located within the walled Old City of Jerusalem, the ground on which the church stands is believed to be Golgotha, the Hill of Calvary, where the Bible says that Jesus was crucified. It is also contains the place where Jesus was buried and resurrected. (The Sepulchre).

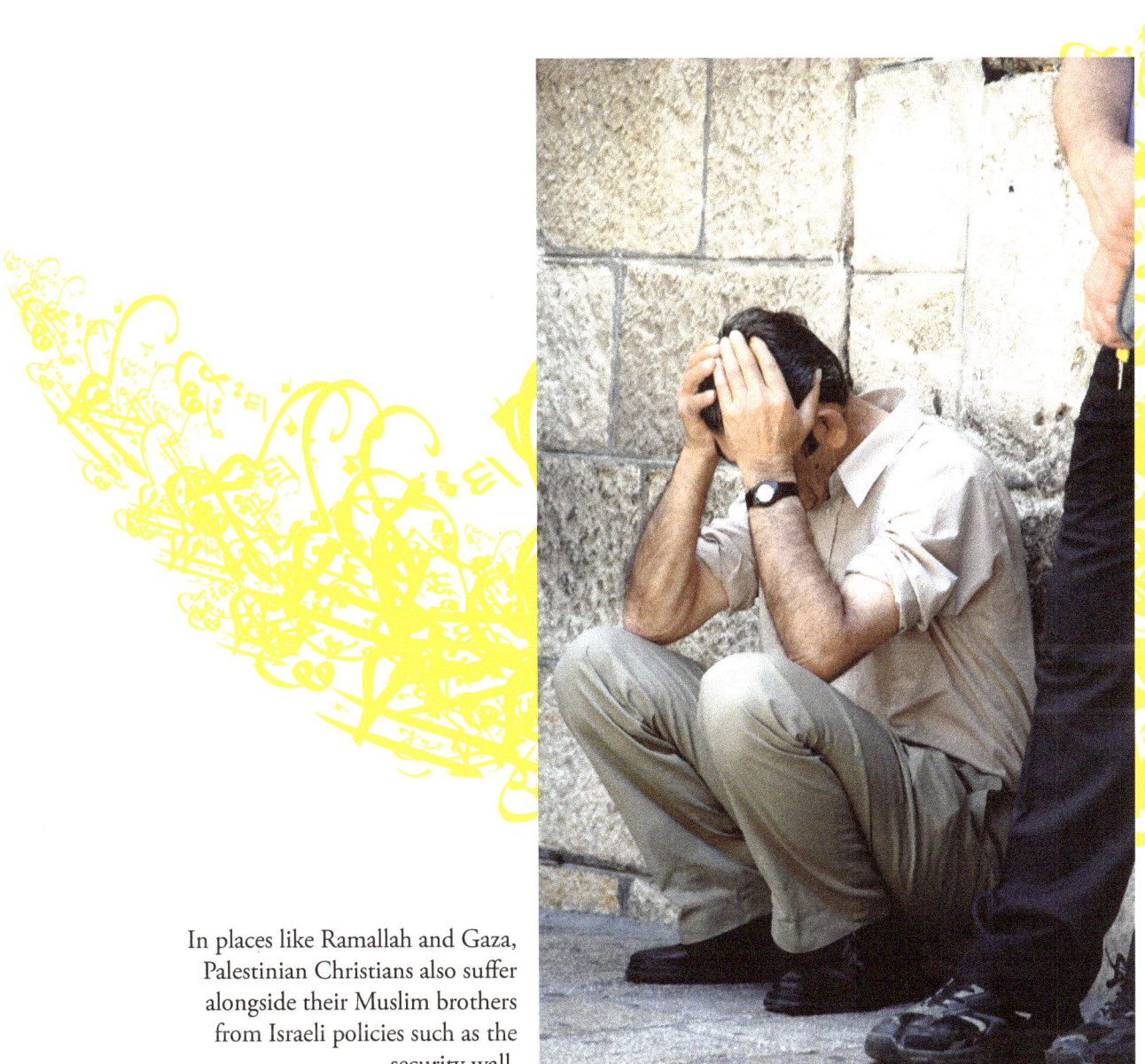

In places like Ramallah and Gaza, Palestinian Christians also suffer alongside their Muslim brothers from Israeli policies such as the security wall.

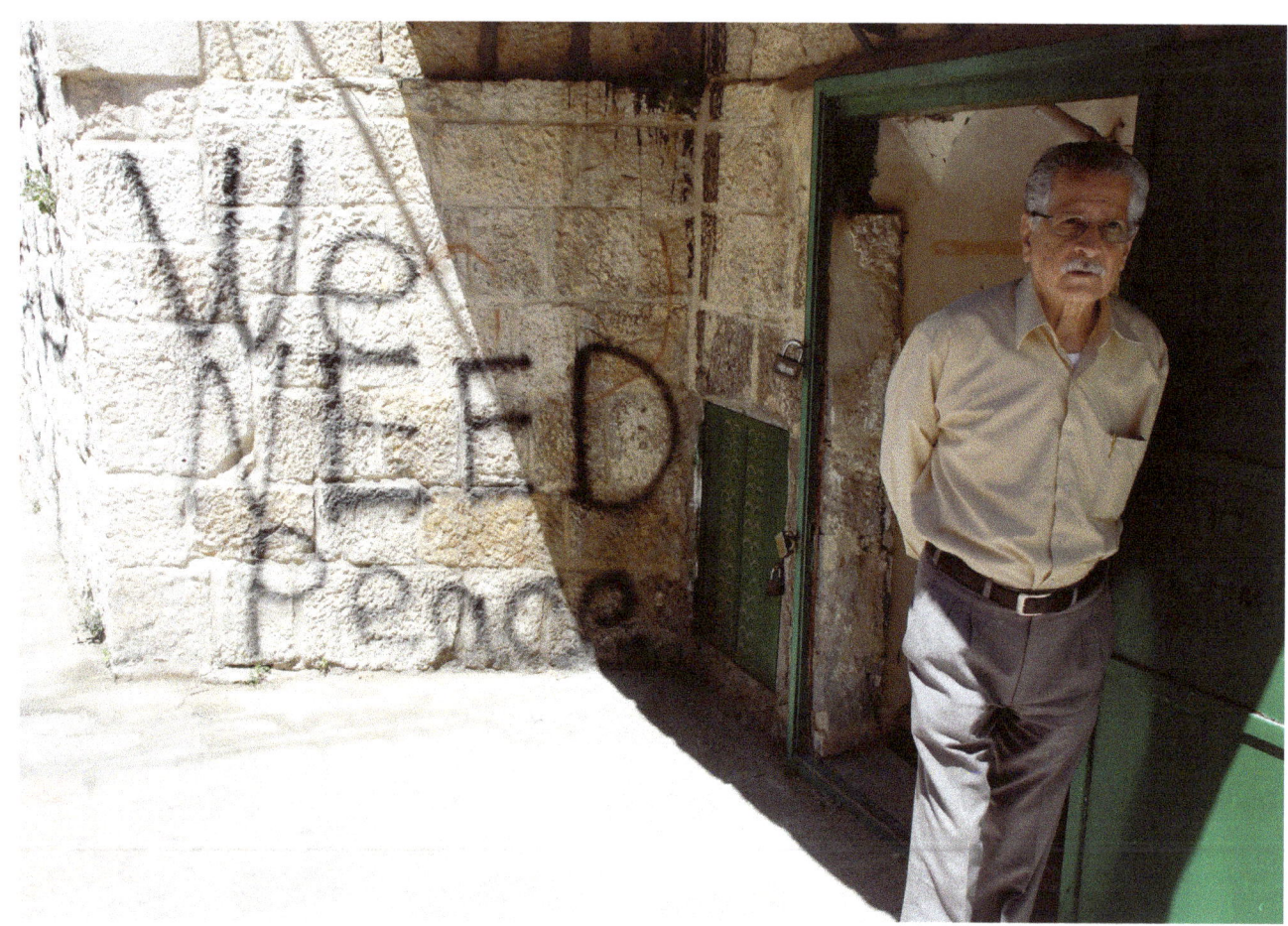

A Palestinian man outside a shop in the Arab Quarter in Jerusalem.

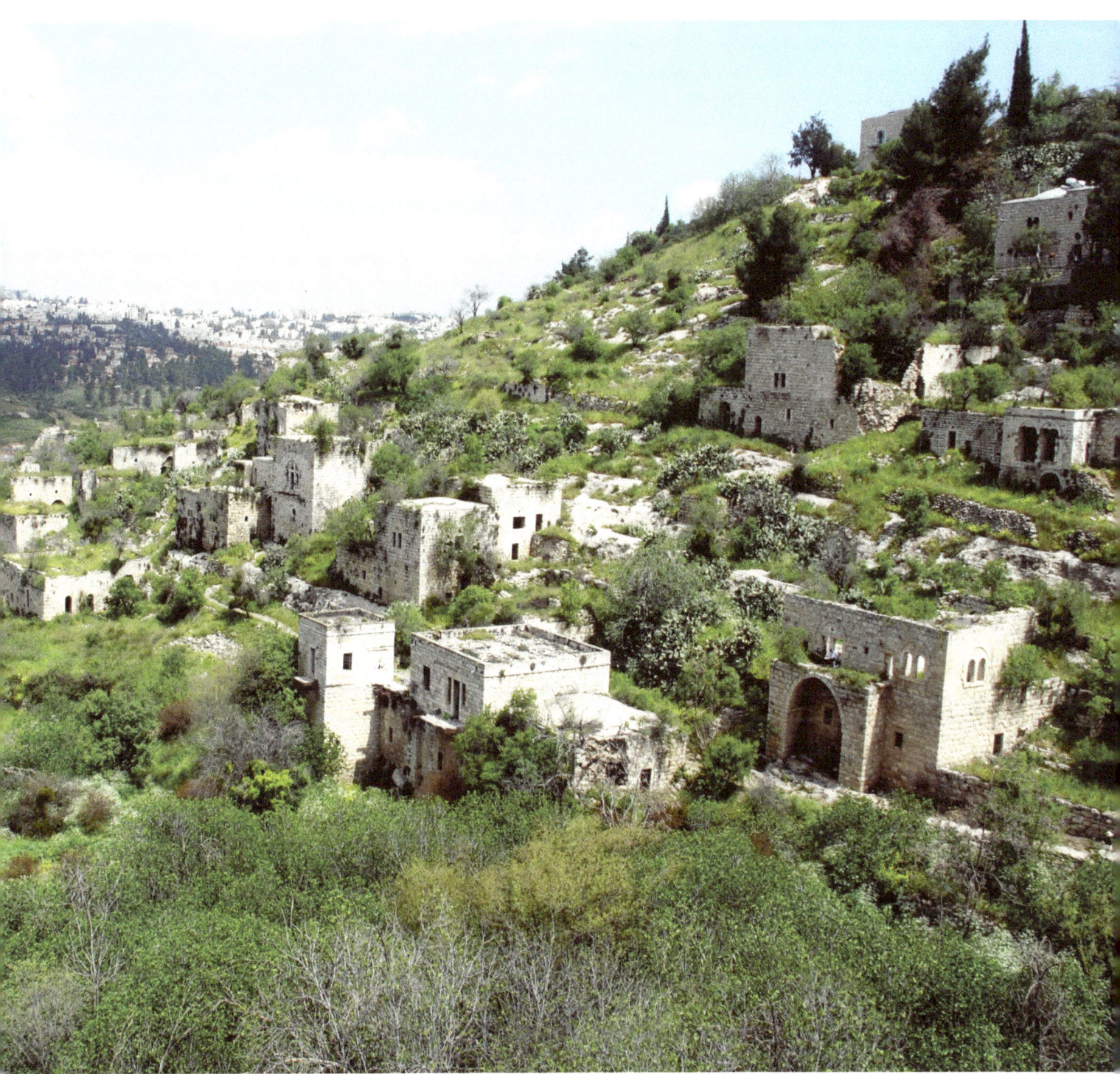
Abandoned Palestinian village. Jerusalem, Israel.

المصباح الهادي

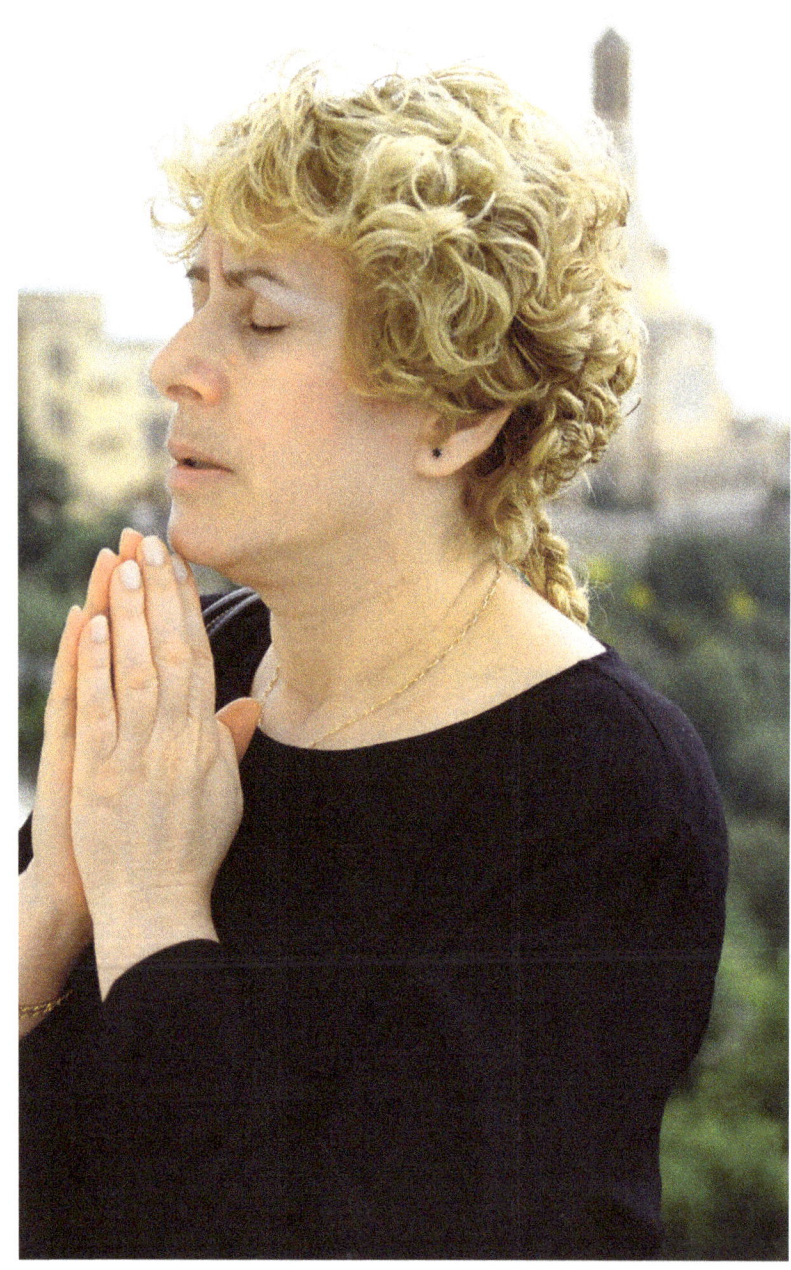

A Lebanese woman prays at the Our lady of Lebanon pilgrimage site located in Harissa - a village which is located 650 meters above sea level. The pilgrimage site has a 15-ton white statue of the Virgin Mary that was made at the end of the 19th century. Inside the statue's base there is a small chapel. A huge modernistic Maronite cathedral built of concrete and glass stands right beside the statue.

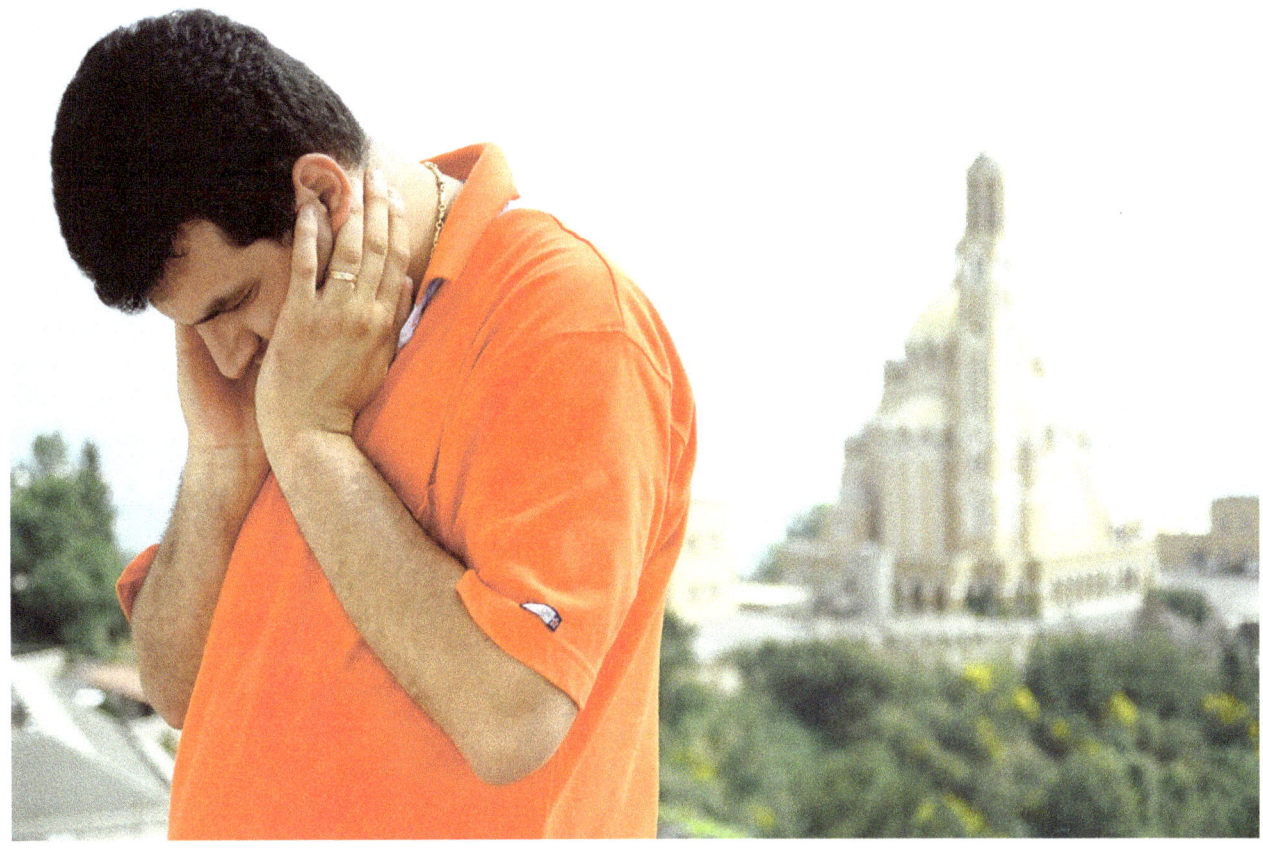

Lebanon's constitution dictates that the President is always a Christian, the Prime Minister a Sunni Muslim, and the parliamentary speaker a Shia Muslim. Lebanese Christianity is made up of two denominations; the largest are the Maronites, who traces their origins to a fourth century Syrian hermit called St. Maron. Though they have their own rites, the Maronites are in full communion with the Holy See in Rome. Beirut, Lebanon.

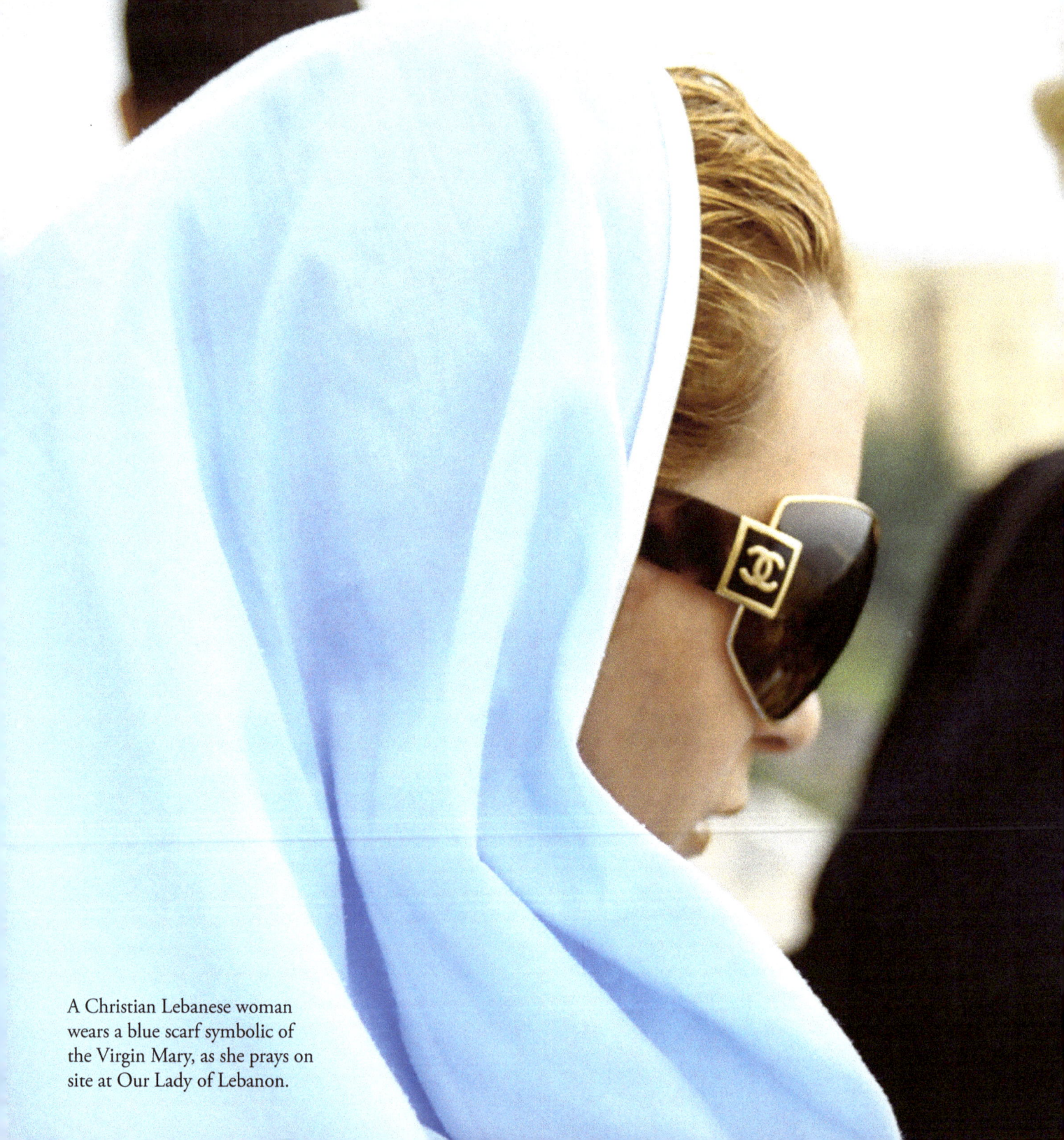

A Christian Lebanese woman wears a blue scarf symbolic of the Virgin Mary, as she prays on site at Our Lady of Lebanon.

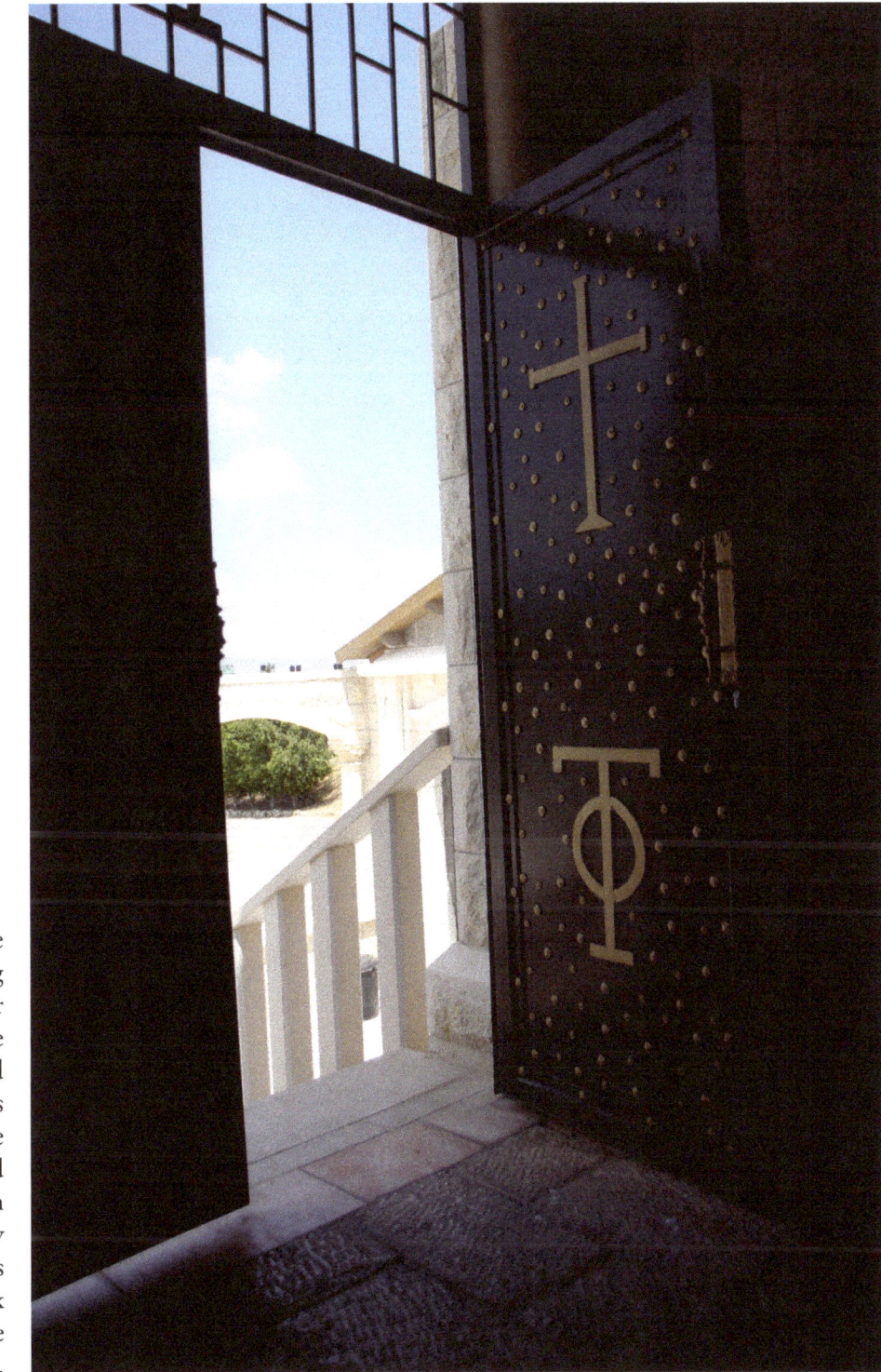

The Orthodox Church is quite strong in the Holy Land, along with a wide range of other denominations which all operate freely. This location pictured is also the place where Jesus performed his first miracle at a wedding where he turned water into wine. In the 17th century Kafr Kana was officially recognized by the Vatican as Cana of the Galilee. The Greek Orthodox church of St. George was built in 1886.

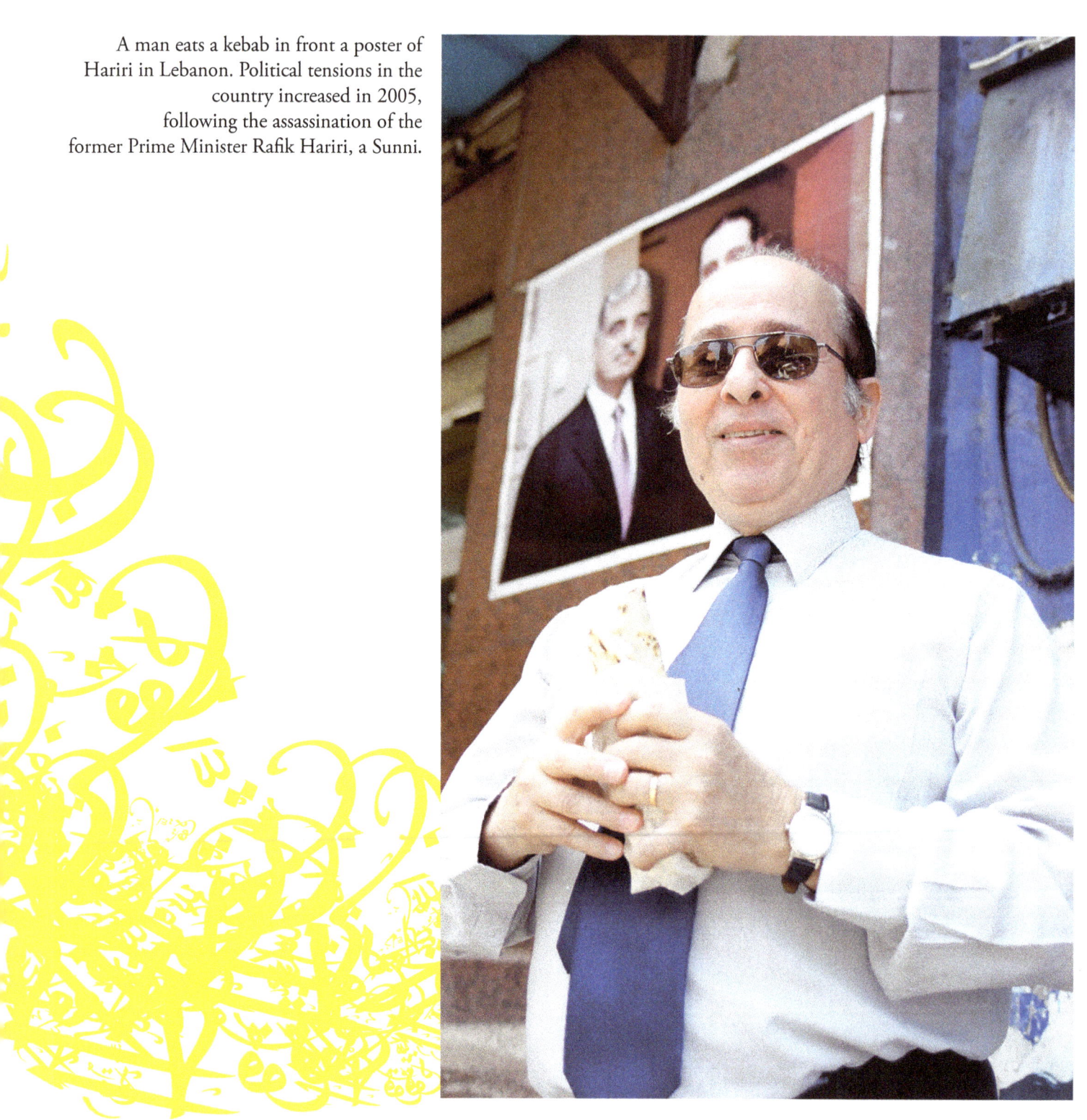

A man eats a kebab in front a poster of Hariri in Lebanon. Political tensions in the country increased in 2005, following the assassination of the former Prime Minister Rafik Hariri, a Sunni.

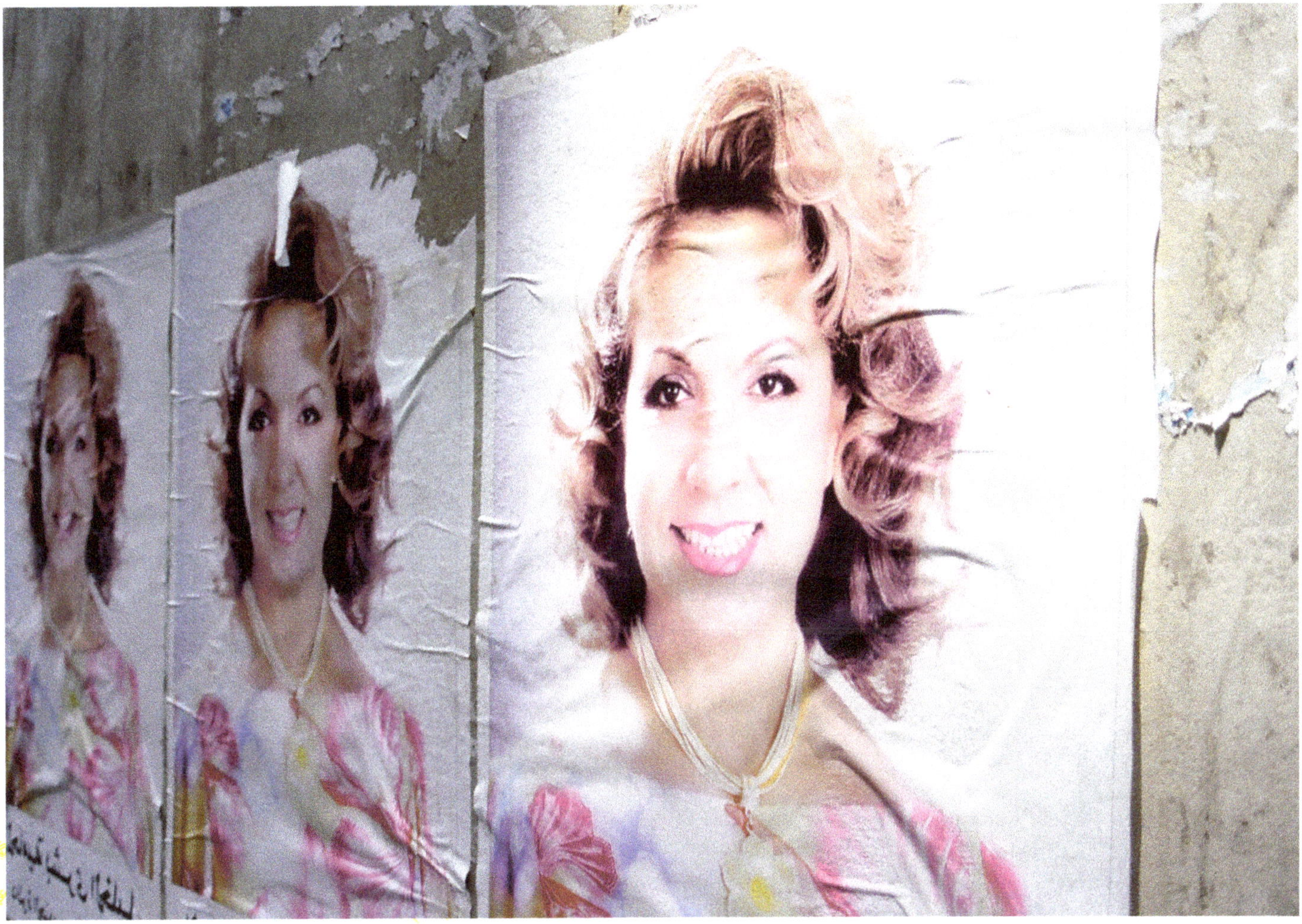

Political posters line the streets of Beirut, Lebanon.

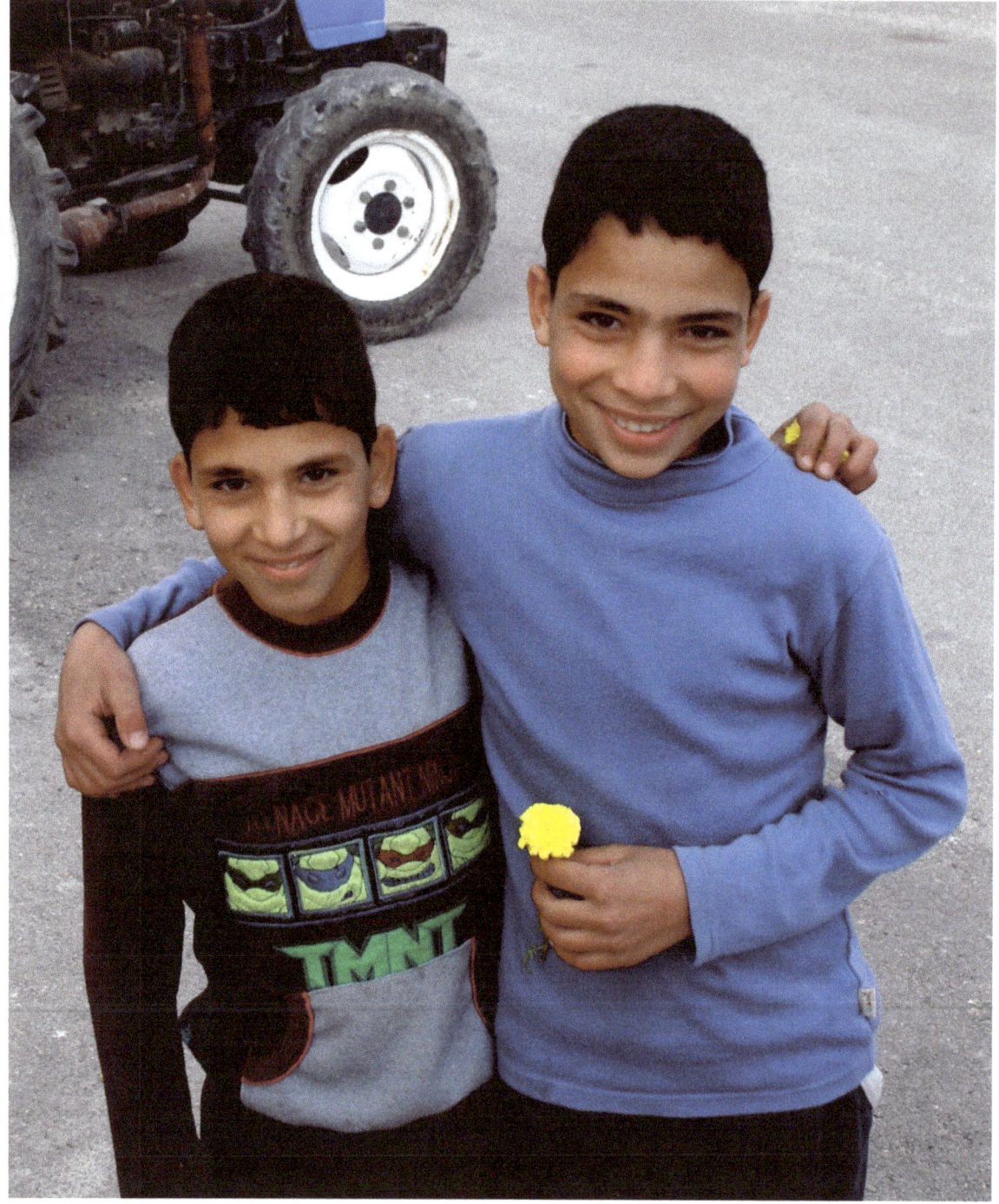

In Syria, the Christian minority makes up at least ten percent of the population, with the town of Malula, in the mountains some forty miles northwest of Damascus, being a cornerstone for the preservation and teaching of Aramaic, the language spoken by Jesus Christ.

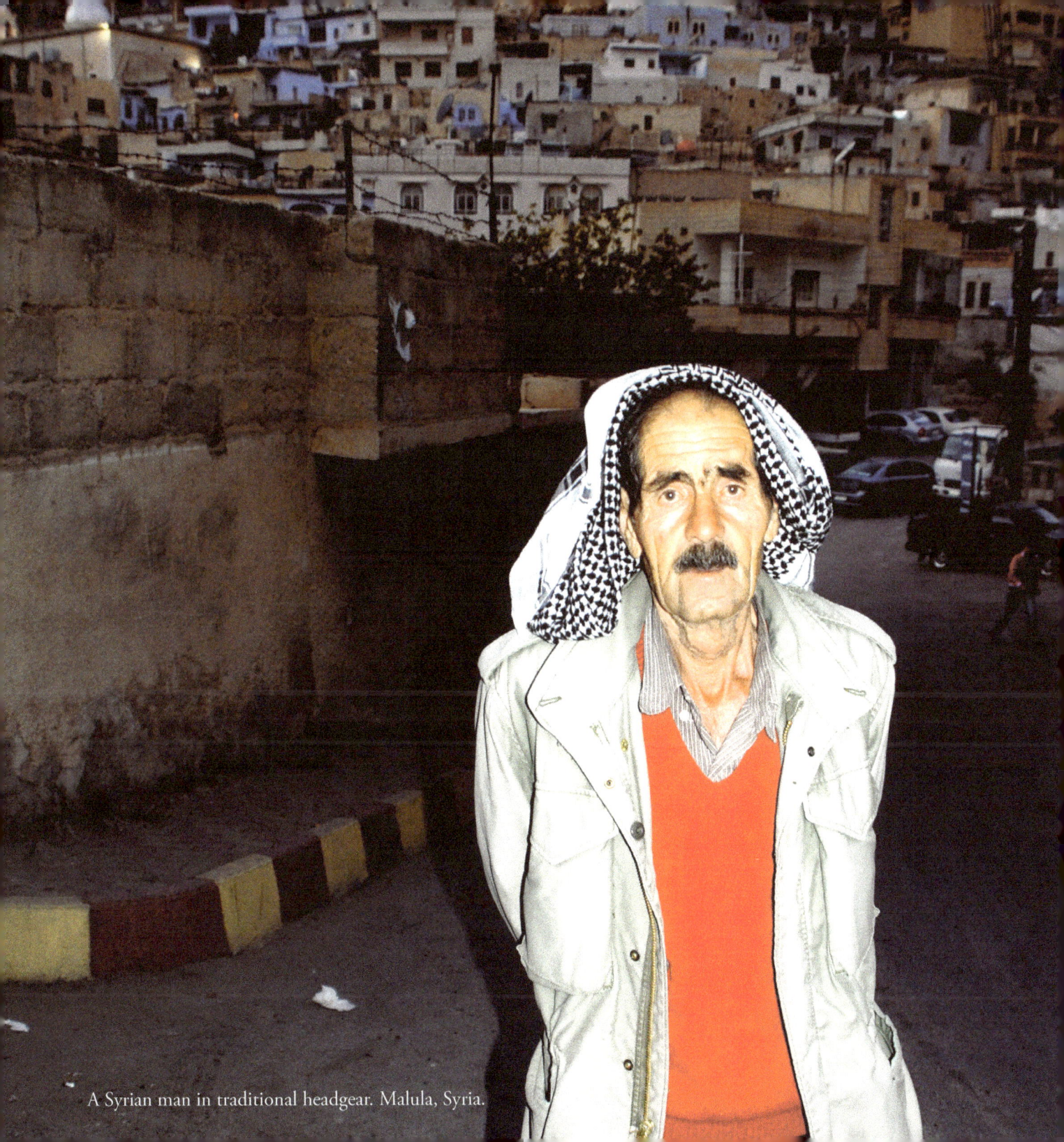
A Syrian man in traditional headgear. Malula, Syria.

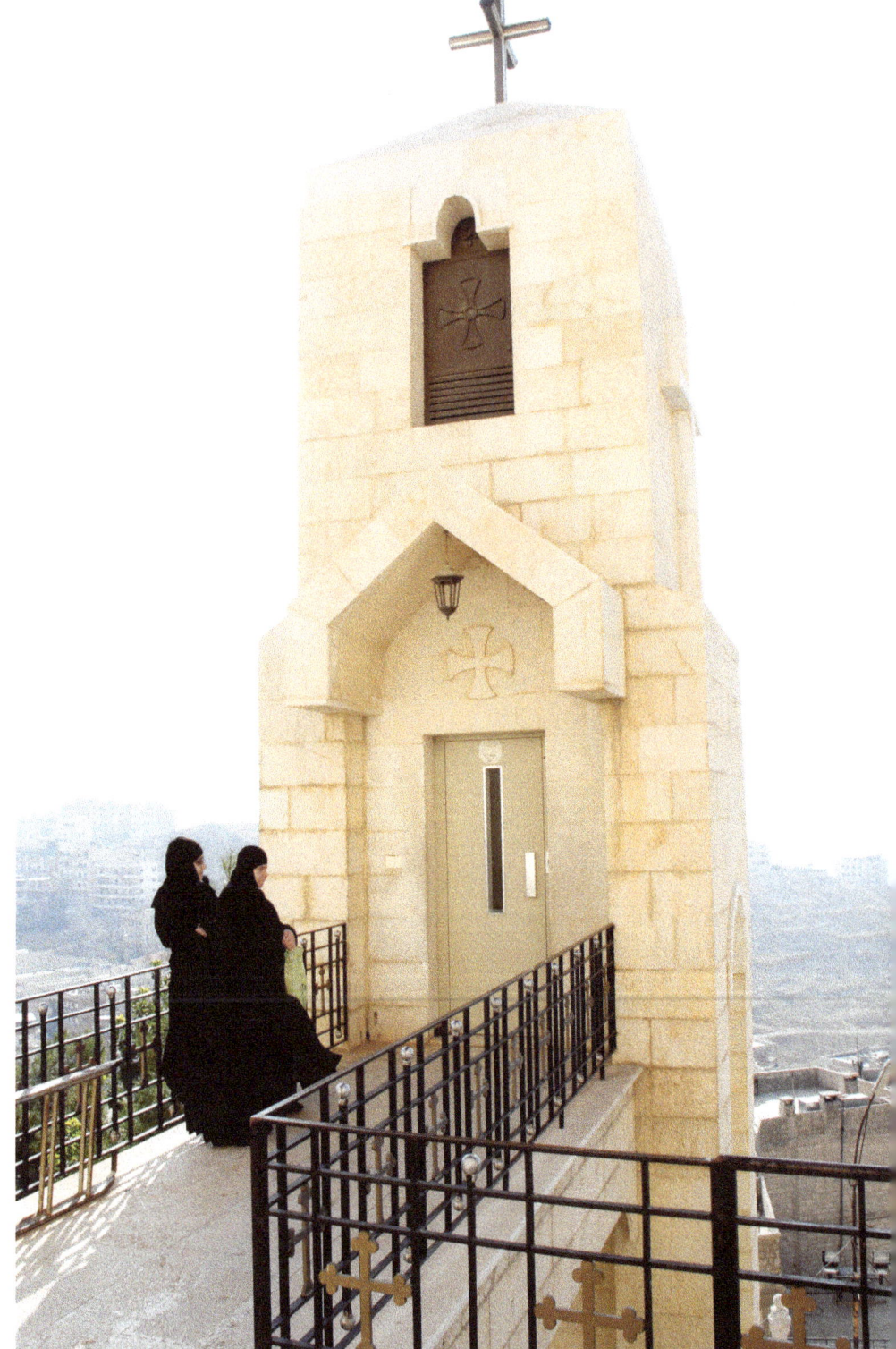

Hidden in the crevices of mountainous caves (in the time of Nero's Rome, these were hideouts for persecuted Christians) are several churches and a small community of some six thousand residents. These Christian nuns still speak Aramaic and use the churches as places of worship and also as a shelter for orphans. Malula, Syria.

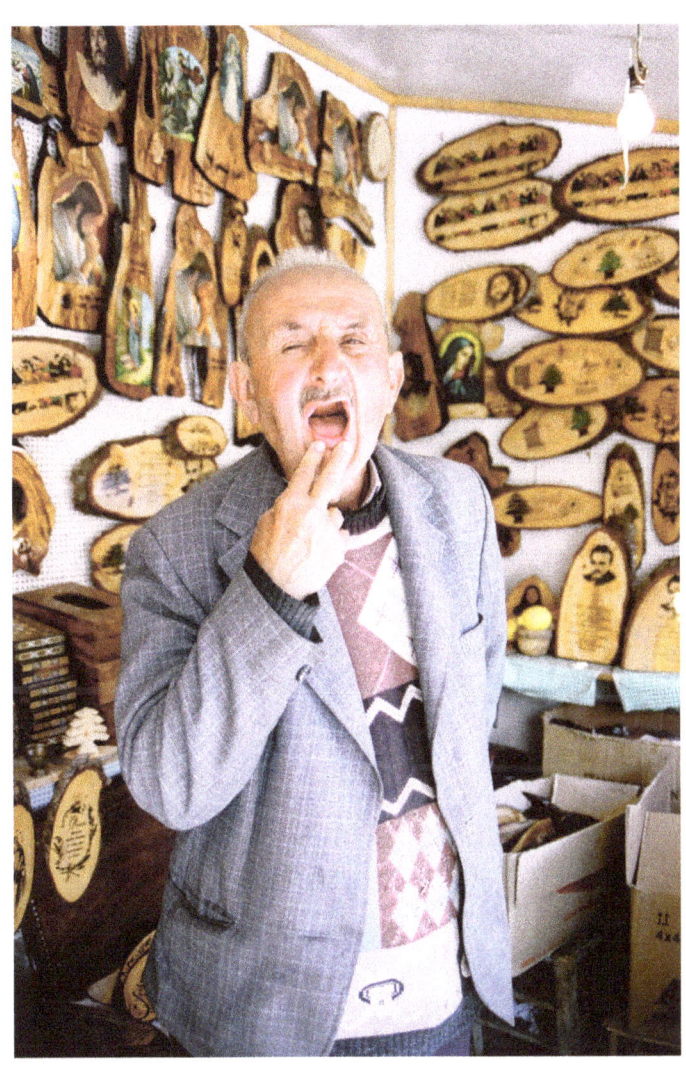 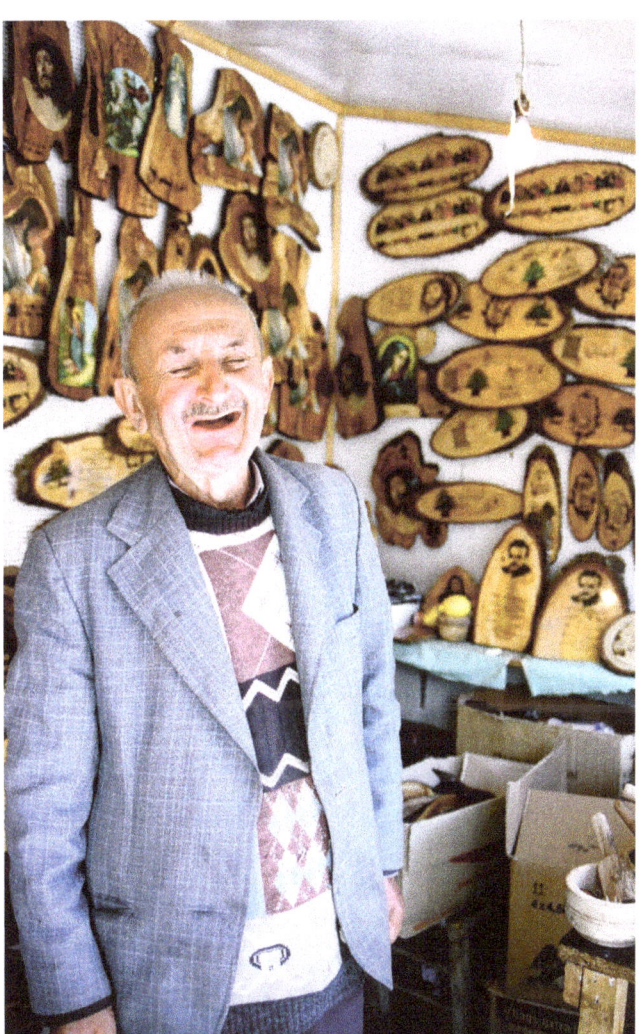

This man explains where he was shot, during clashes in Lebanon.

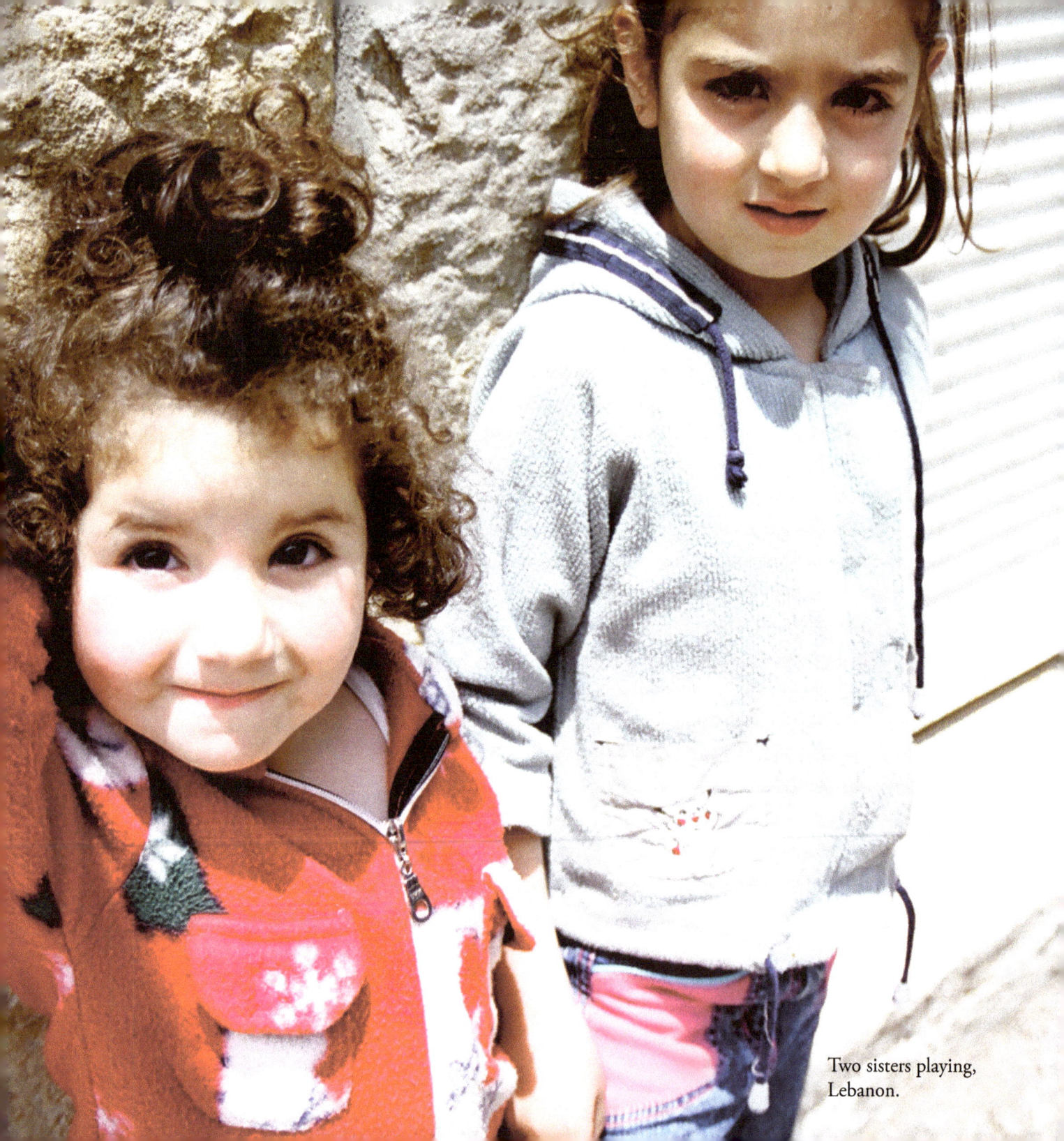
Two sisters playing, Lebanon.

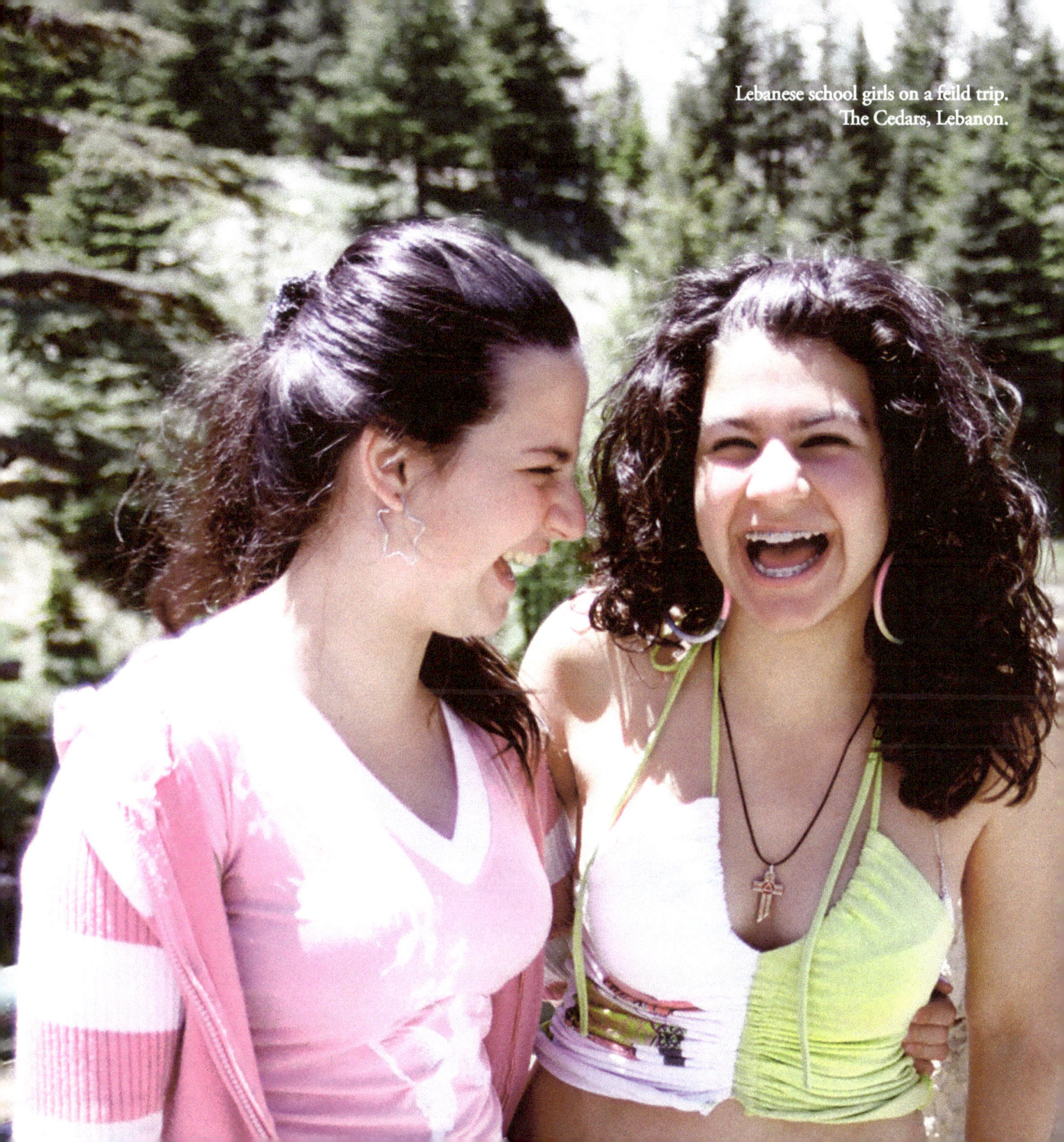
Lebanese school girls on a feild trip.
The Cedars, Lebanon.

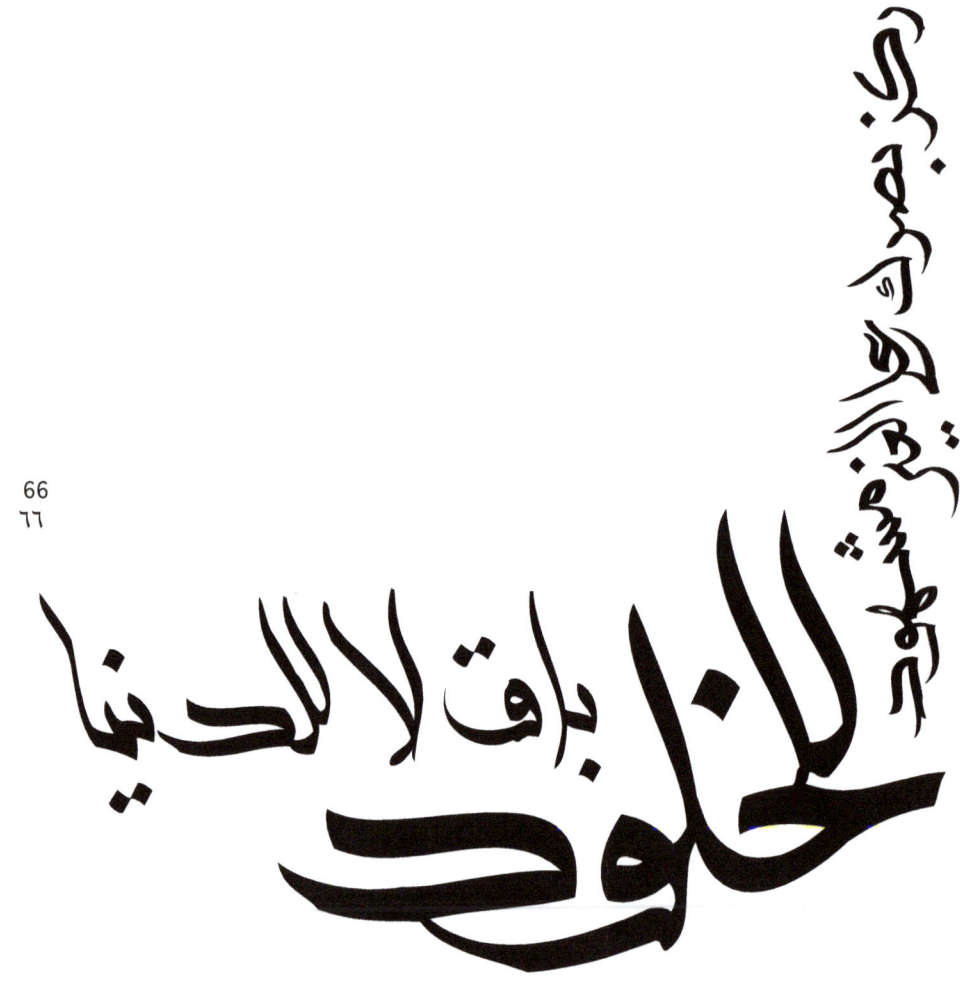

الخلوة باق لا الدنيا

Cairo, Egypt.

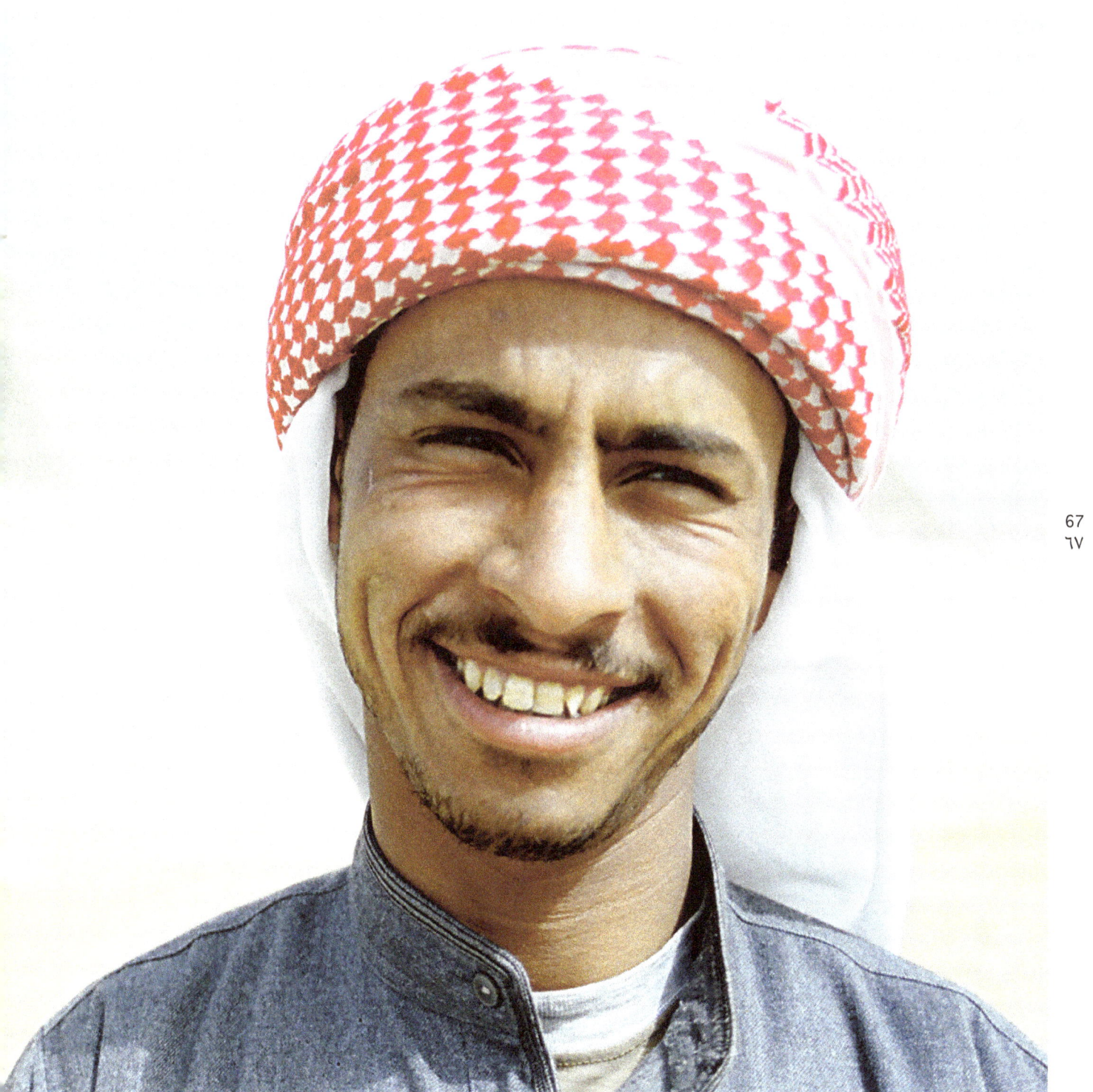

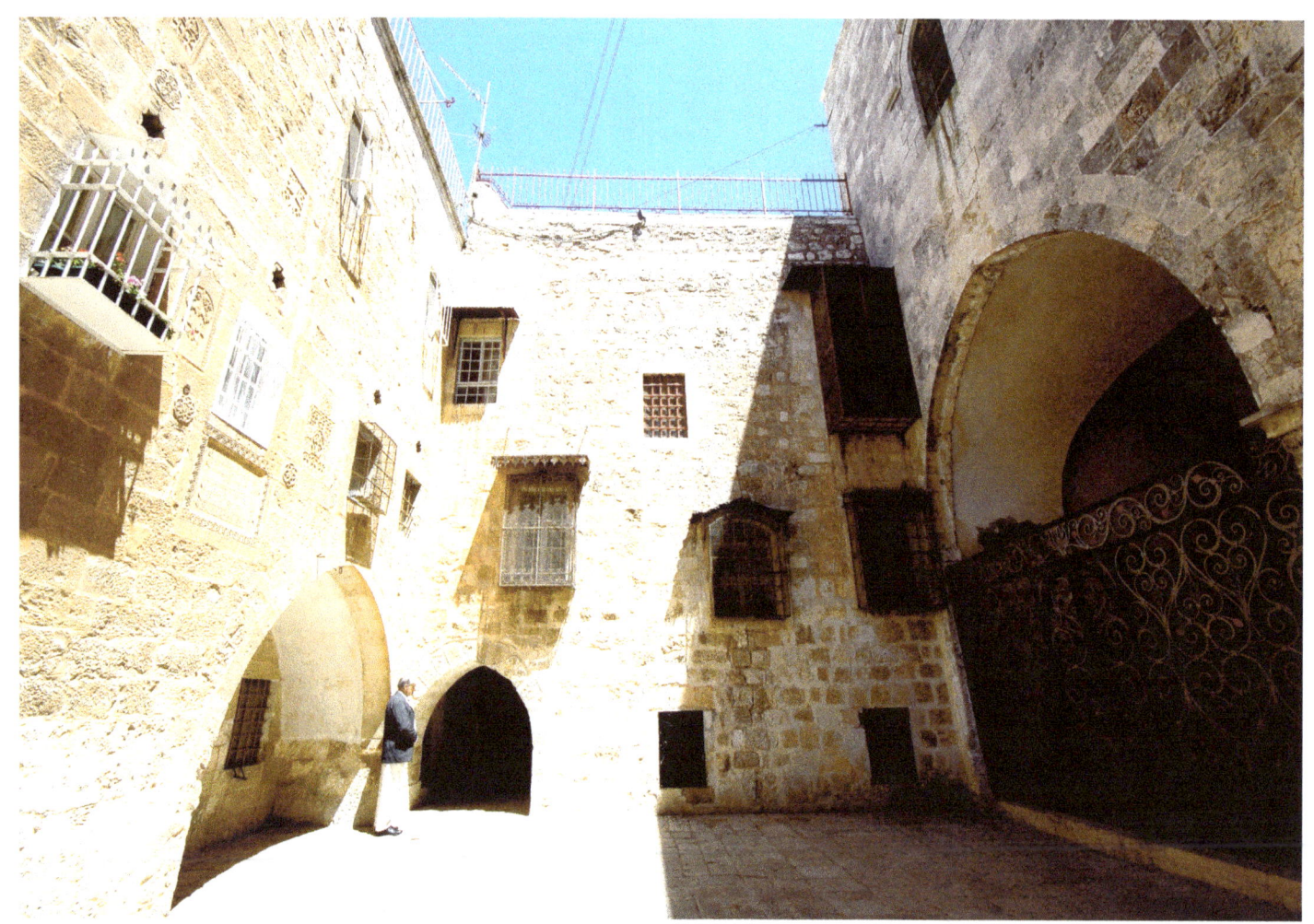

This man enjoys a moment of solitude in the Armenian quarter. Jerusalem, Israel.

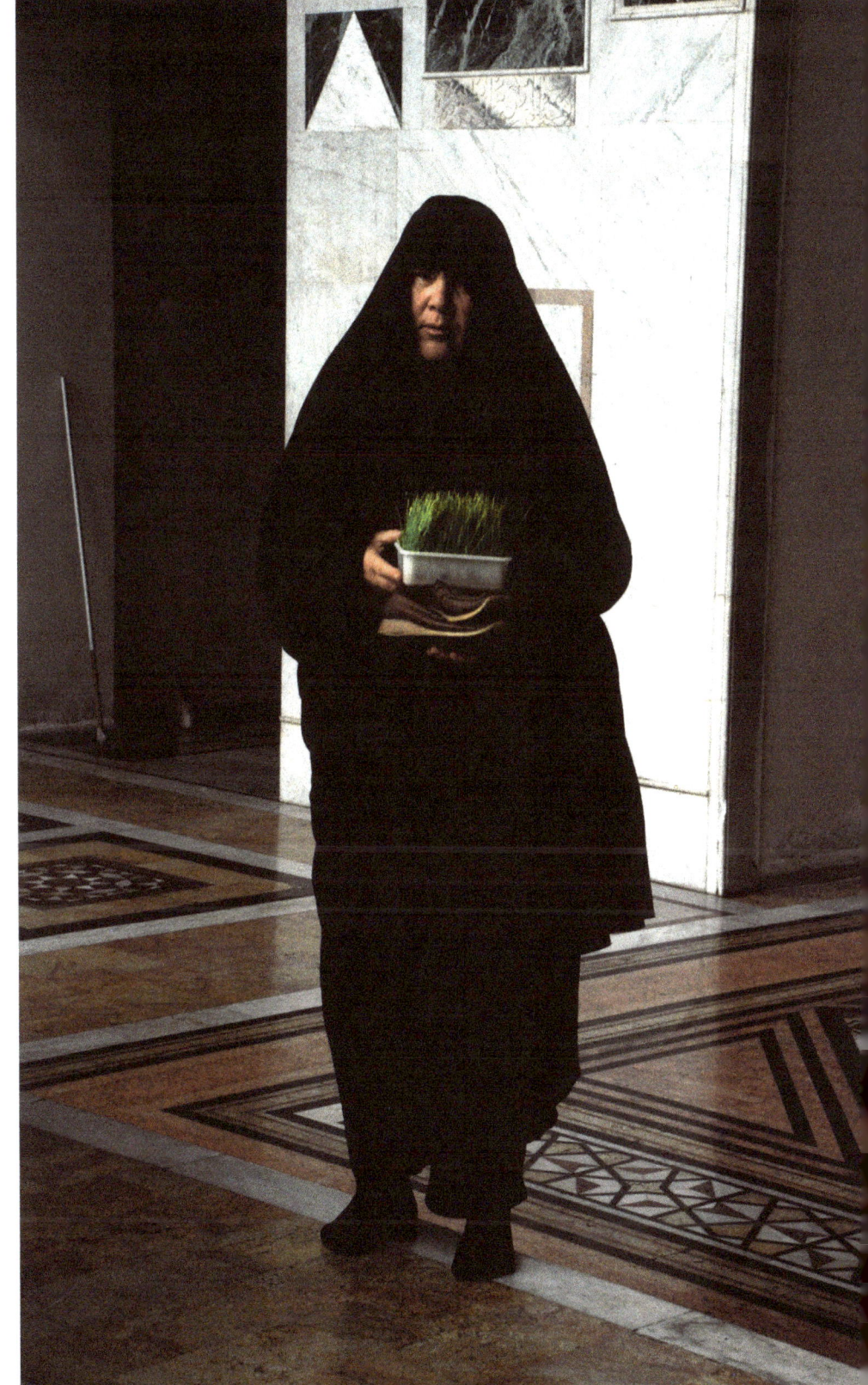

As soon as Saddam Hussein's regime was crushed in 2003, thousands of Iranian and Iraqi muslims were able to openly visit the holy sites of Islam in Syria. Once the border was open many poor and elderly women crossed from Iran to Iraq, some with all their worldly possessions and a piece of their homeland.

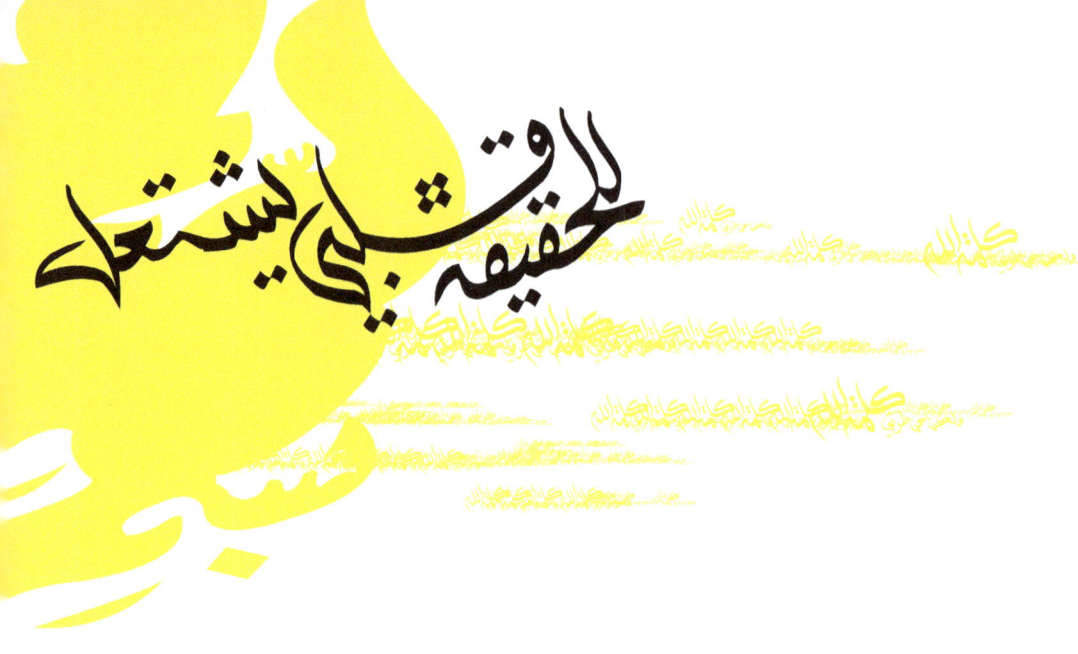

للحقيقة شعلي يشتعل

These Shiaa pilgrims are also spiritual leaders within the Shiaa community.
Their black or white turbans symbolize a superior level of spiritual education.
Damascus, Syria.

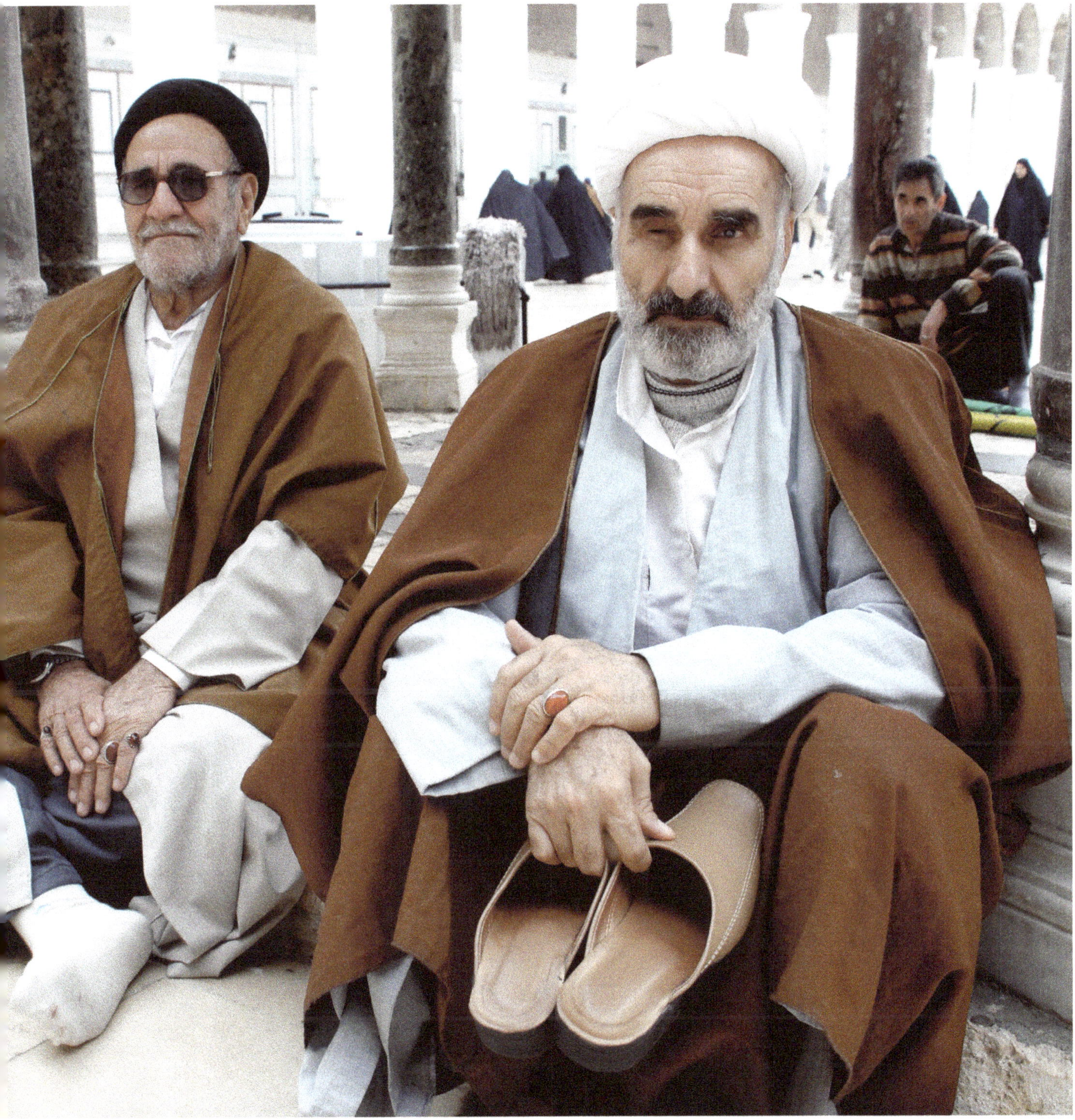

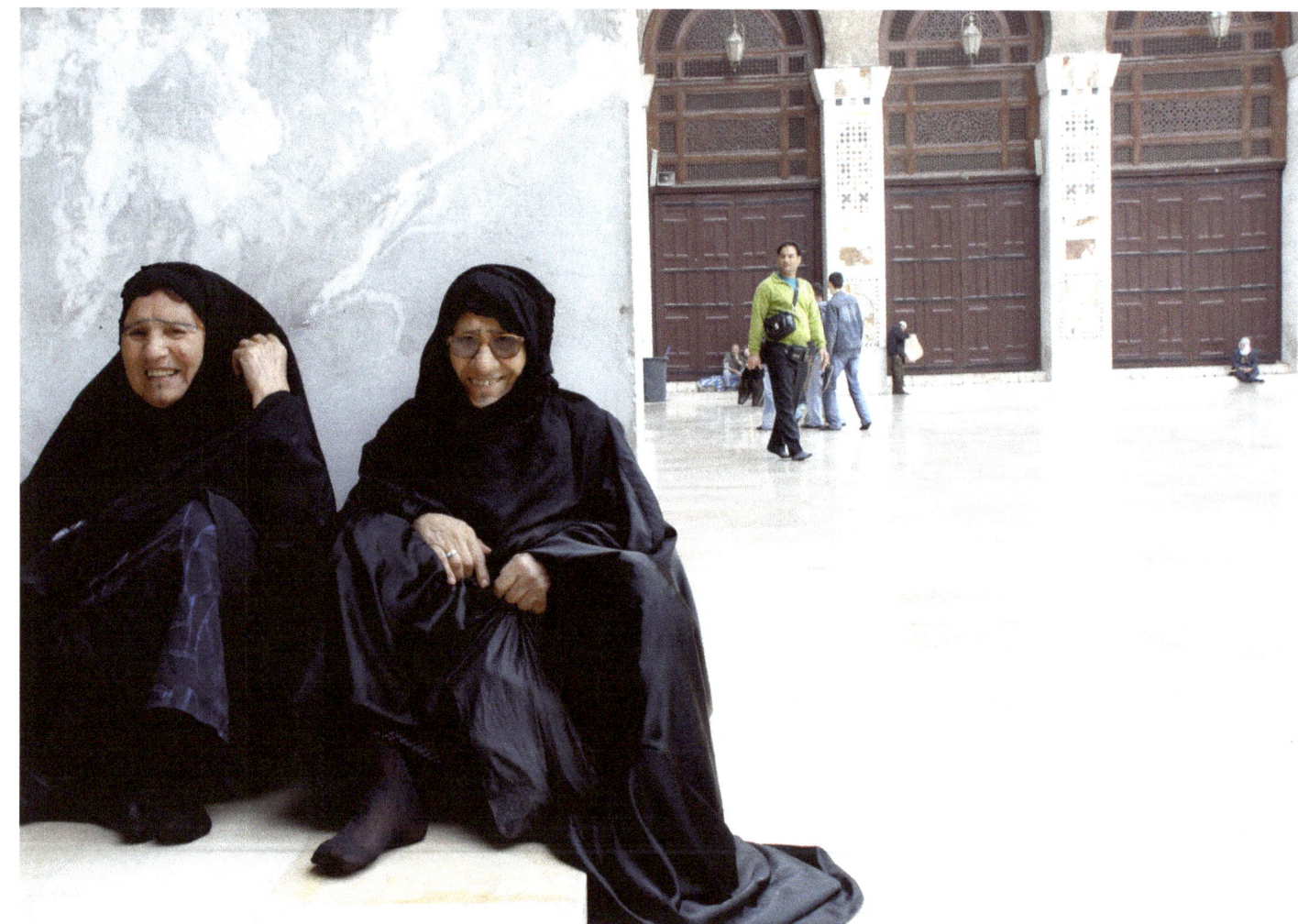

These two pilgrims take a well-earned break after walking for hours to various holy sites in Damascus. Umayyad Mosque, Syria.

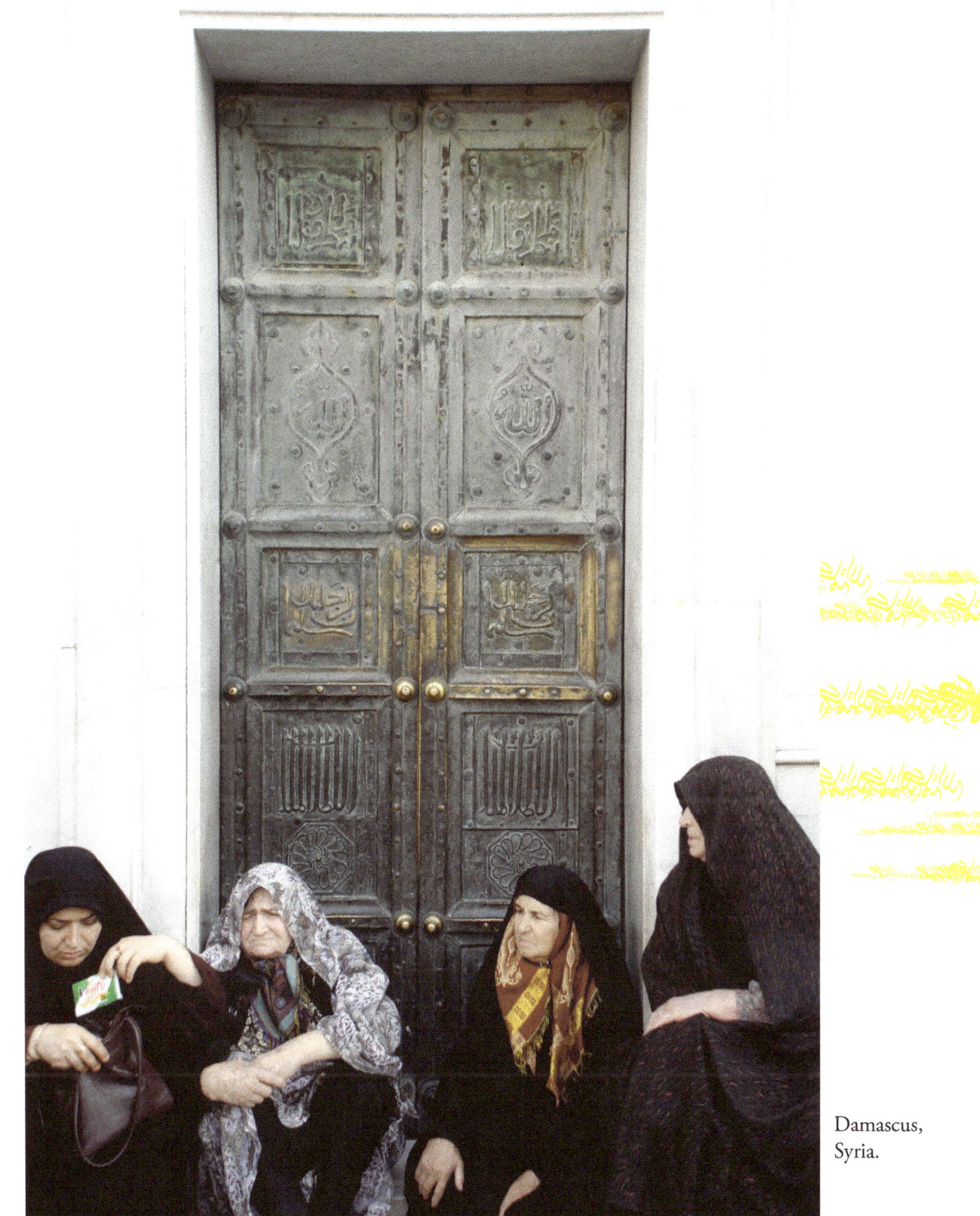

Damascus, Syria.

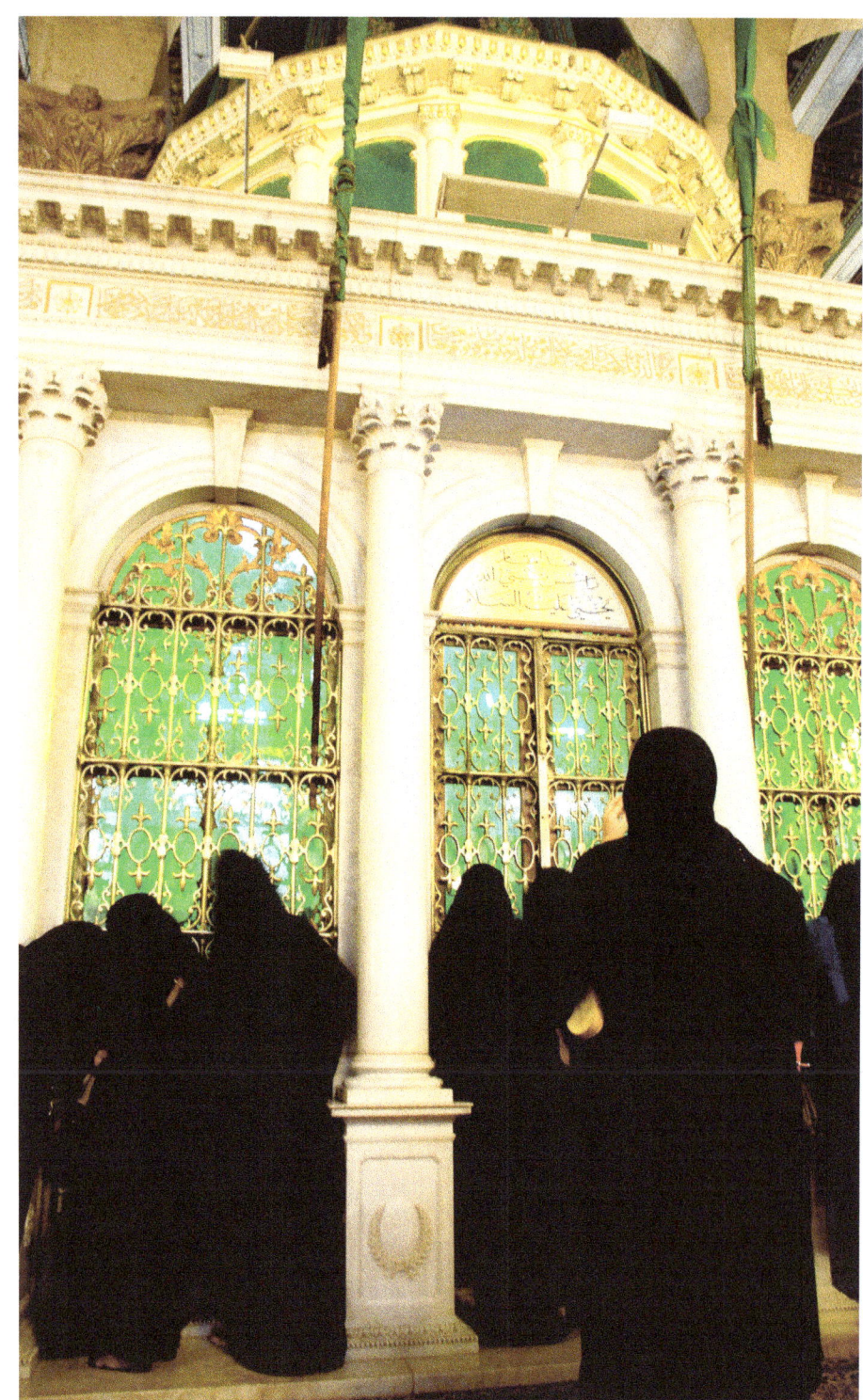

Shrine of John The Baptist.
Umayyad Mosque, Syria.

طريق النور

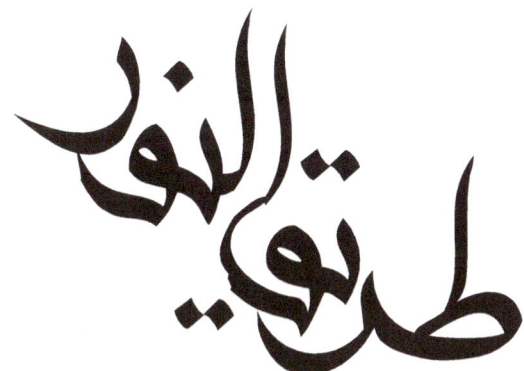

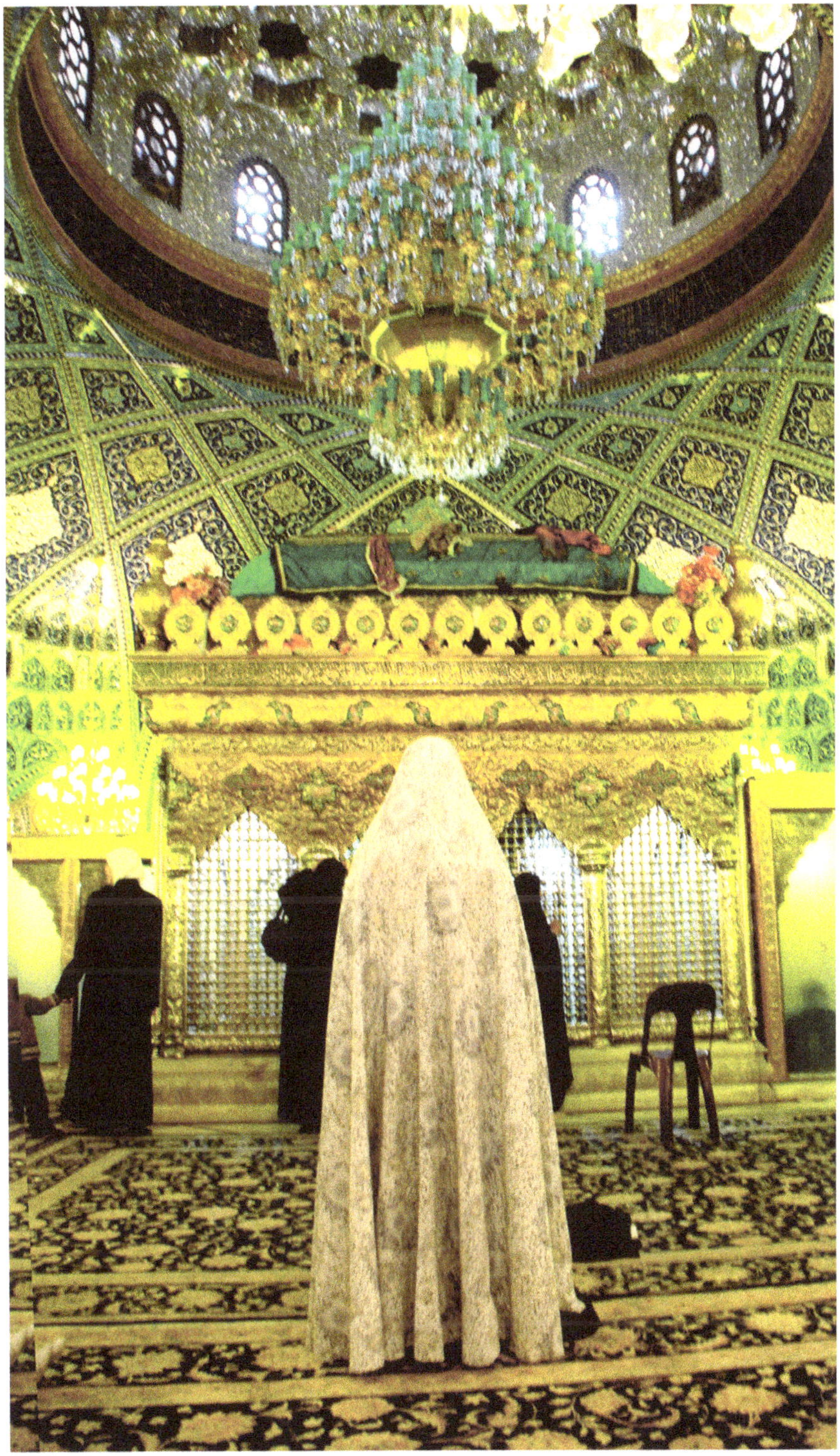

Sayidda Zeinab Mosque. Damascus, Syria.

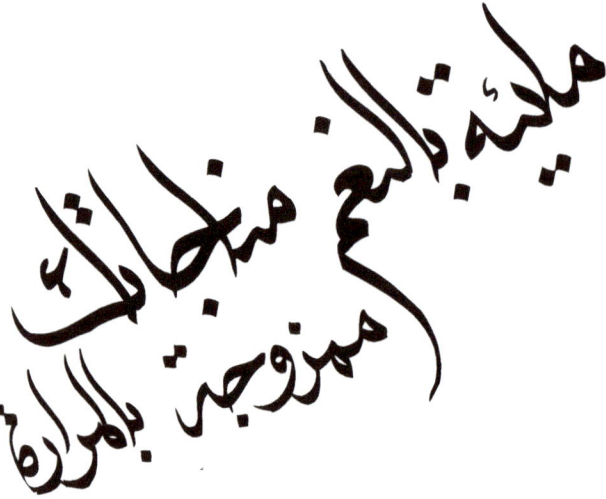

مليئة بالنعم منجاتك ممزوجة بالمرارة

The Druze are a religious community of about two million followers globally. They are found primarily in Syria, Lebanon and Jordan. This man seen here is wearing a traditional Druze dress. Beirut, Lebanon.

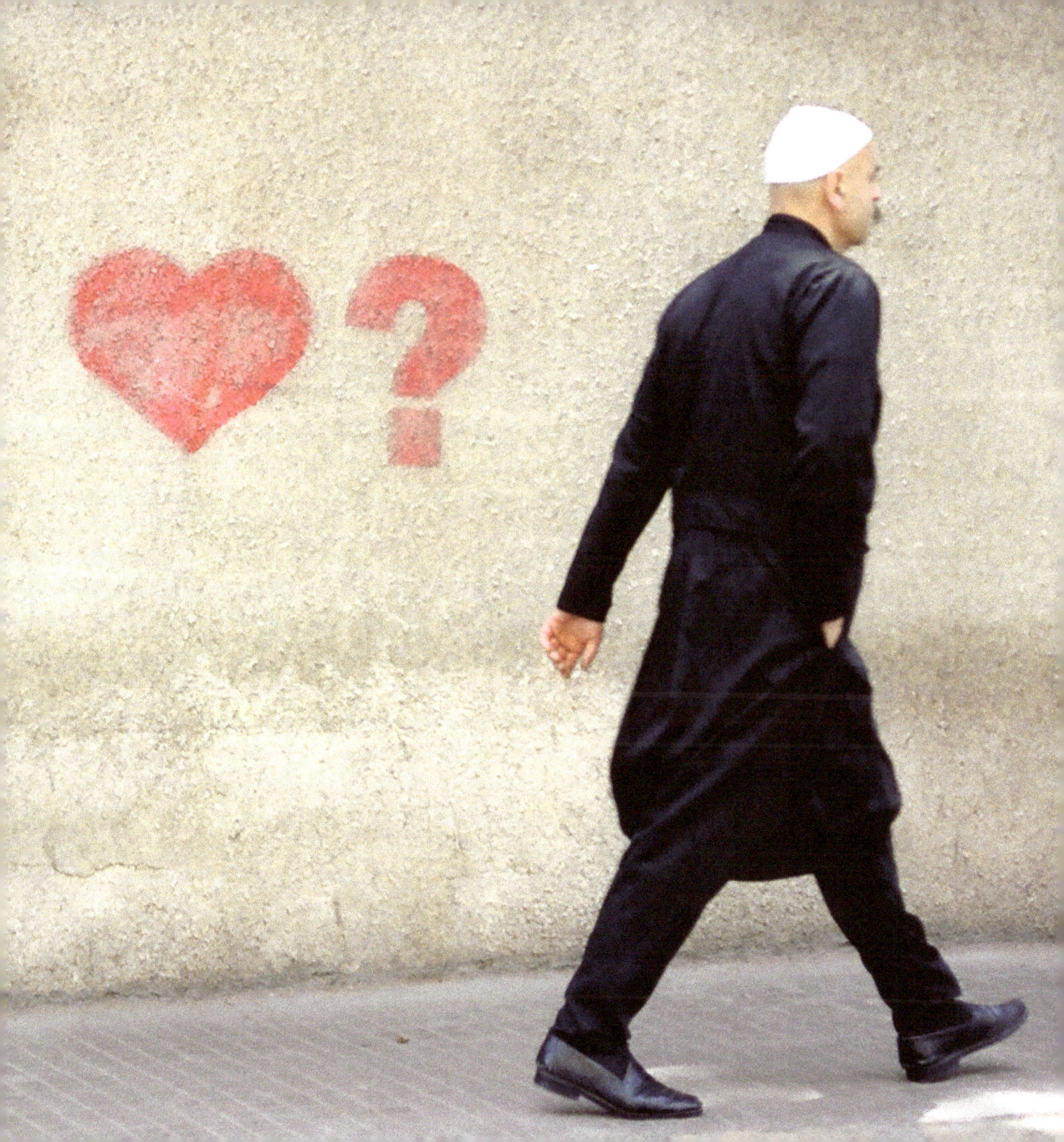

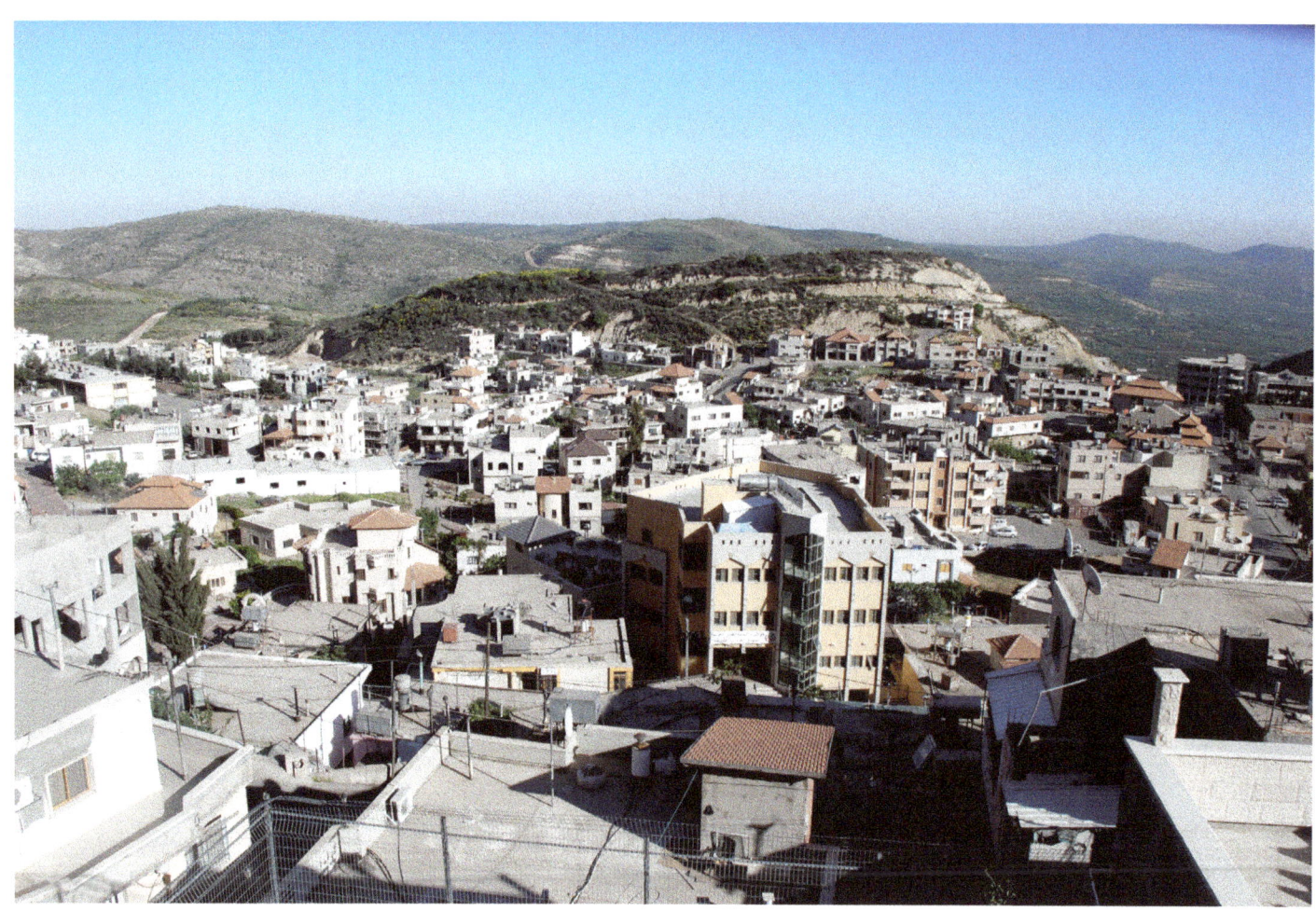

Druze village. Golan Heights, Israel.

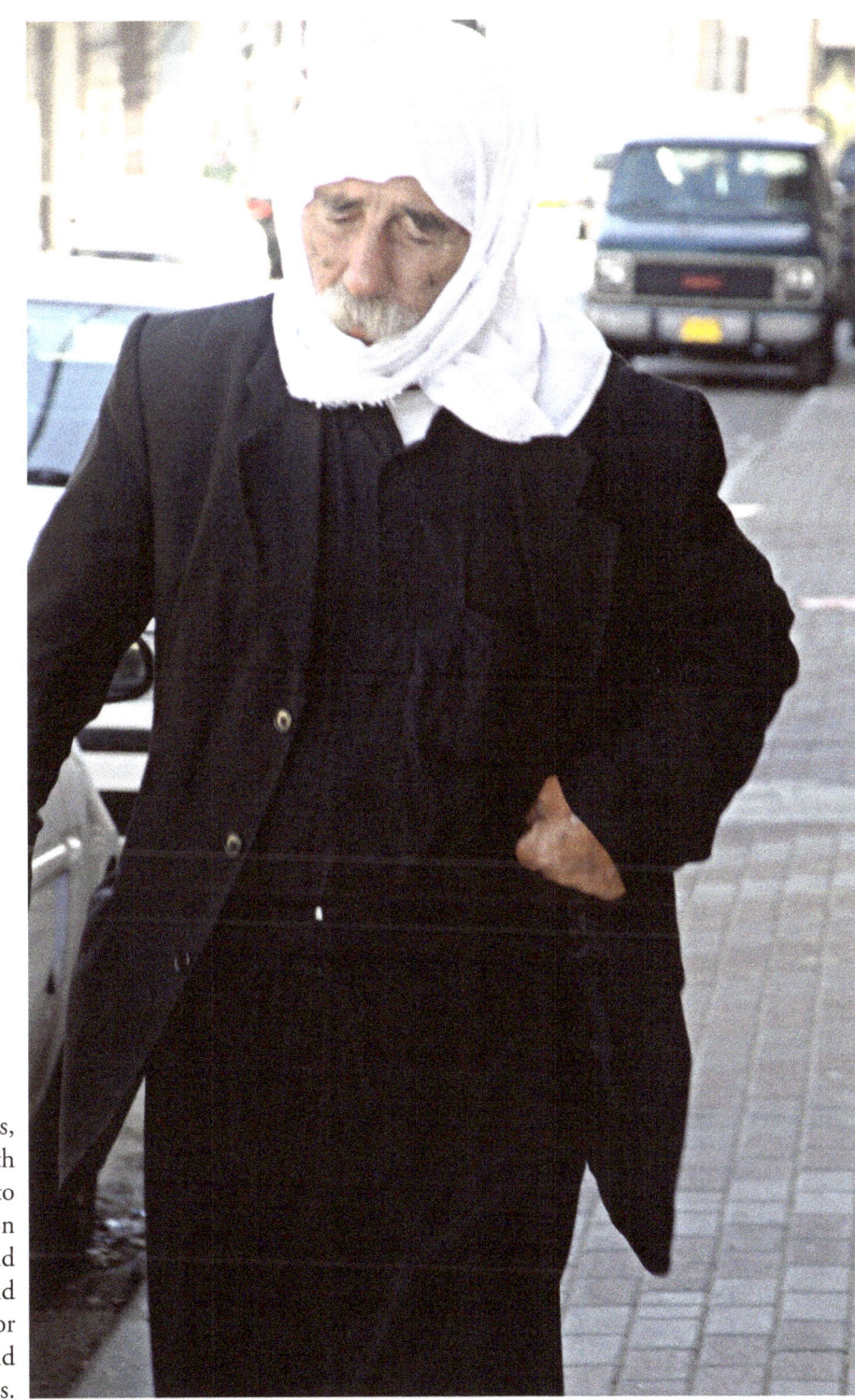

Many Druze men grow mustaches, and wear dark traditional dresses, with white turbans that vary according to the community hierarchy. Conversion to the religion is not allowed and marriage between Druze and non-Druze is strongly discouraged for religious, political and historical reasons.

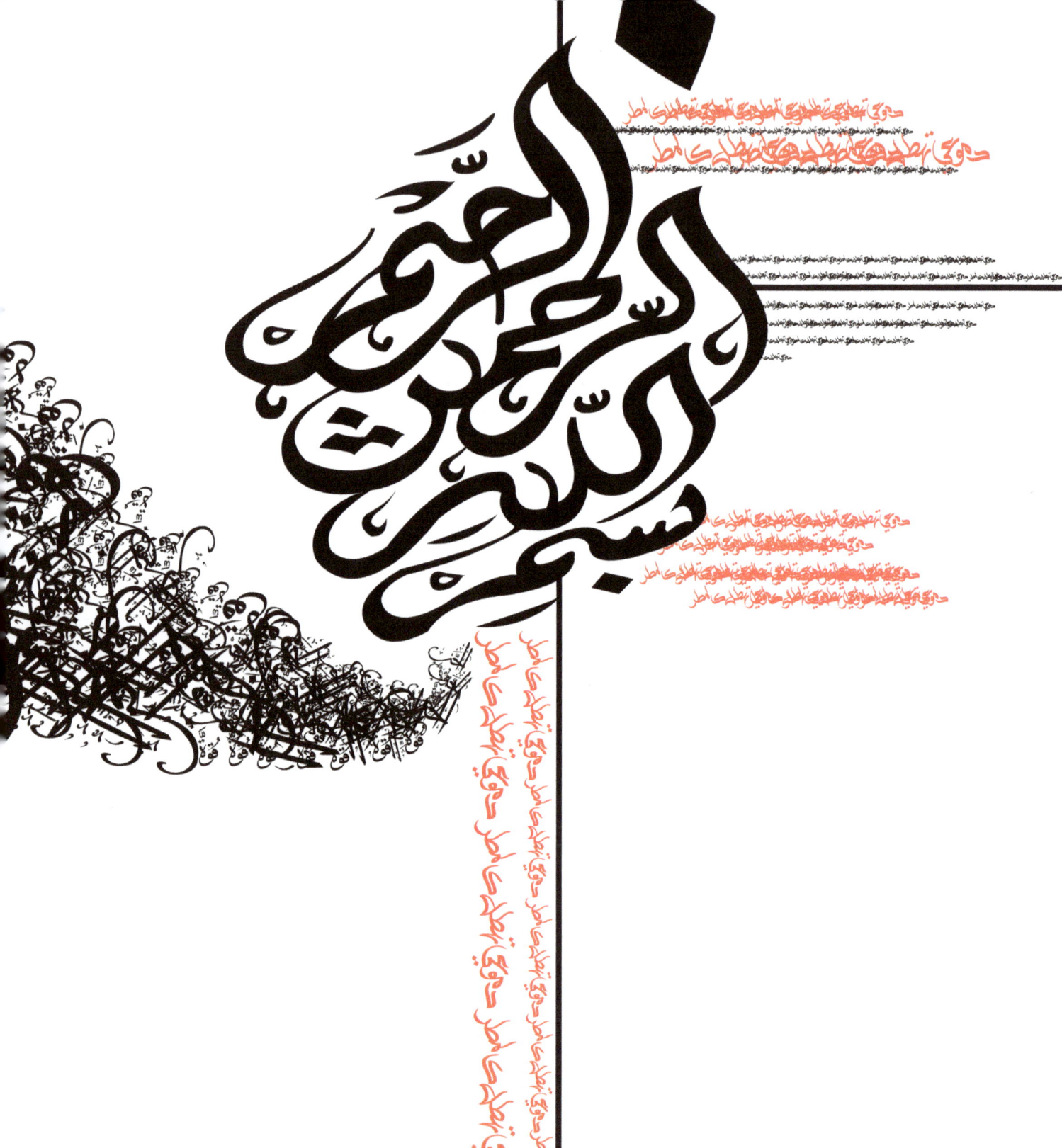

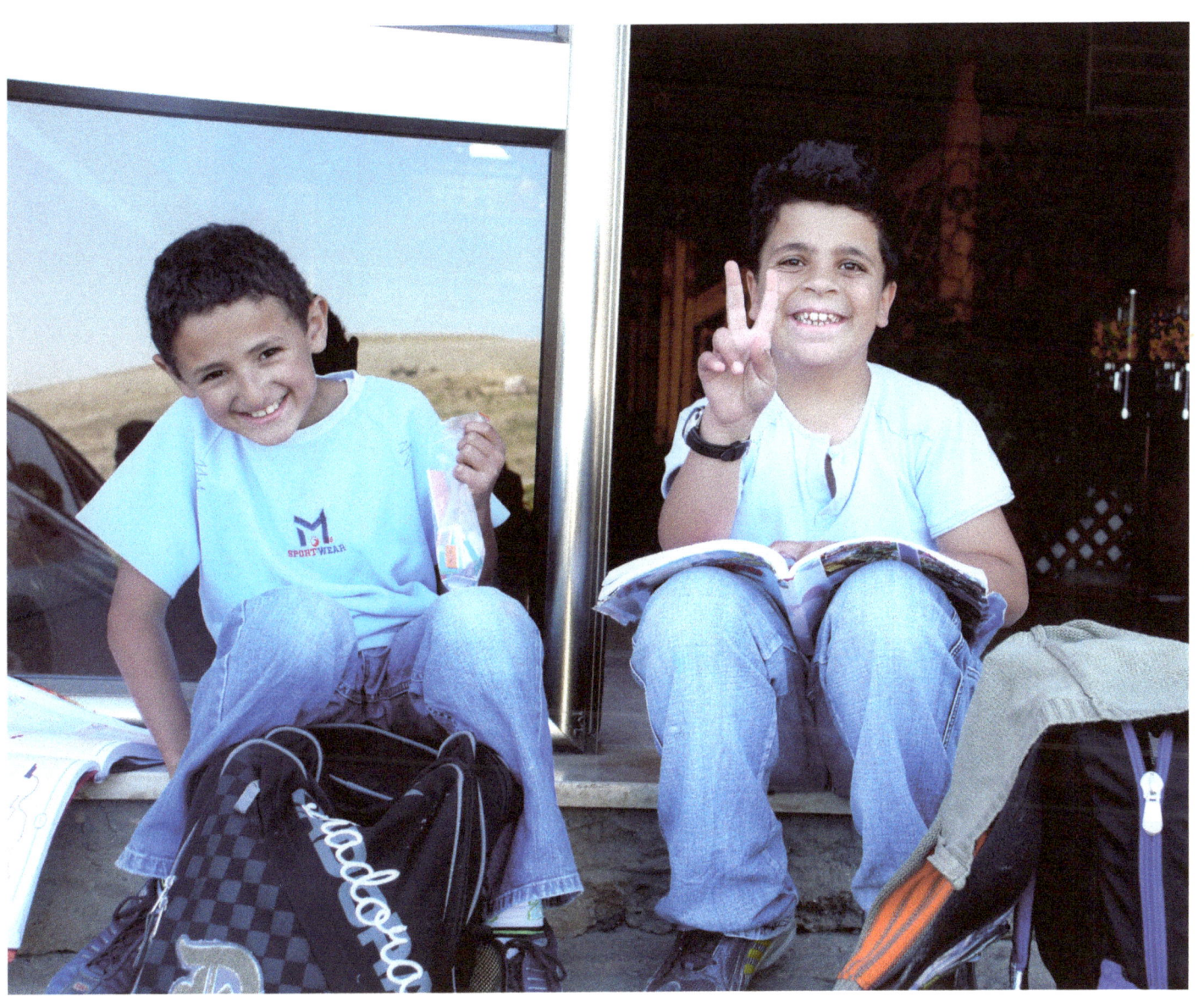

Druze school boys. Golan Heights, Israel.

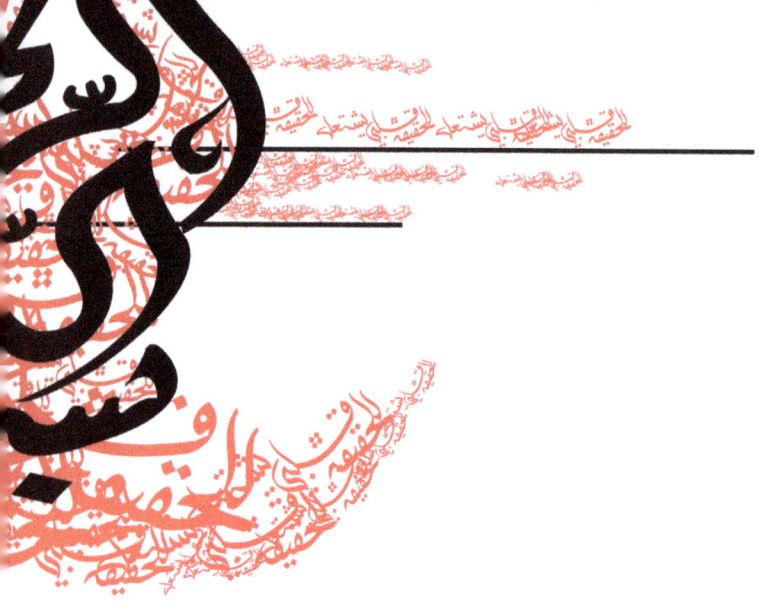

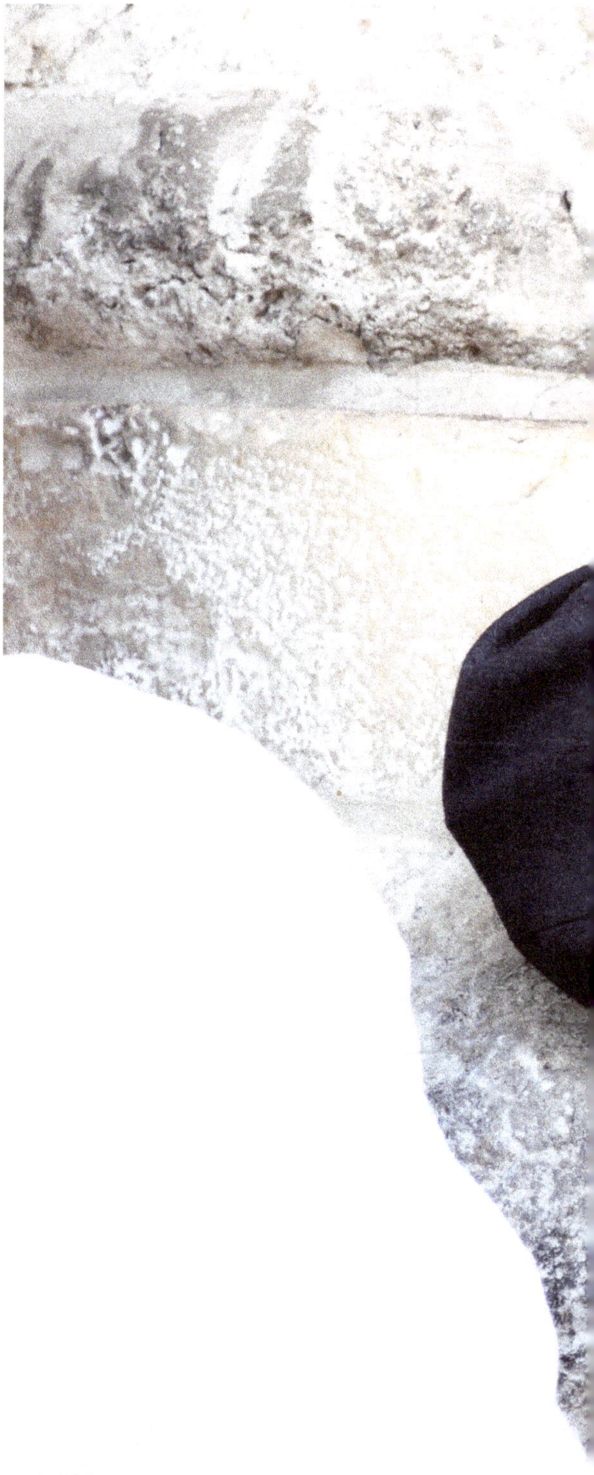

The total Palestinian population is estimated at approximately twelve million, with less than half of this number found within the boundaries of Palestine.

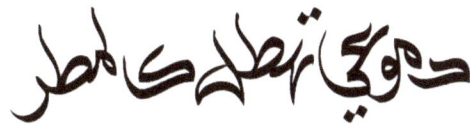
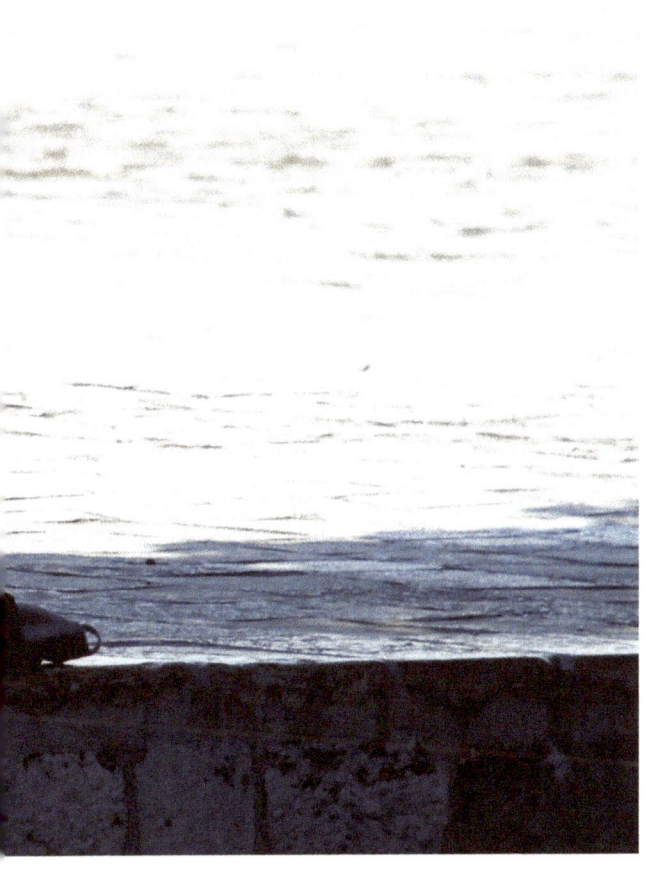

In terms of religious affiliation, most Palestinians are Muslims from the Sunni branch of Islam. There is also a significant Christian minority, as well as some that are Druze.

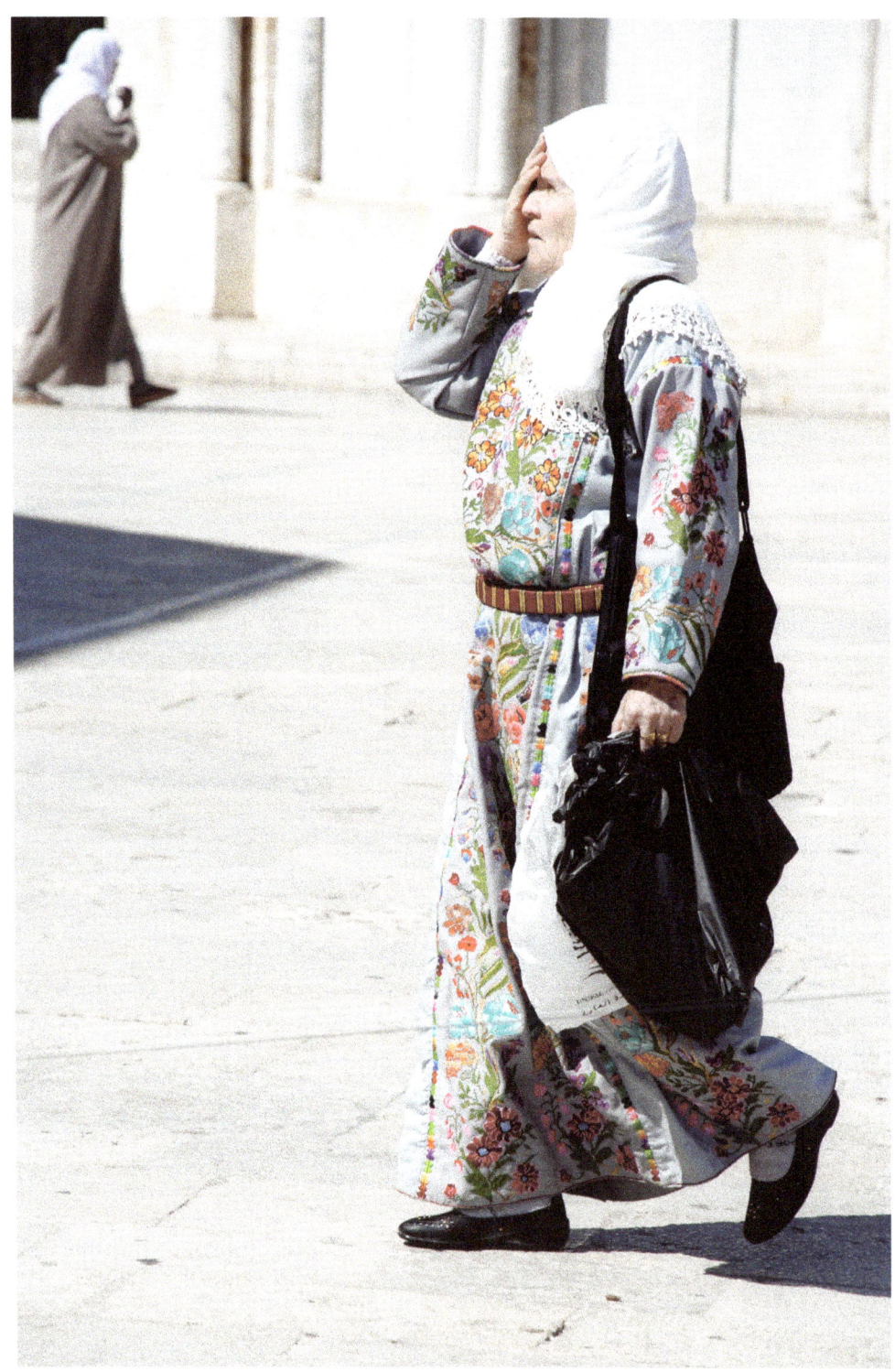

Woman in traditional Palestinian dress. Temple Mount, Jerusalem.

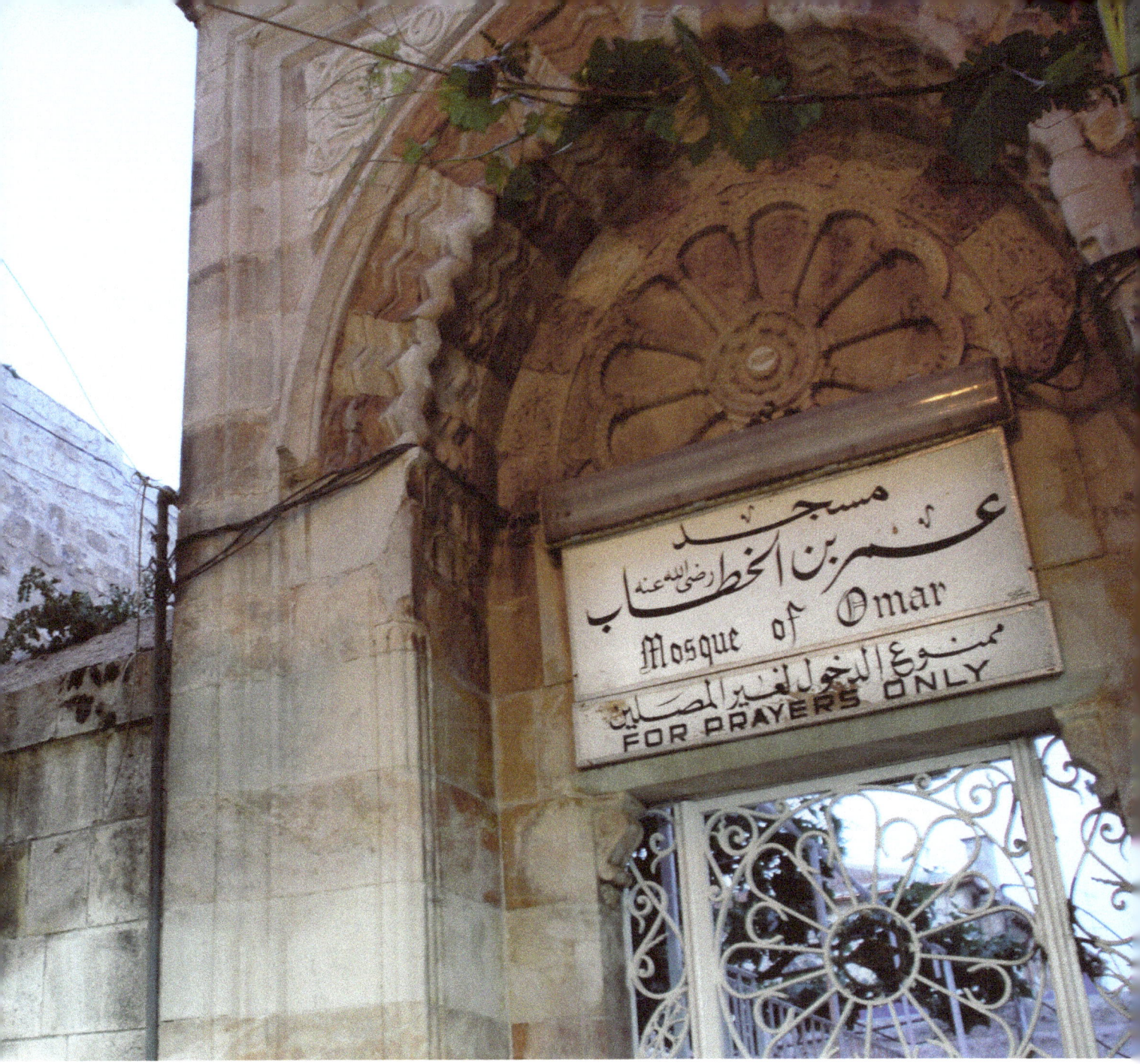

After the Siege of Jerusalem by the Rashidun army, Caliph Omar traveled to Jerusalem to accept the surrender. He then visited the Church of the Holy Sepulchre where he was invited to pray. Omar declined, as he did not want to endanger the Church's status as a Christian site. Instead he prayed outside in the courtyard, in a place where David was believed to have prayed.

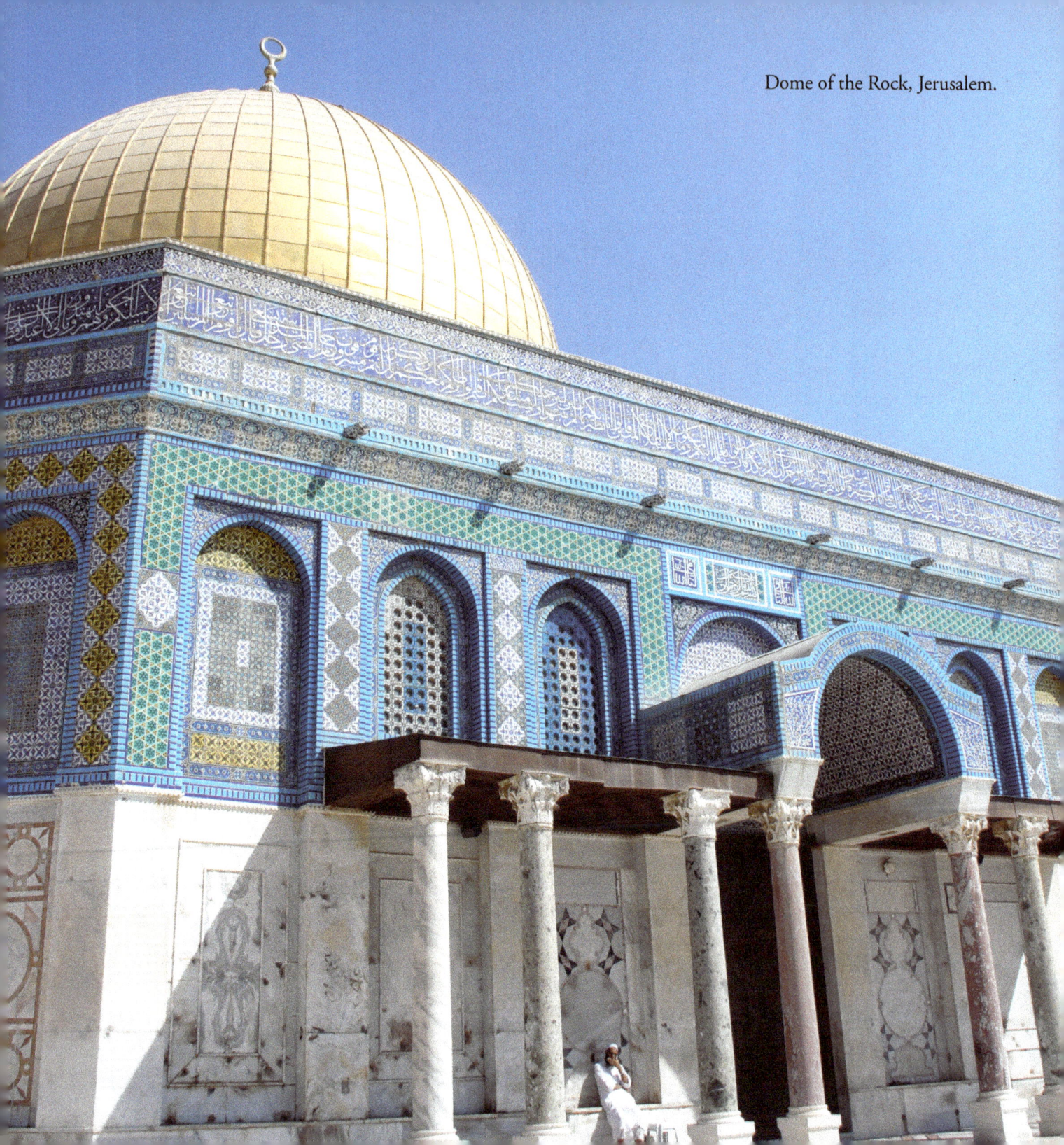

Dome of the Rock, Jerusalem.

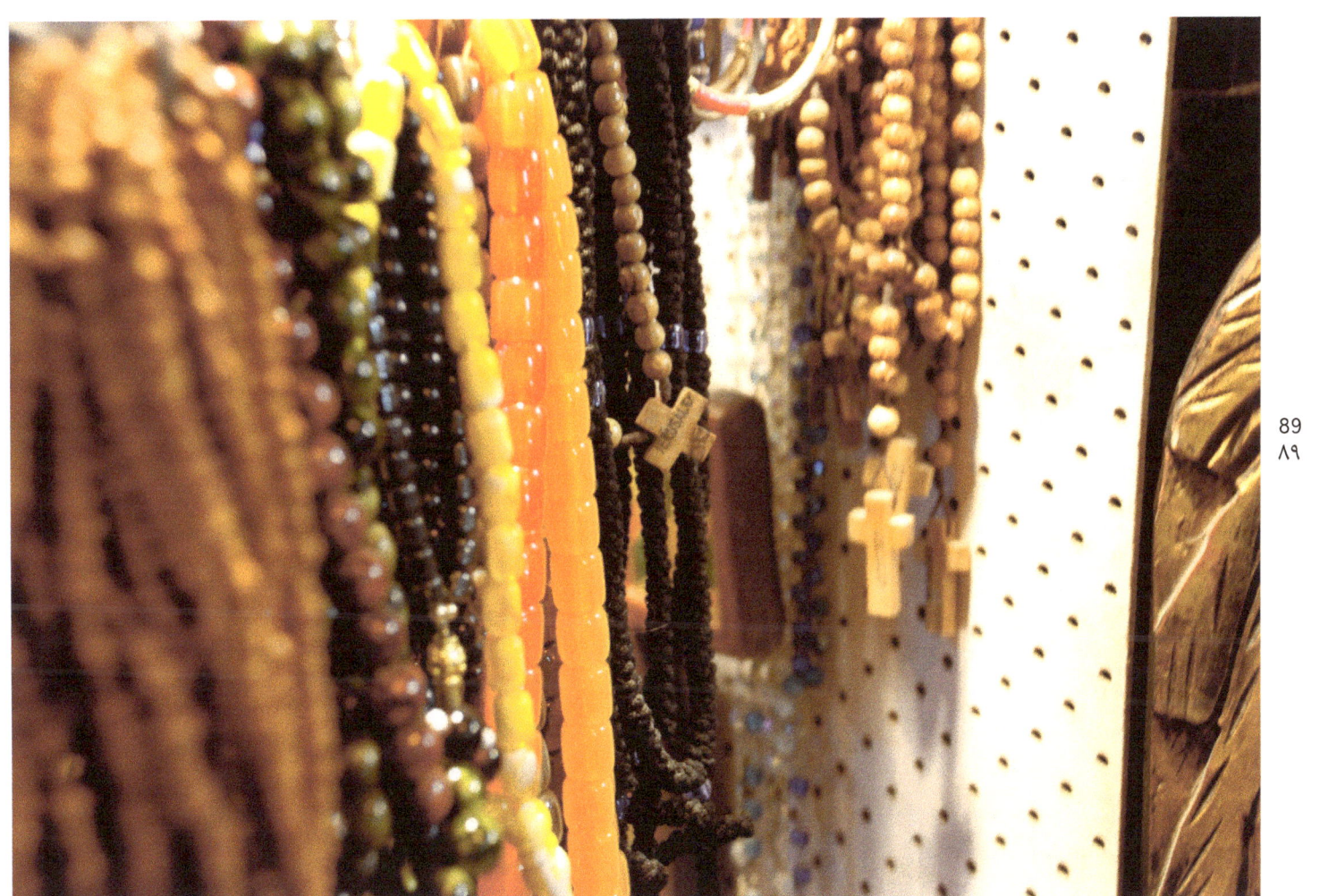

Prayer beads, Jerusalem.

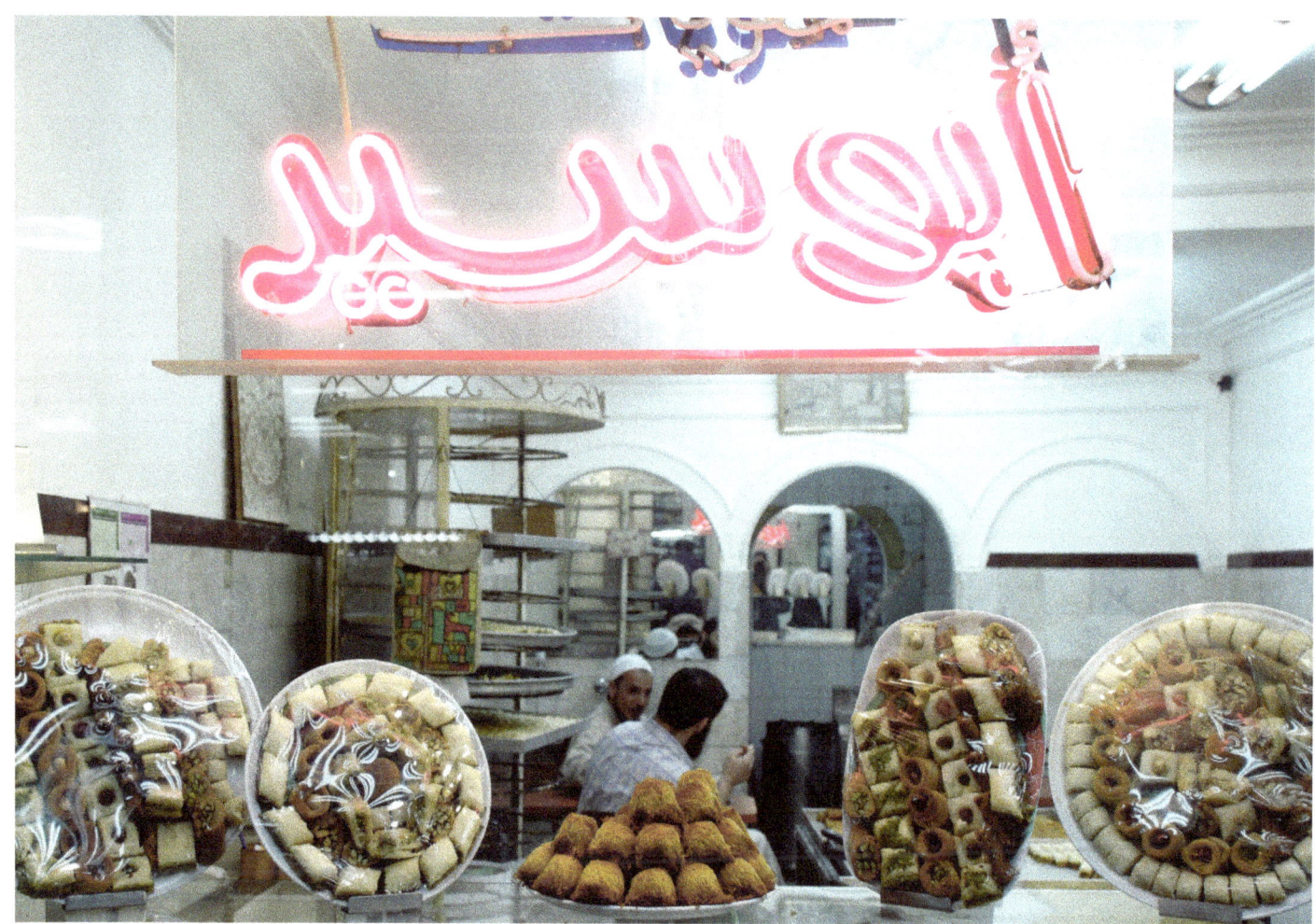

Traditional Palestinian sweets for sale in the Arab Quarter of Jerusalem.

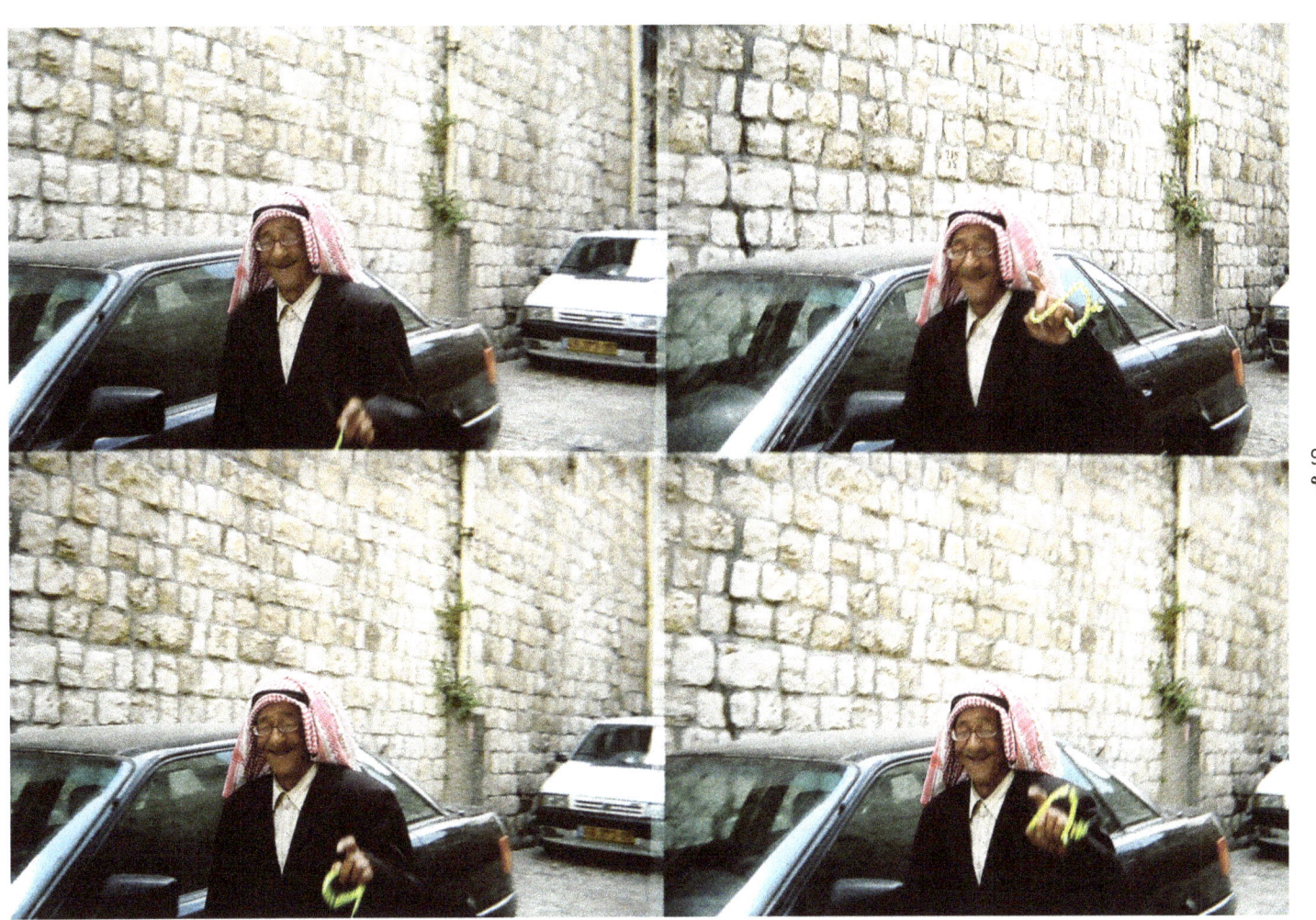

Old Palestinian man waving. Muslim Quarter, Jerusalem.

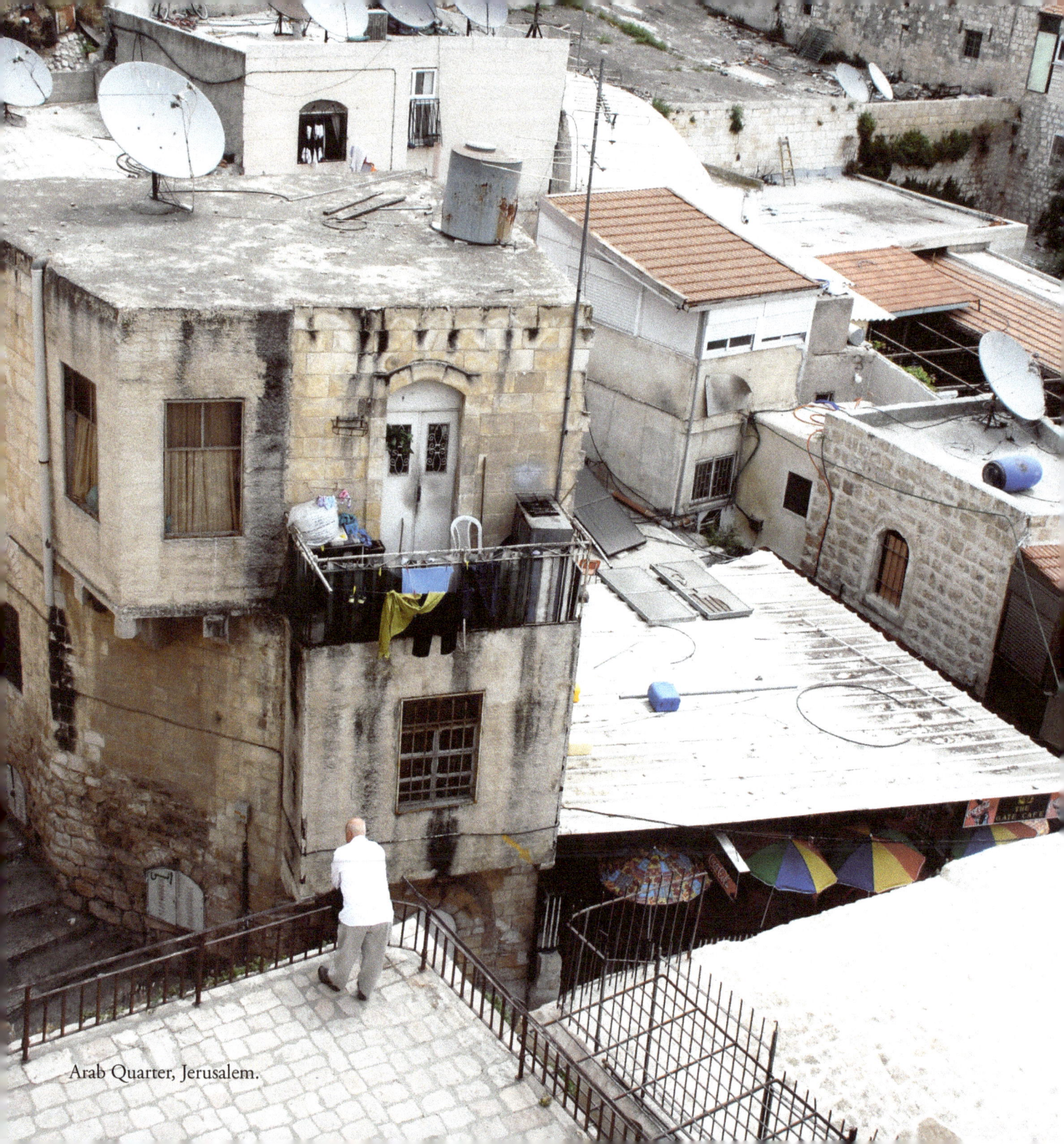

Arab Quarter, Jerusalem.

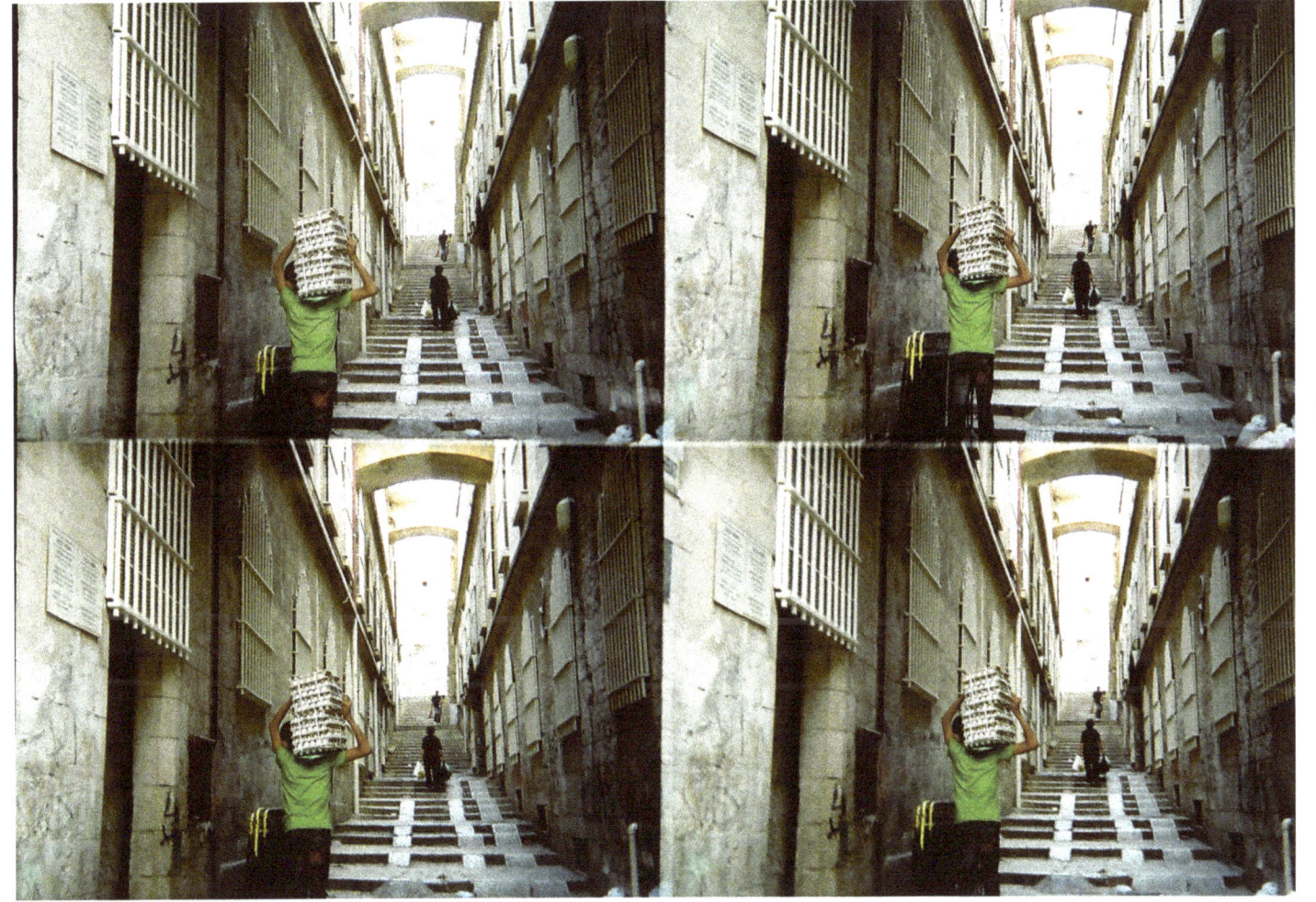

An increasing number of Palestinian children are now working to support their families instead of attending school. Arab Quarter, Jerusalem.

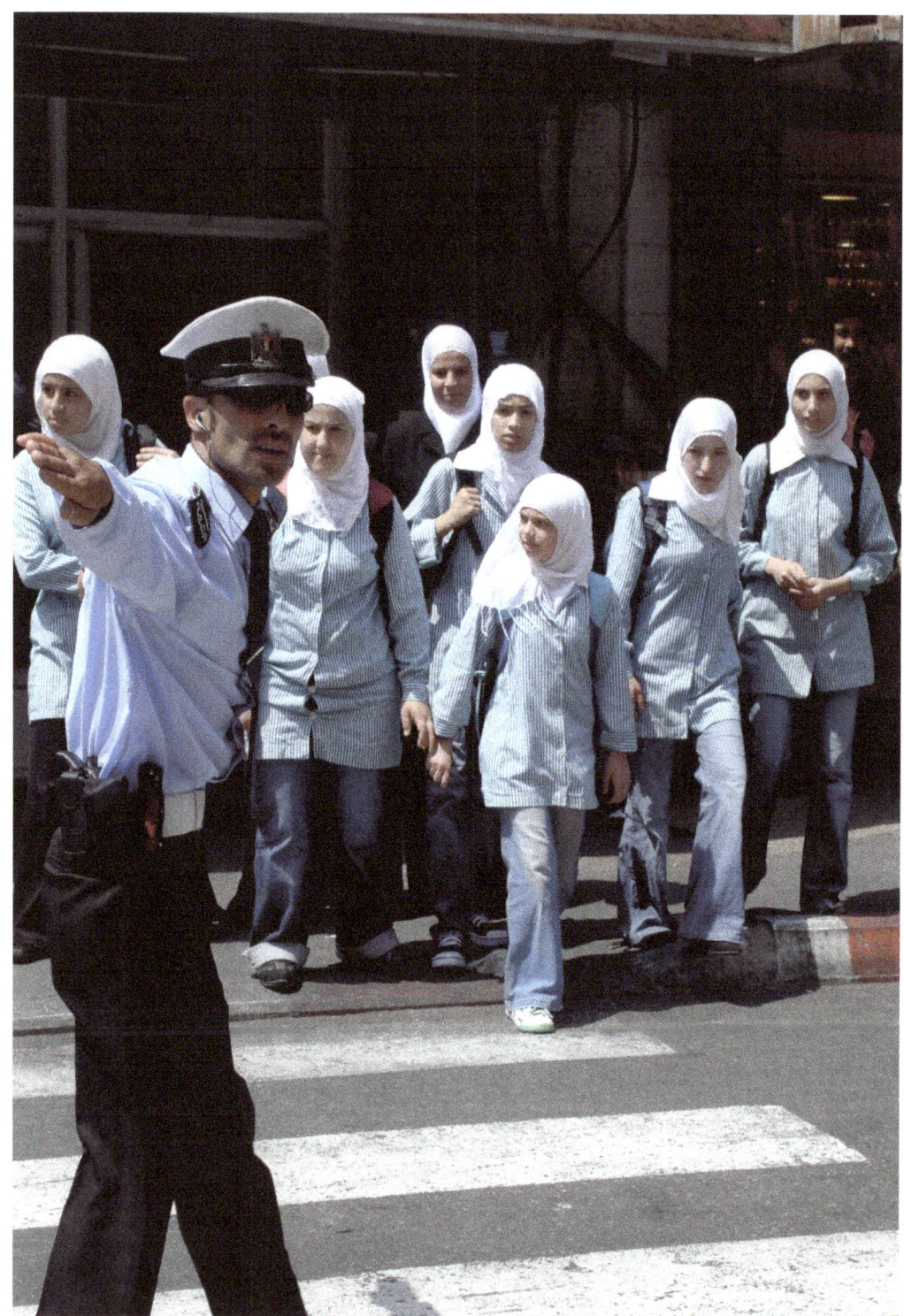

Dancing policeman.
Ramallah, Palestine.

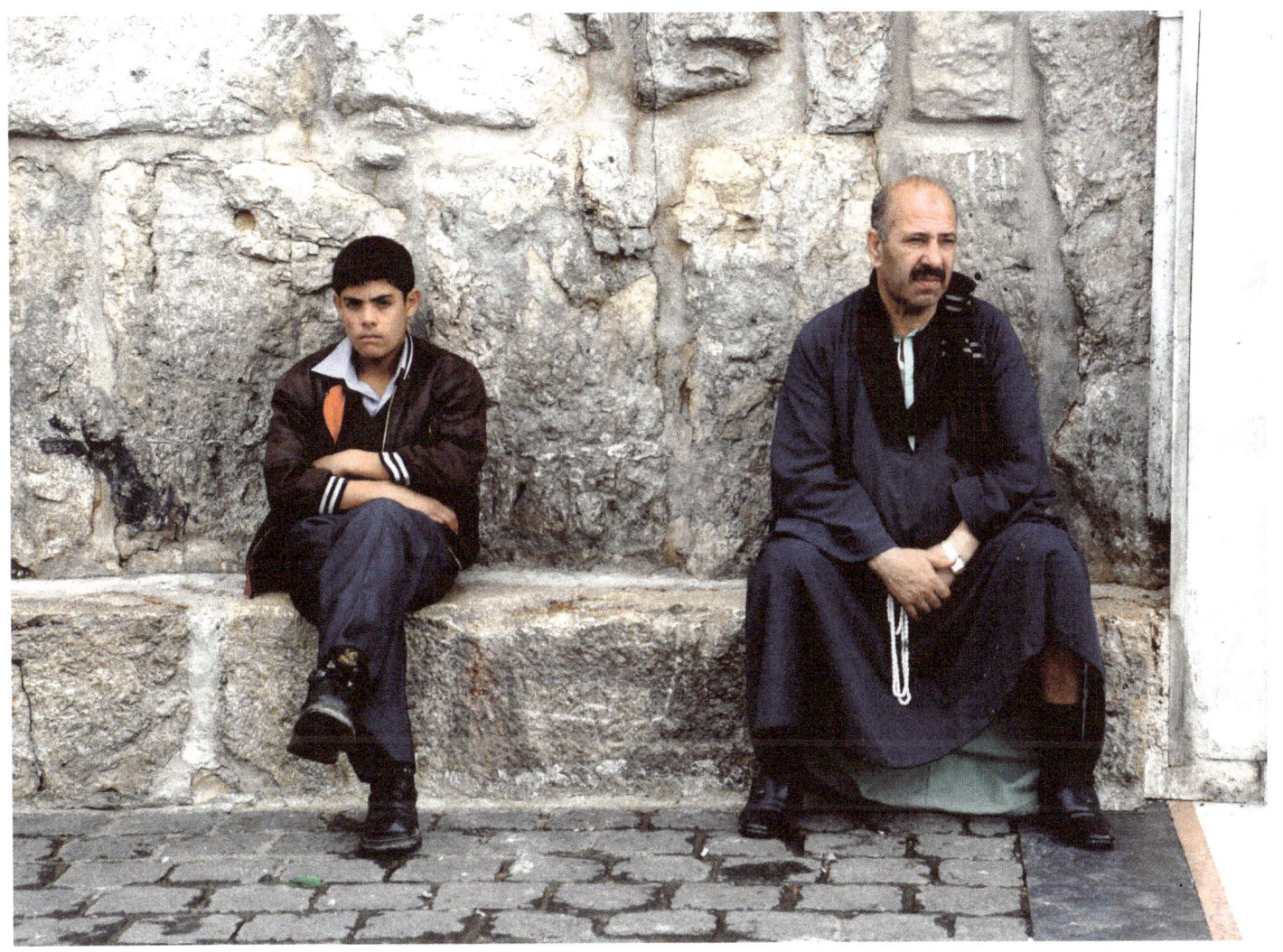

Religious freedom among the monotheistic faiths is also respected and debated openly: Syria is one of the few countries in the Arab world where Jews, Christian and Muslims live, work and socialize in peace, side by side.

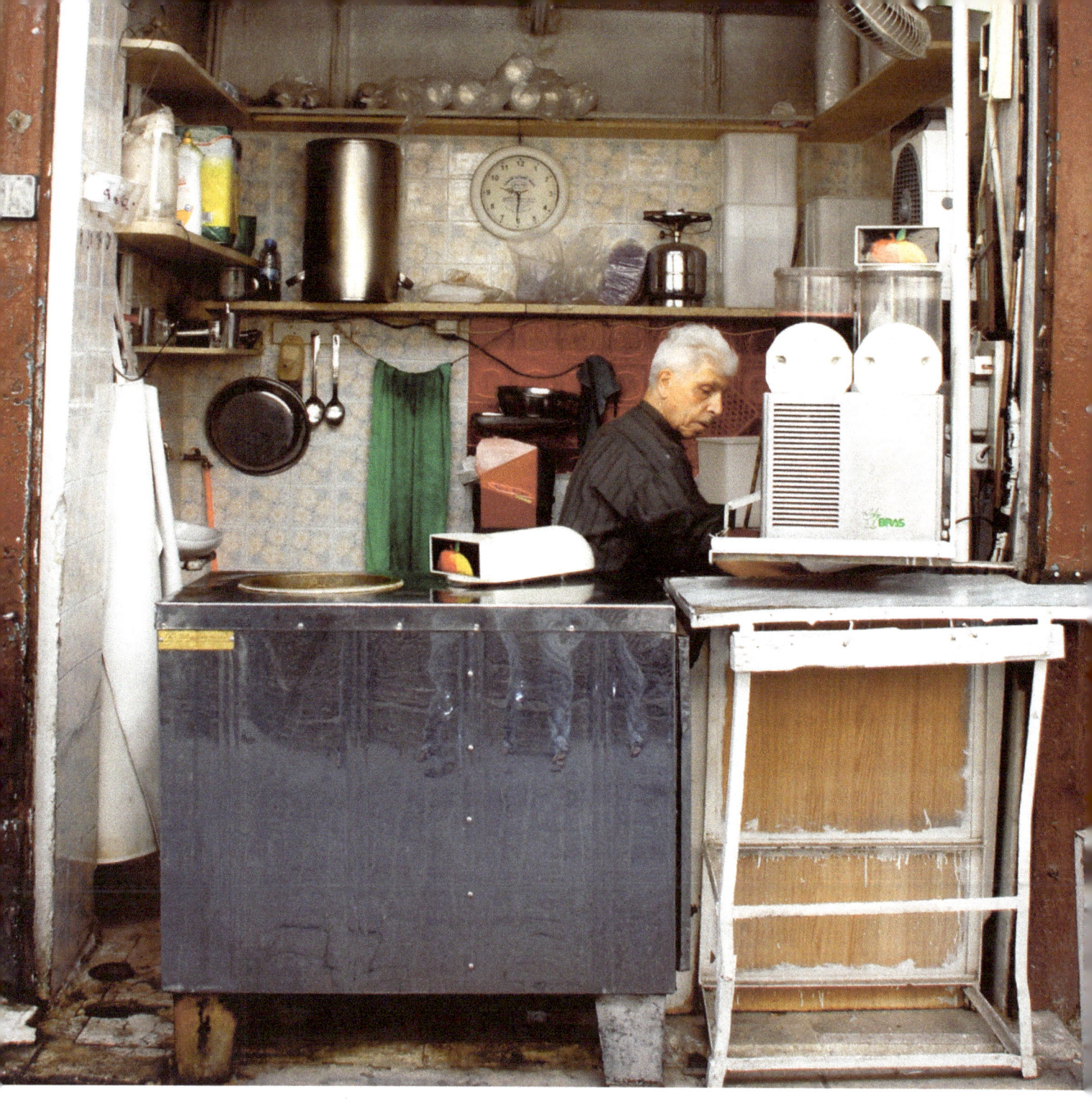

A Syrian man prepares morning meals. Damascus, Syria.

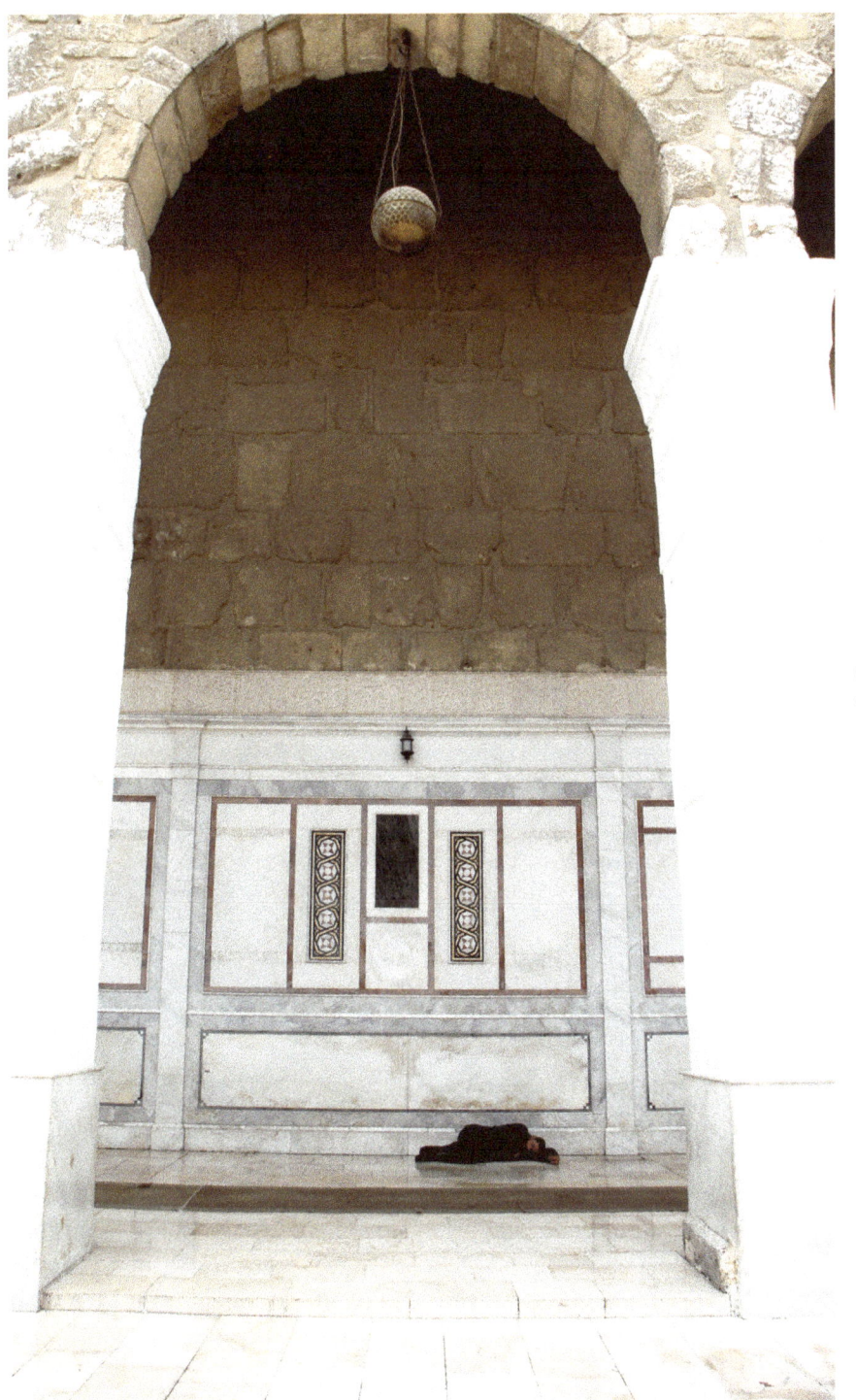

'Displaced' is the formal description of the homeless according to Article 600 of the Syrian Penal code, which defines homeless people as a healthy person with no home and no job for a month or more. But while there are no official reports dealing with homeless issues in Syria, workers say that displaced people are increasing daily, not only in the streets and public gardens of Damascus, but more noticeably in other government organizations and state run facilities. Places of worship also support many street dwellers.

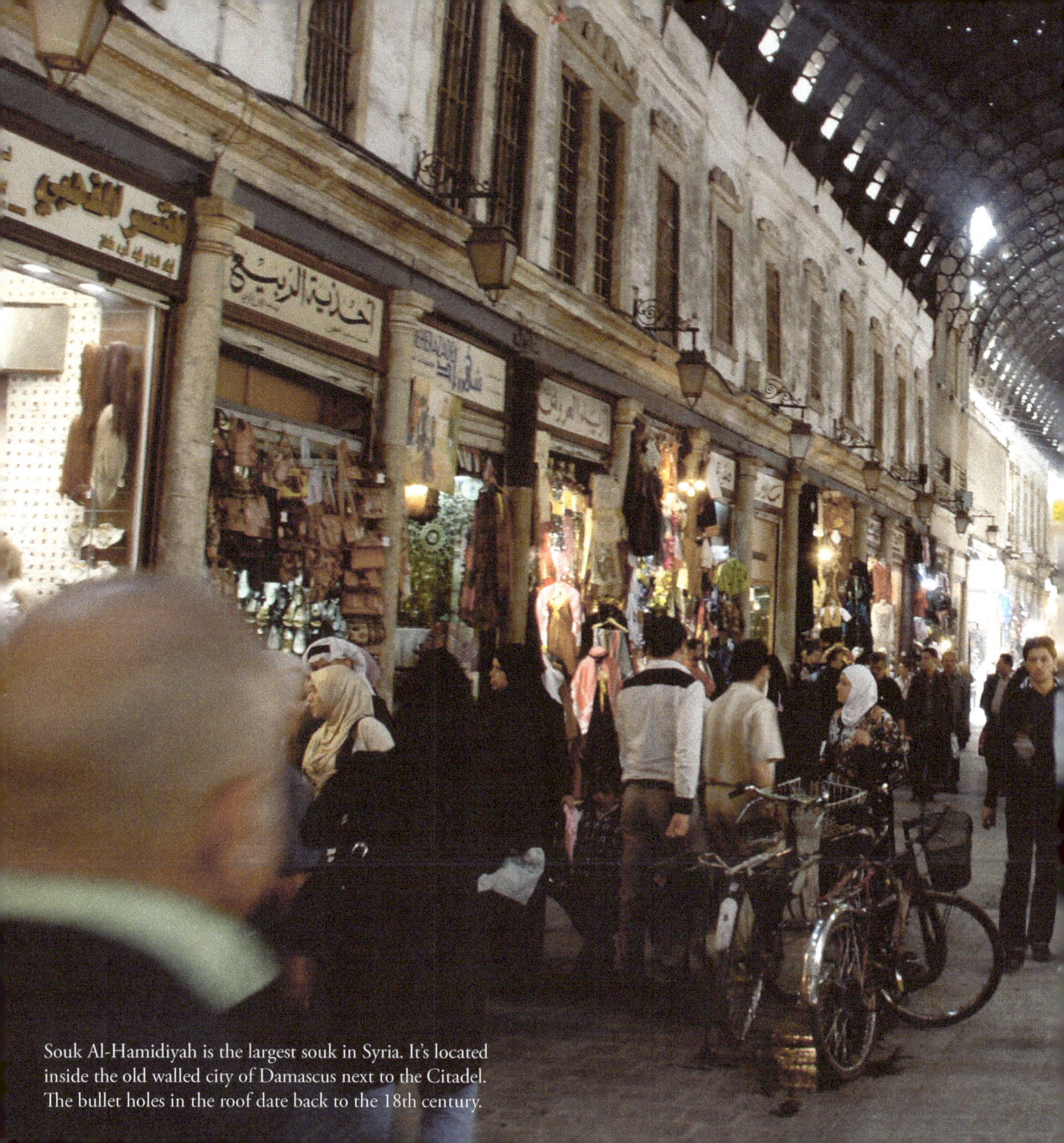

Souk Al-Hamidiyah is the largest souk in Syria. It's located inside the old walled city of Damascus next to the Citadel. The bullet holes in the roof date back to the 18th century.

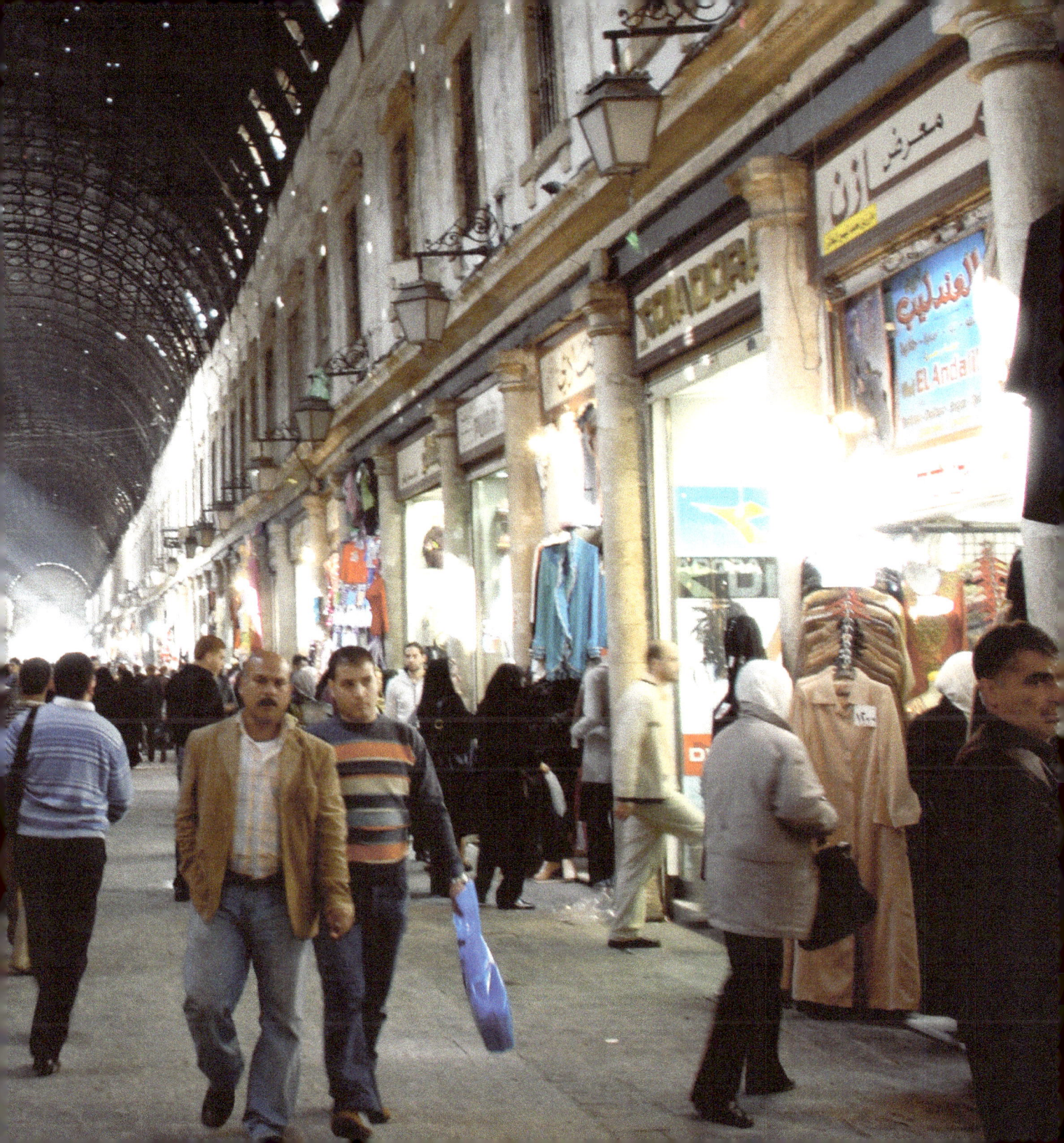

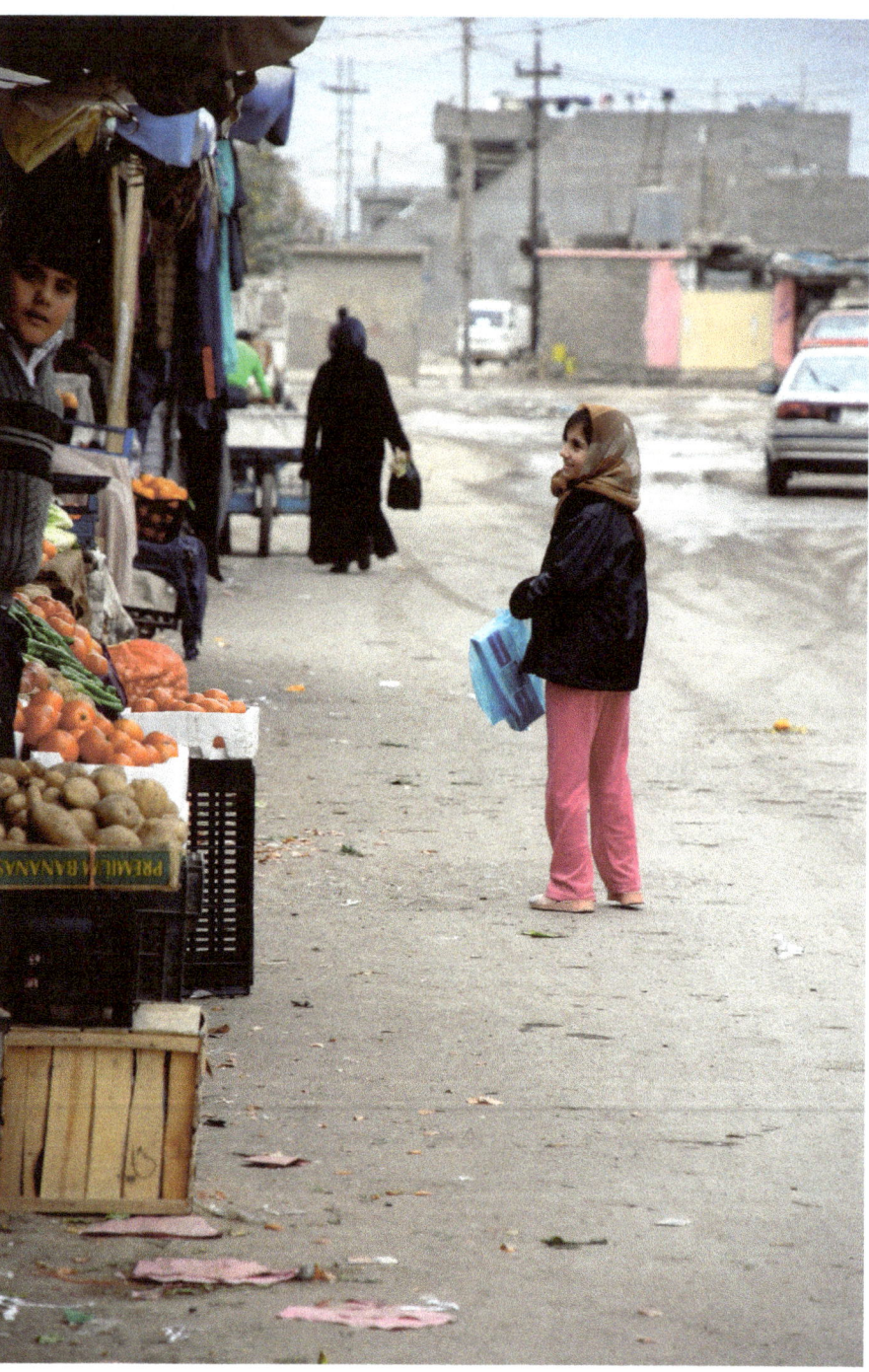

Frequently identified by Westerners as Arabs, the Kurds are actually a separate people who continue to preserve their culture and heritage amidst years of intense persecution and attempted genocide. Mountain Village, Iraq.

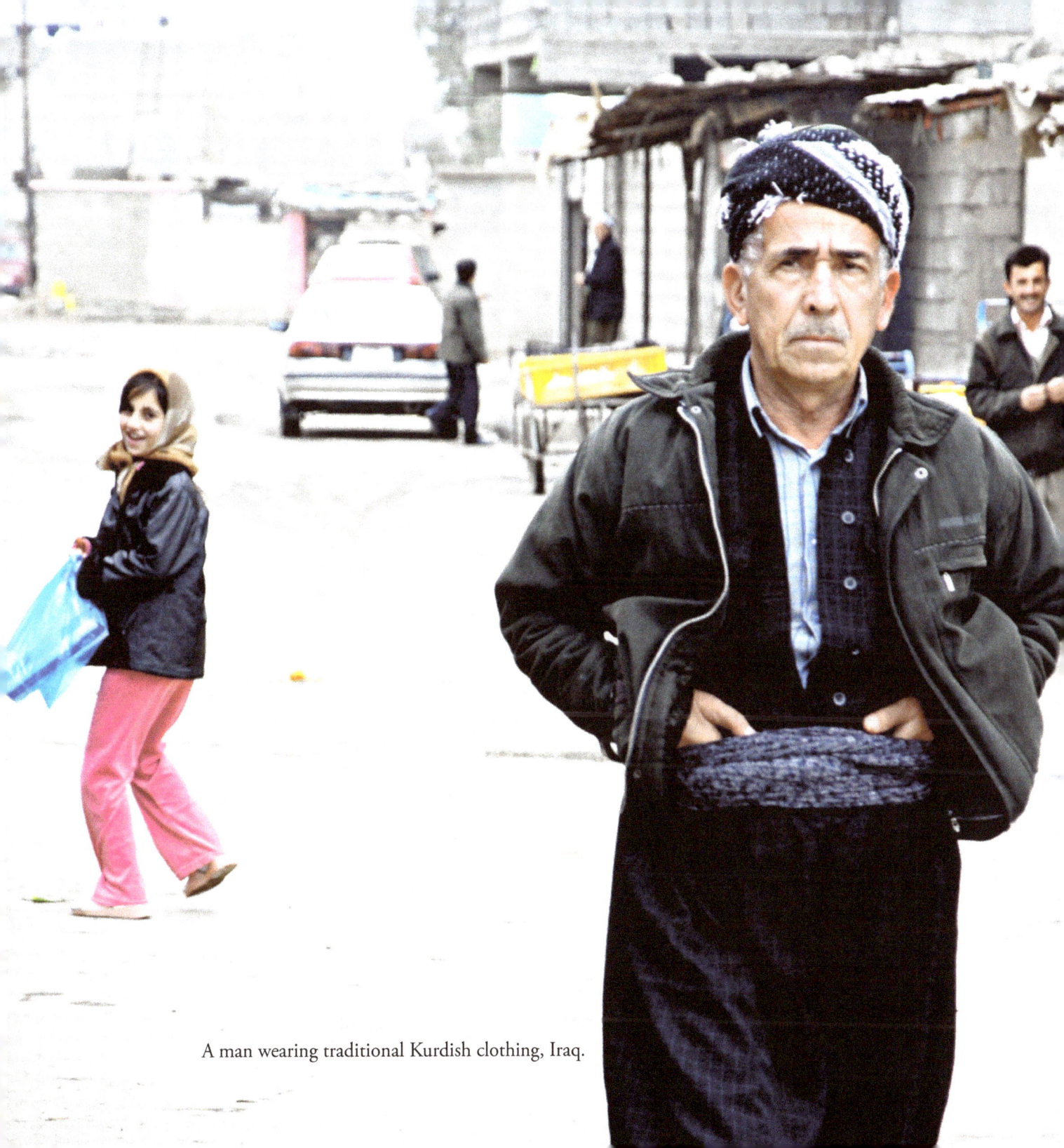
A man wearing traditional Kurdish clothing, Iraq.

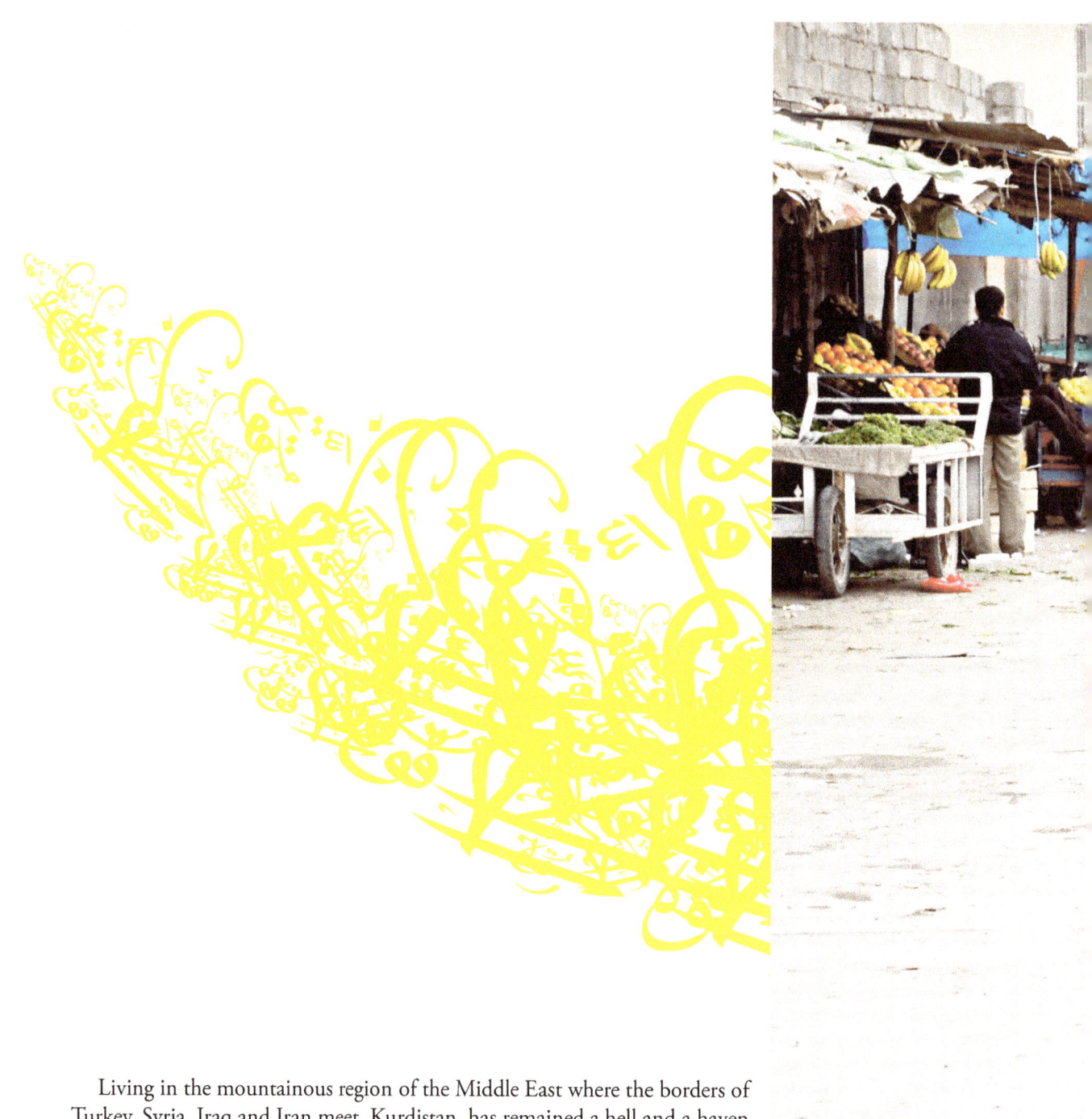

Living in the mountainous region of the Middle East where the borders of Turkey, Syria, Iraq and Iran meet, Kurdistan, has remained a hell and a haven for the Kurds who have been repeatedly attacked and persecuted by surrounding nations. They trace their language back to the Medes; an ethnic Iranian group that once lived in the northwestern part of Iran.

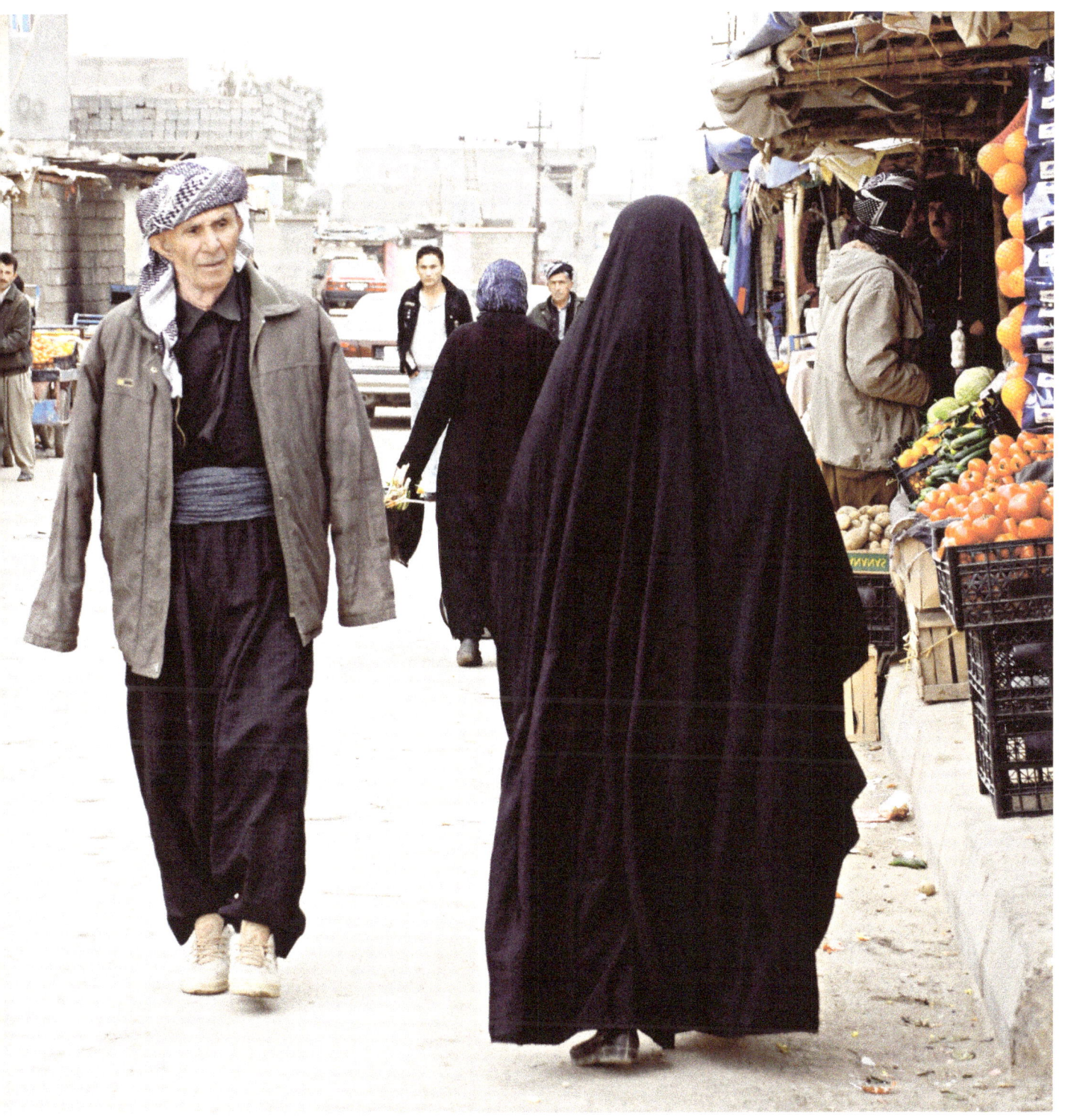

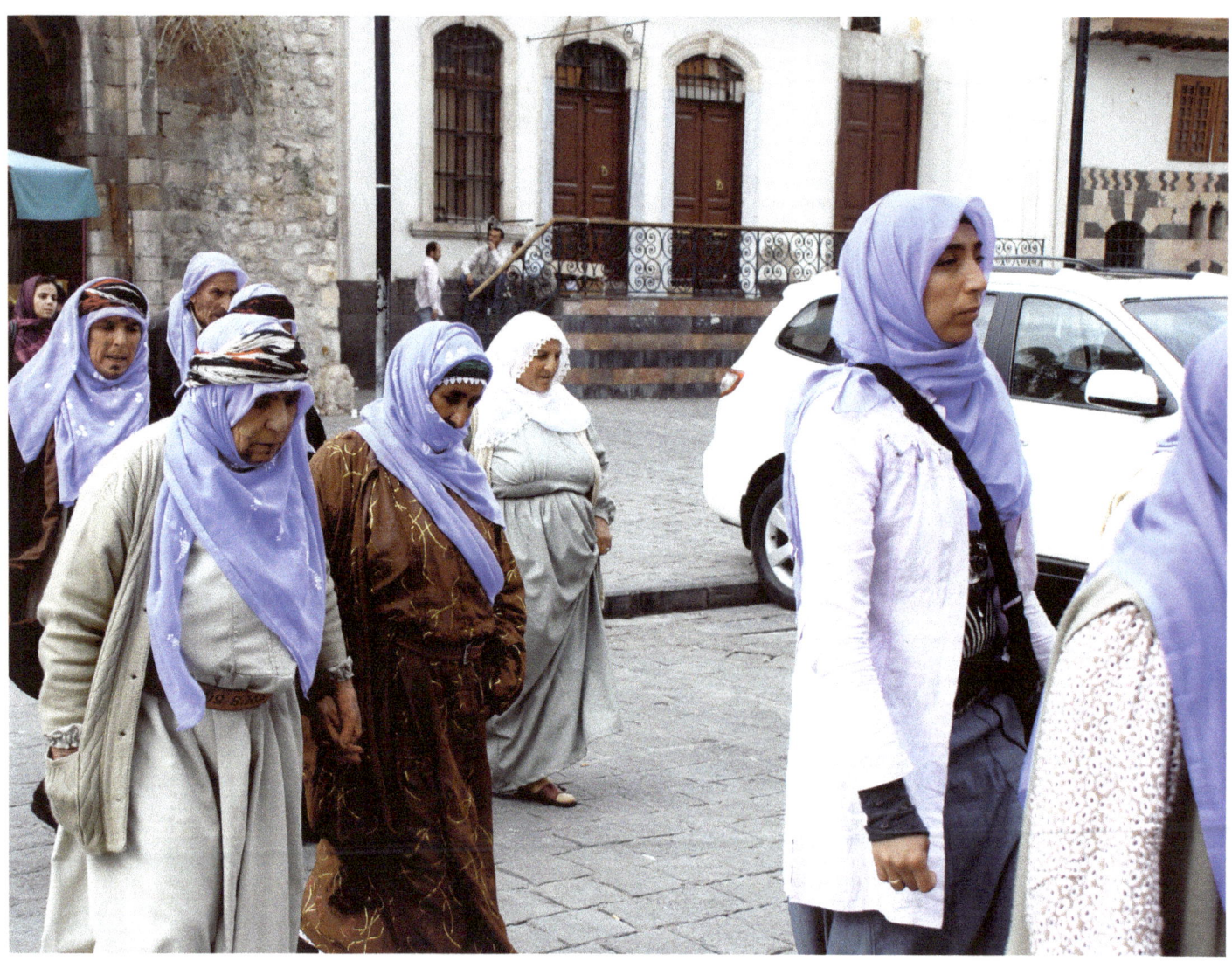

Many Kurds continue to hope for a future of stability and freedom of expression in their own land. The scars of Saddam will remain for years to come as families seek out their loved ones, still buried in unknown mass graves across the wilderness of Iraq. These Kurdish pilgrims have just arrived in Damascus, Syria.

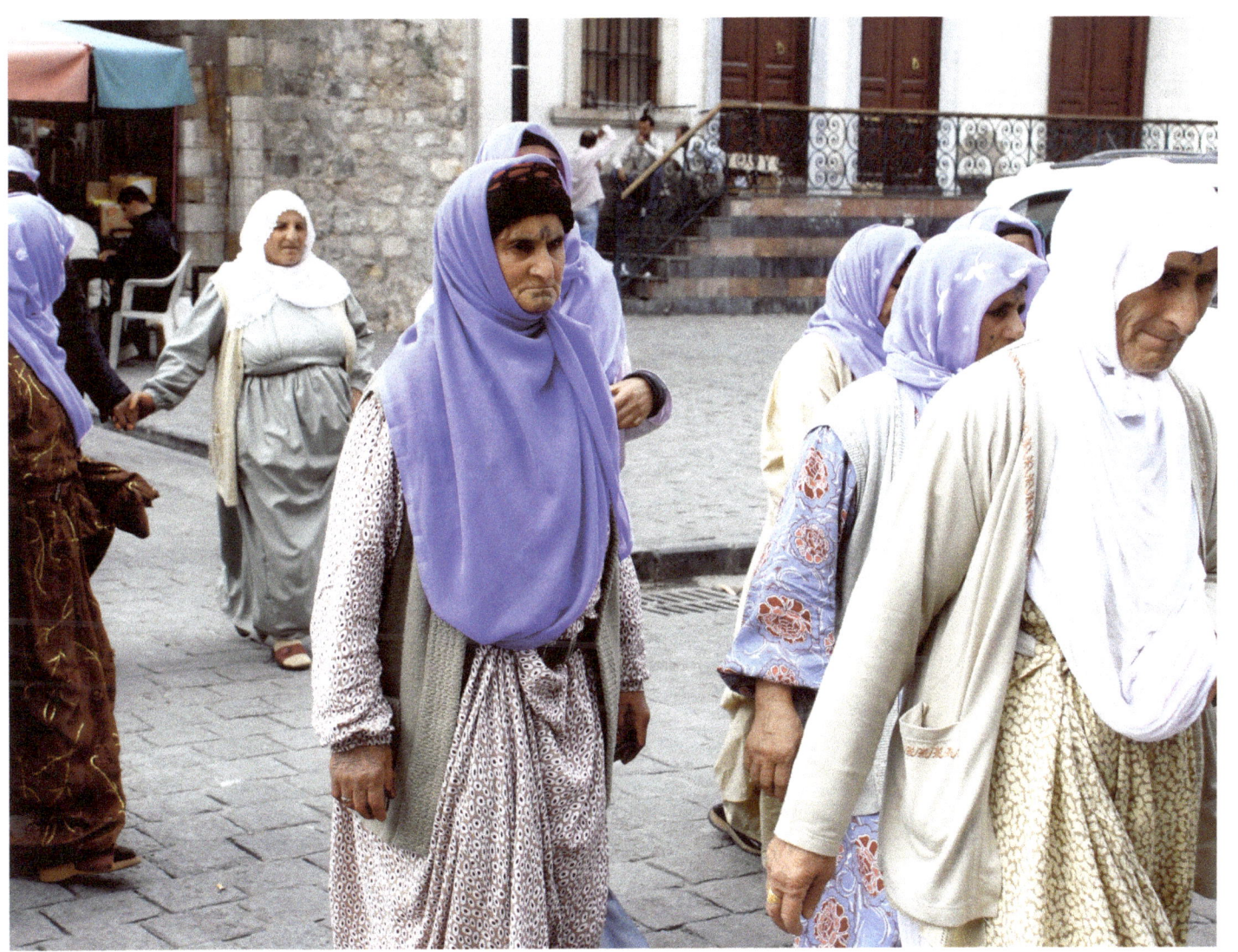

These Kurdish pilgrims in Damascus also have small tattoos on their foreheads and chins, which identifies which tribe they come from.

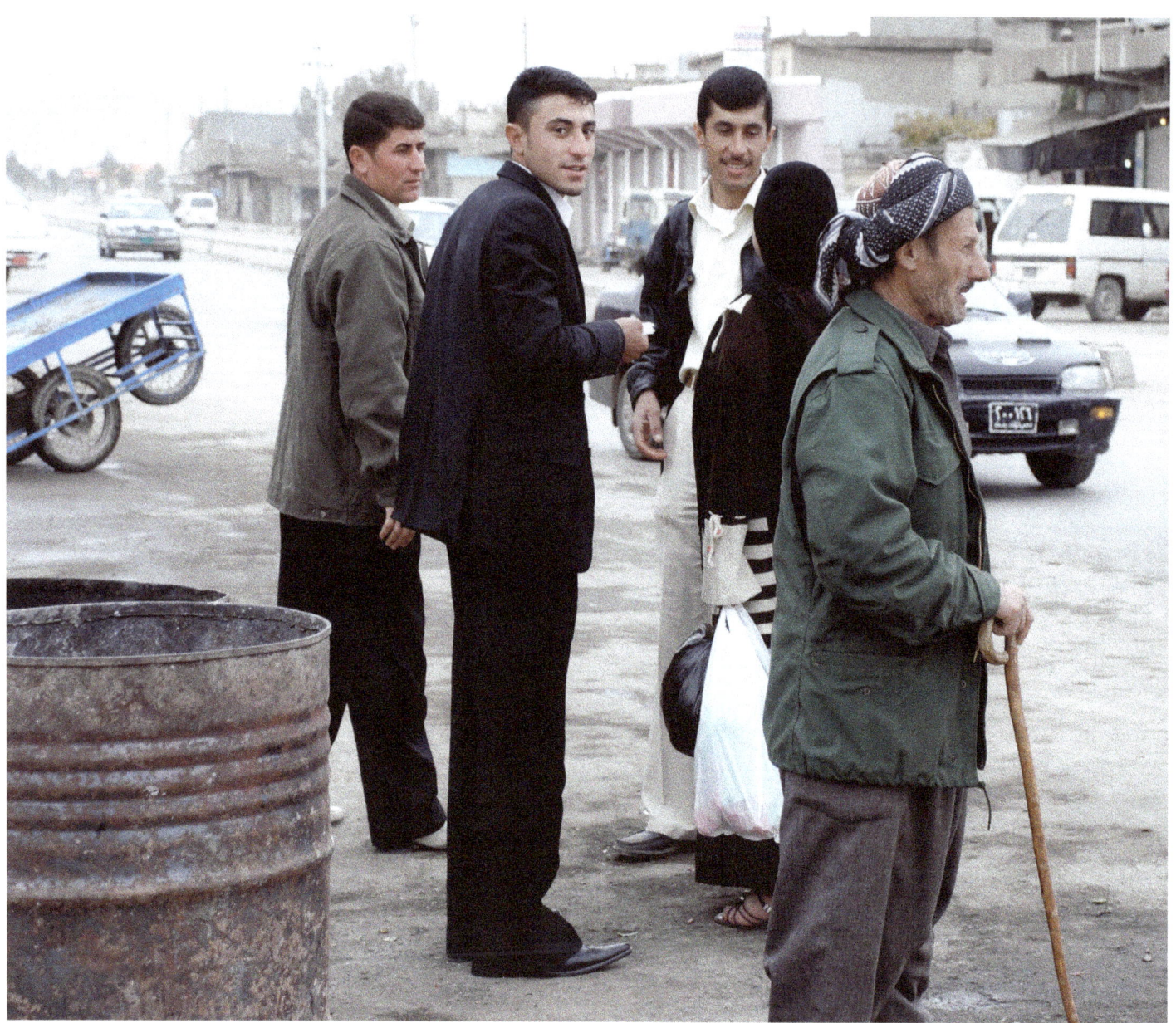

Kurdish men in modern and traditional attire, Iraq.

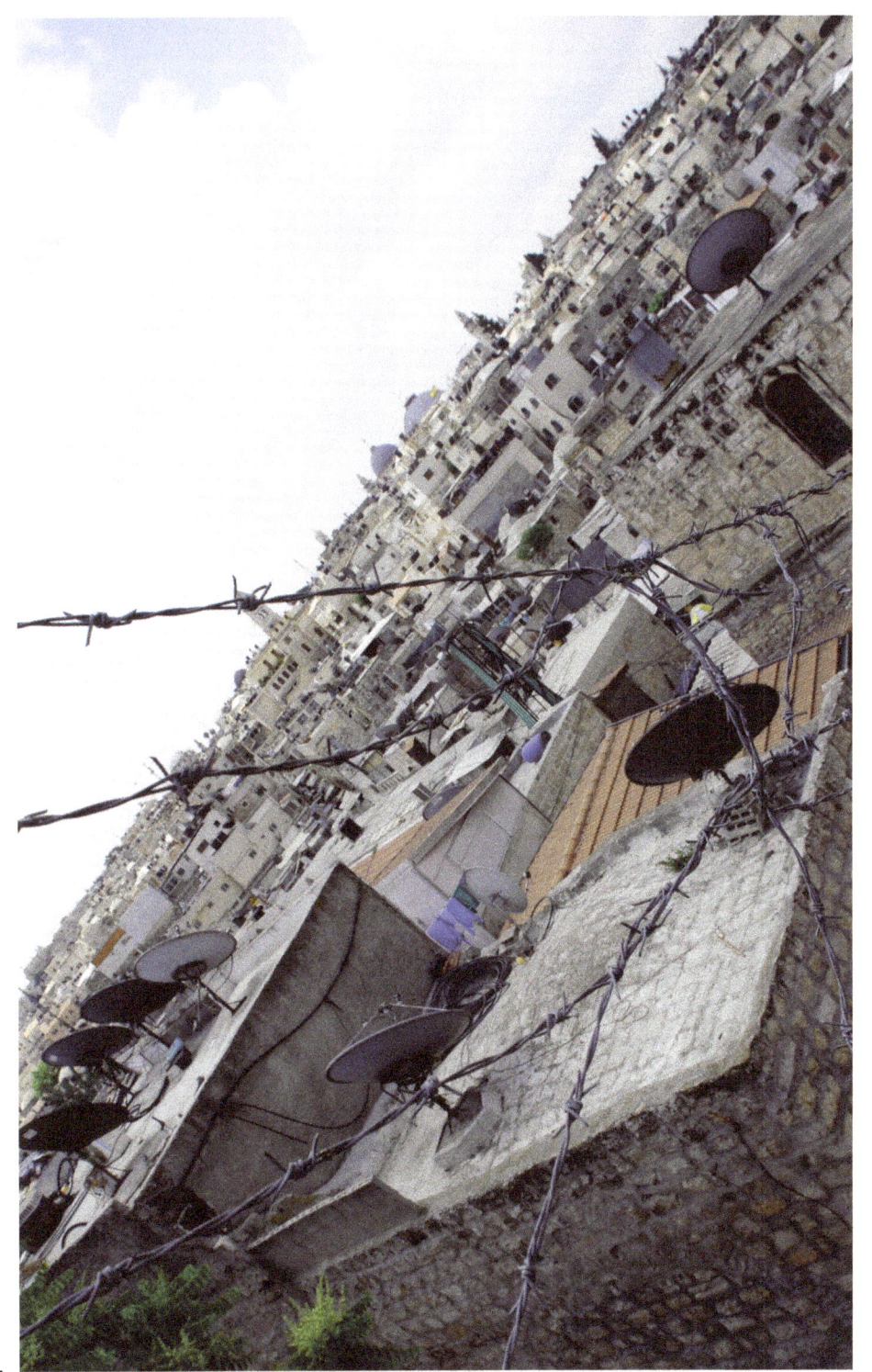

Rooftop, Jerusalem.

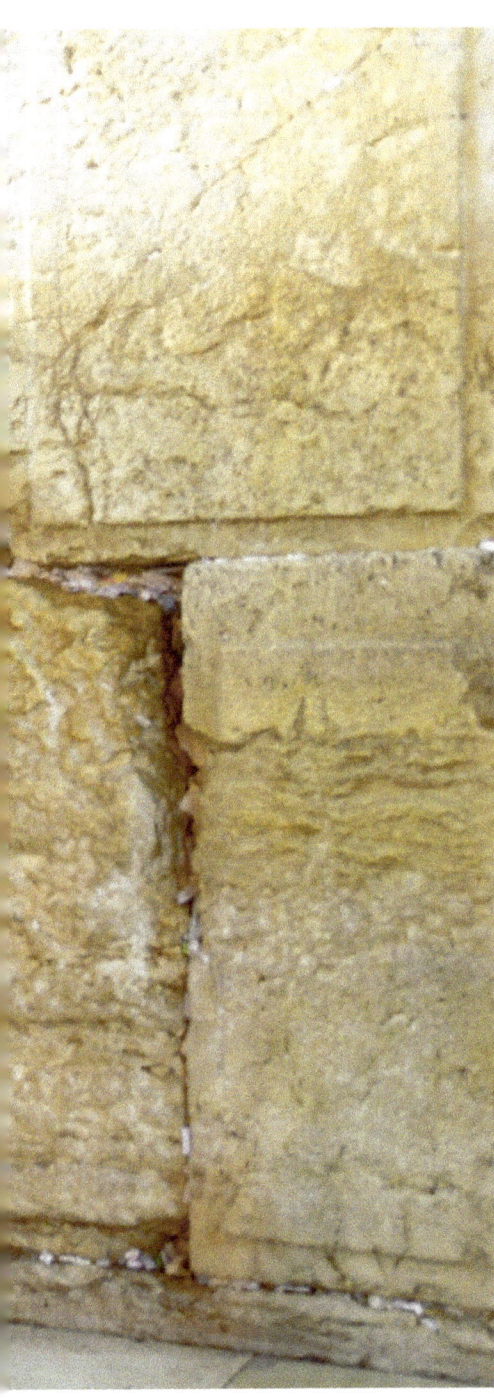

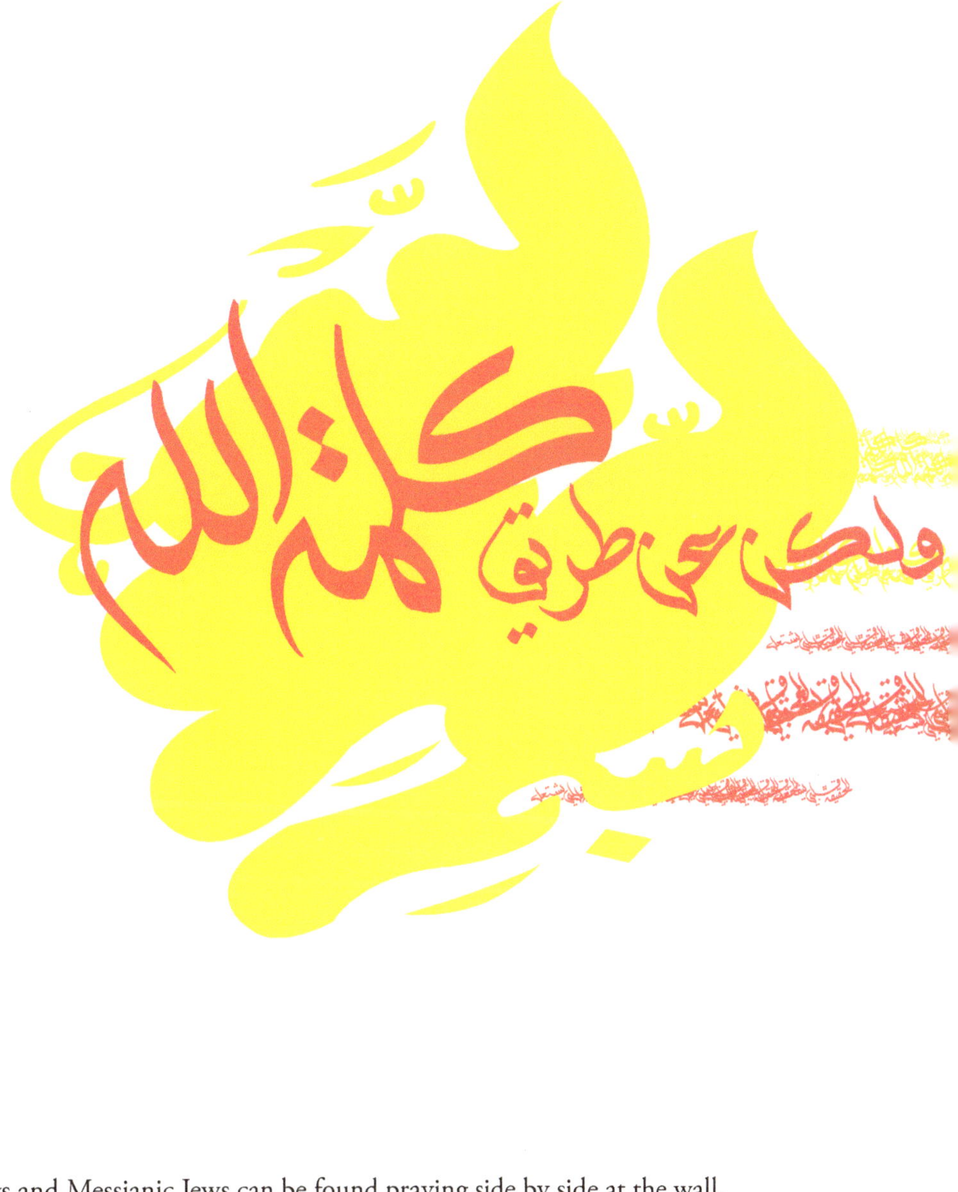

Jews and Messianic Jews can be found praying side by side at the wall, sometimes unknown to each other, as they continue to petition for the peace of Jerusalem; that she will be made complete, perfect, and whole, as well as be restored to the One, to whom the city belongs.

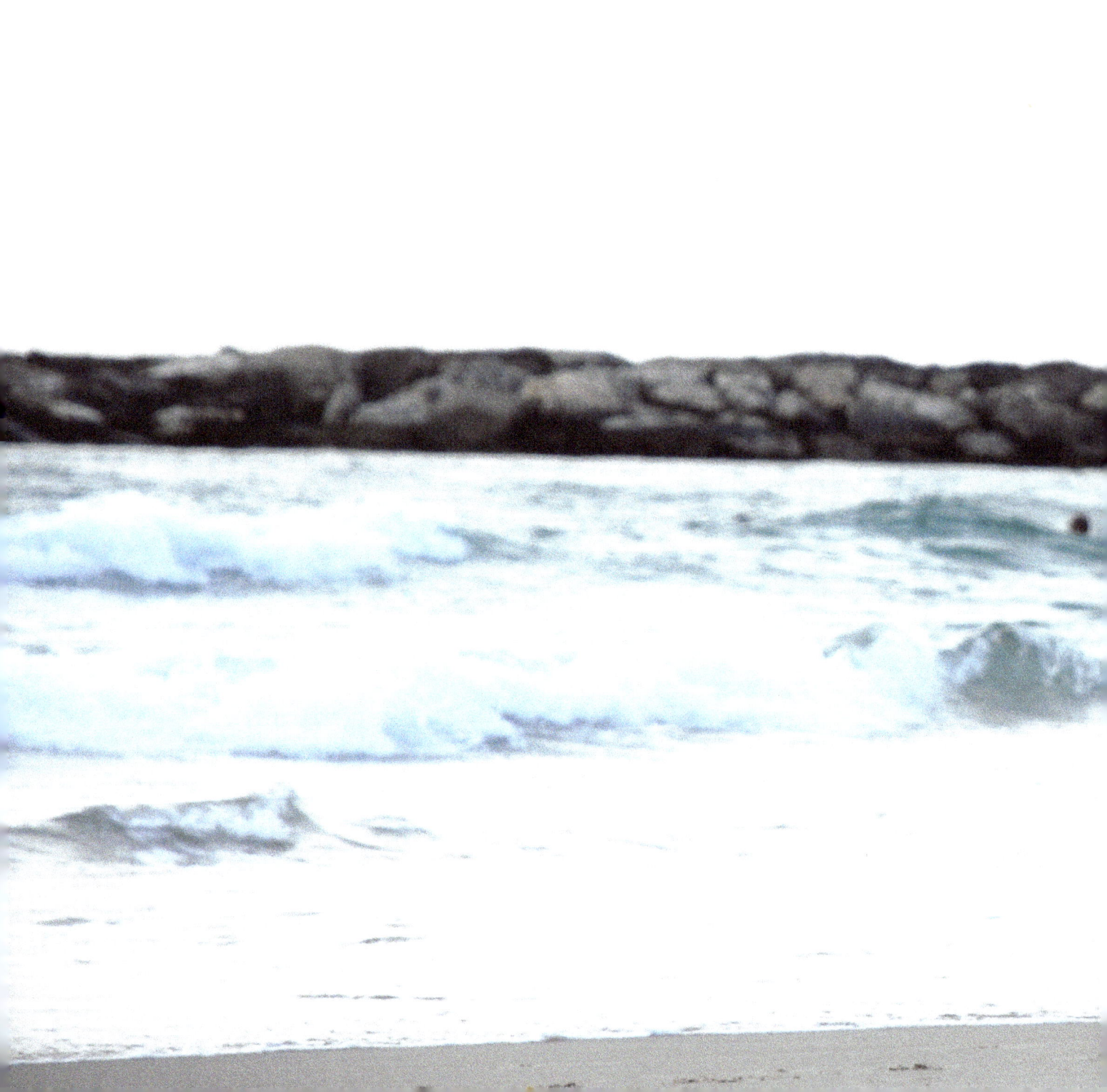

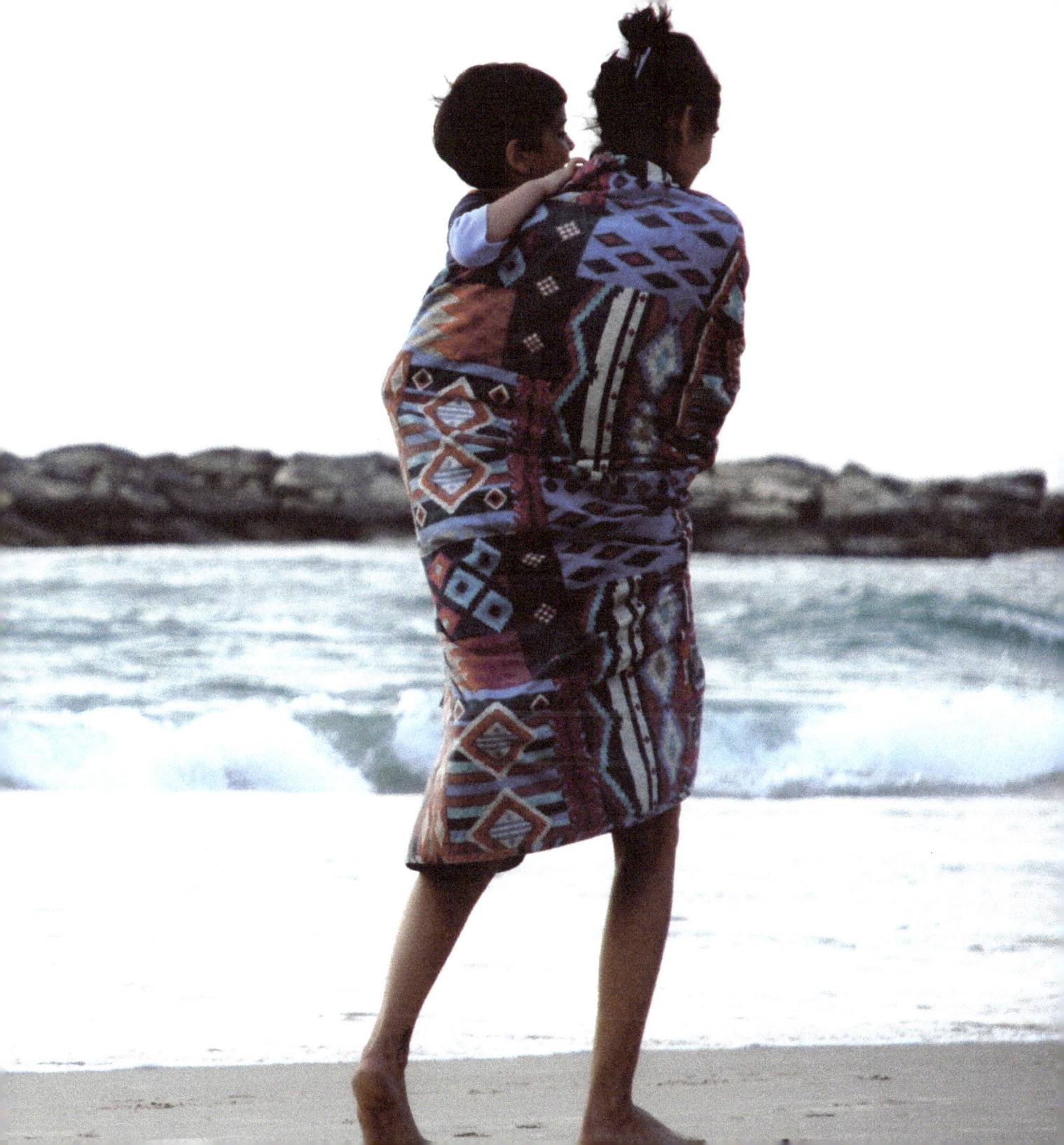

About the Author:

Hermoine Macura is the first Australian female English speaking TV news anchor in the Middle East and North Africa region (MENA), and also one of the area's most recognized faces.

Currently the CEO of Straight Street Media, Hermoine's portfolio includes the delivery of live-to-air news bulletins, frequently whilst being in the midst of breaking stories both locally and across the Middle East. Hermoine has also hosted a variety of other shows including the 3 hour live launch of the Burj Khalifa and Maak Ya Lebanon, which featured exclusive interviews with several key players in aid programs in Lebanon. The program was a part of a series that raised 55 Million Dirhams to help people caught in the 2006 conflict.

Complimenting her role as an anchor, Hermoine has also interviewed a variety of decision makers, and people in the know. From the Duchess of York to Hollywood Actor Michael Douglas, Hermoine has interviewed a wide variety of personalities and government officials in the country.

Born in Sydney, Australia, Hermoine began her career in Journalism as a graduate of the University of Wollongong where she was also trained in photography. Originally a Print Journalist, her works have been published in a wide variety of publications and exhibited across the world.

FACES OF THE MIDDLE EAST is her first book. It was born out of her passion for photography and the arts, and her deep desire to see peace in the Middle East.

www.FacesoftheMiddleEast.com

Join us: FacesoftheMiddleEast FacesMiddleEast

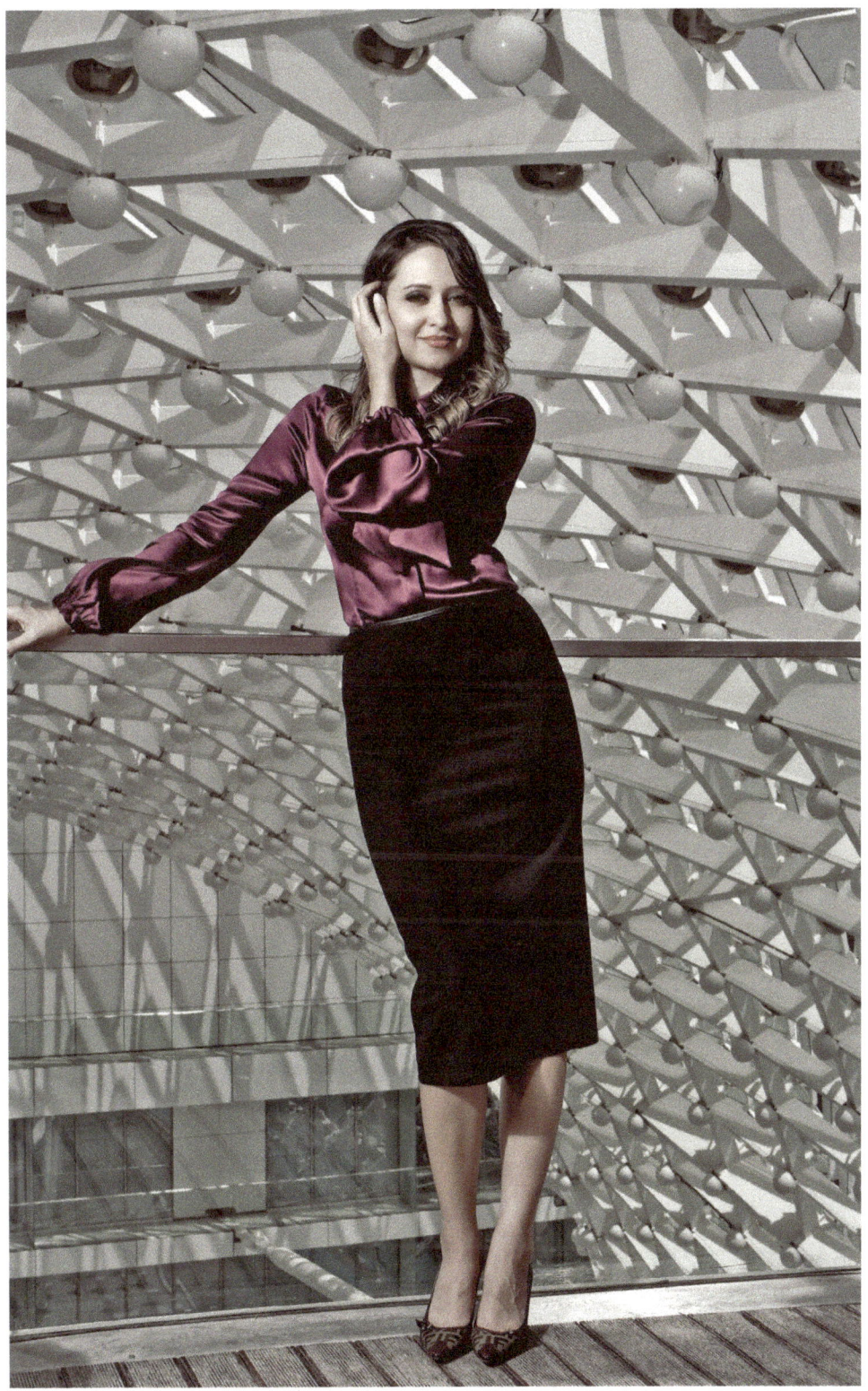

113
١١٣

Image:
by Martin Beck.
Location: Yas Hotel,
Abu Dhabi, UAE.

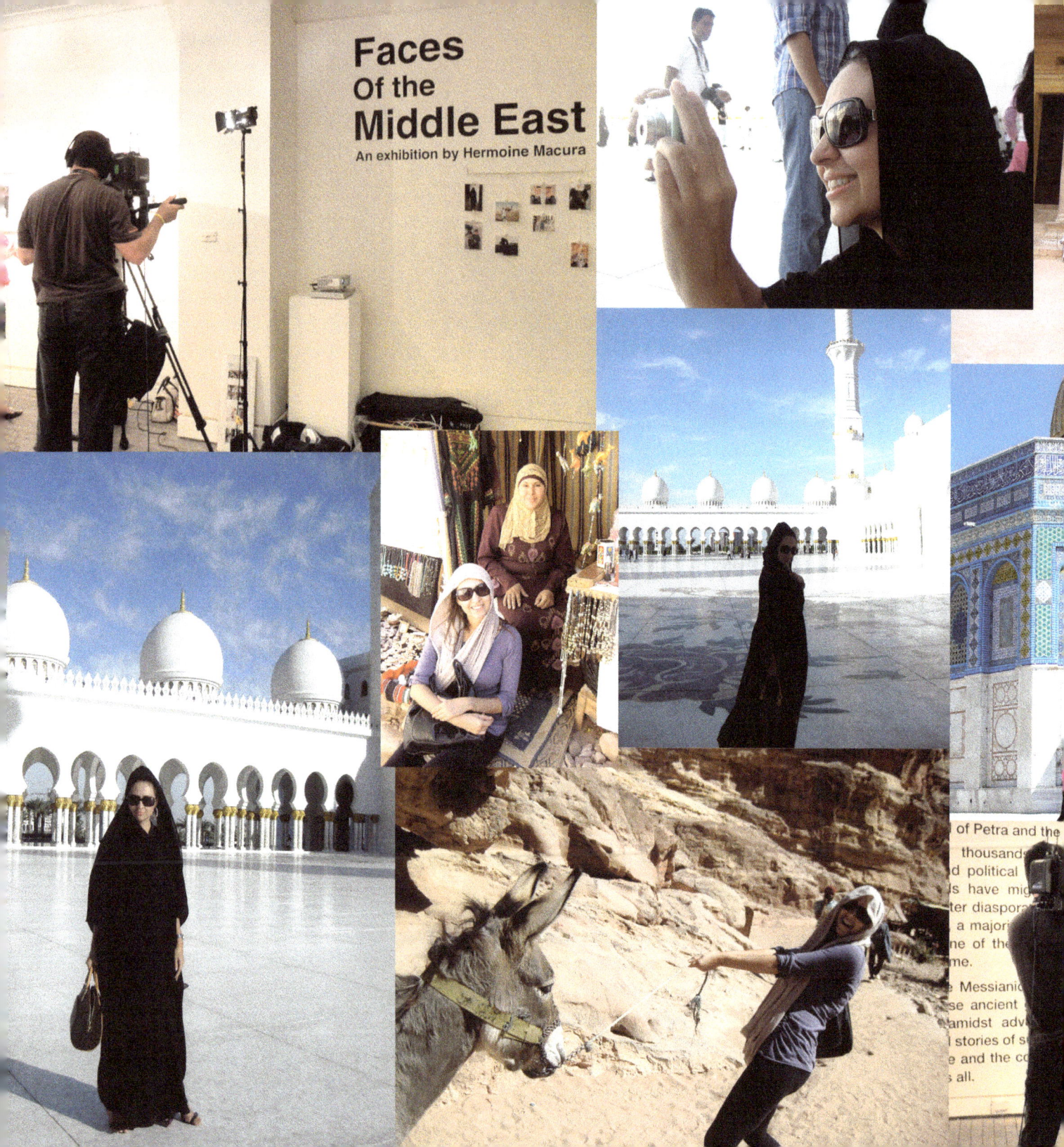

www.ingramcontent.com/pod-product-compliance
Lightning Source LLC
Chambersburg PA
CBHW040543220526
45473CB00016B/3006